$47

The Assemblies of God

The Assemblies of God

Godly Love and the Revitalization of American Pentecostalism

Margaret M. Poloma and John C. Green

NEW YORK UNIVERSITY PRESS
New York and London

NEW YORK UNIVERSITY PRESS
New York and London
www.nyupress.org

Library of Congress Cataloging-in-Publication Data
Poloma, Margaret M.
The Assemblies of God : godly love and the revitalization of American Pentecostalism / Margaret M. Poloma and John C. Green.
p. cm.
Includes bibliographical references (p.) and index.
ISBN 978-0-8147-6783-2 (cl : alk. paper) — ISBN 978-0-8147-6784-9 (ebook)
1. Assemblies of God. 2. Christian sociology—Assemblies of God.
3. United States—Religious life and customs. 4. Christian sociology—United States. I. Green, John Clifford, 1953– II. Title.
BX8765.5.A4P66 2010
289.9'4—dc22 2010024129

New York University Press books are printed on acid-free paper, and their binding materials are chosen for strength and durability. We strive to use environmentally responsible suppliers and materials to the greatest extent possible in publishing our books.

Manufactured in the United States of America
10 9 8 7 6 5 4 3 2 1

Contents

Acknowledgments

This book revisits Margaret Poloma's (1989) pioneering sociological research on the Assemblies of God. We wish to acknowledge the role that the late Dr. Thomas F. Zimmerman, then General Superintendent of the Assemblies of God (AG), played in graciously listening to Poloma's proposal and encouraging pastors to participate in the original study. Although not always agreeing with its sociological assessments, many in the denomination continue to demonstrate the spirit of Dr. Zimmerman's gracious acceptance of Poloma and her research.

A scholarly and systematic introduction to the AG was provided by Russell Spittler at Fuller Theological Seminary shortly after Poloma decided to embark on the original study. At Fuller she also met Cecil M. Robeck; both Russ and Mel have traveled with her through the years as insiders, helping this outsider to better understand issues and events as they unfolded in the denomination. They were soon joined by Murray W. Dempster of Vanguard University of Southern California (an AG university), who invited her to attend one of the earliest conferences on the globalization of Pentecostalism (see Dempster, Klaus, and Petersen 1999) and offered her the opportunity to teach courses at Vanguard while commuting from her Ohio home. Many other significant collegial relationships developed and continue at Vanguard, including those with Byron D. Klaus (now President of the Assemblies of God Theological Seminary), Sherilyn Benvenuti, Roger Heuser, Elizabeth Leonard, Frank Macchia, Jesse Miranda, Douglas Petersen, Phil Robinette, Edmund Rybarczyk, as well as other faculty and students too numerous to mention. While teaching at Vanguard and doing research for the present work, she met Margarita Lima, a friend and colleague who translated our questionnaire into Spanish, and Pastor Fernando Tamara, who located the Hispanic churches, interviewed the pastors, and administered the surveys to Hispanic congregations. It was also at Vanguard that she encountered the Superintendent of the Southern California District, Ray Rachels, who had enrolled in one of her classes and from whom she learned much.

This book originated because while teaching at Vanguard University in the late 1990s, Poloma was approached by David A. Roozen and James R. Nieman (Hartford Seminary's Institute for Religious Research) to conduct a small study on the AG as part of a comprehensive project entitled "Organizing Religious Work for the Twenty-first Century" (ORW). Thinking that she had moved on from research on the AG to studies on the sociology of prayer and religious revivals, she was reluctant to accept this invitation. It was Murray Dempster's enthusiastic encouragement that led her to sign on with the ORW project. There she had the privilege of joining the AG historian William Menzies and the late missiologist Gary McGee, who had also been invited to provide accounts of the AG. The research conducted on AG pastors allowed her to revisit *Crossroads* and proved to be foundational for the present work. With permission granted by the editors and the publisher of *Church, Identity, and Change: Theology and Denominational Structures in Unsettled Times,* the major findings from the ORW survey of AG pastors have been drawn upon in chapters 3 and 4. A special note of appreciation to David Roozen for his insightful comments on earlier drafts; to Scott Thumma, who assisted with questionnaire construction, distribution, and data entry; and to William B. Eerdmans Publishing Company for granting permission to use modified sections of the original work.

When we initially attempted to revisit *Crossroads* using the ORW pastoral data and secondary materials, we realized that such an endeavor would be wanting without a new survey of AG congregations. With the assistance of Jim Lewis and a generous grant from the Louisville Institute, a Lilly Endowment–funded program based at Louisville Seminary supporting those who lead and study American religious institutions, we were able to collect the new congregational survey data that is at the core of this book. We also wish to acknowledge Baffour Takyi of the Pan African Studies Program at the University of Akron for conducting the survey at a Ghanaian congregation, and the Bliss Institute at the University of Akron, where Janet Bolois provided administrative assistance and other staff offered technical support and data entry. Appreciation is also extended to the Institute for Research on Unlimited Love (IRUL), which provided the funding for an earlier work and a publishing subvention for this one, and to its co-principal investigator, Ralph W. Hood, Jr. It was in writing *Blood and Fire* (2008) together that Ralph and Poloma developed a preliminary theory of Godly Love that proved central to this work. To IRUL's president, Stephen Post, we thank you for reminding us how important it is to take "grace" and theology seriously in reporting on religious ritual and experience. A special word of thanks is offered to Byron Klaus, president of the Assemblies of God Theological Seminary (AGTS), who organized focus groups in Springfield, Missouri, from AGTS, AG Headquarters, Evangel University, and Central Bible College to review an early draft of this manuscript. We appreciate his help and that of members of the three focus groups who participated by sharing their many thoughts and insightful comments.

Our sincere appreciation is also extended to the pastors who completed the ORW surveys, pastors who agreed to be interviewed and to have surveys conducted in their congregations, and all of the AG congregants who completed the surveys. Without their gracious cooperation, there would be no data to report.

Finally, we wish to thank the anonymous reviewers who provided input for revising an earlier version of the manuscript. We especially thank Jennifer Hammer, our editor at New York University Press, who helped us to carry them out. Jennifer worked with us as we sought to present an abundance of rich data collected and mused over for several years without allowing our presentation to get bogged down in tedious details. We trust readers will join us in appreciating her dedicated service.

We are indebted to the numerous other scholars whose works and words have contributed to the development of this study, many of whom are cited in references that appear at the end of this volume. To them and to others whom we have failed to mention by name, we offer another sincere note of gratitude. It goes without saying that this book is a work for which the authors are indebted to many, but for which we bear final responsibility.

Introduction

> As the metal-and-glass doors swing open and the crowd begins to file into the auditorium-sized sanctuary of the Brownsville Assembly of God, moms, ministers, and many more feel they are entering sacred space. As they walk down the wide carpeted aisles—aisles that in a few hours' time will be filled with the lifeless bodies of stricken worshipers—some tread lightly, as if they are walking on holy ground. . . . All told, more than 2.5 million people have visited the church's Wednesday-through-Saturday evening revival services, where they sang rousing worship music and heard old-fashioned sermons on sin and salvation. After the sermons were over, hundreds of thousands accepted the invitation to leave their seats and rush forward to a large area in front of the stage-like altar. Here, they "get right with God." . . . Untold thousands have hit the carpet, where they either writhe in ecstasy or lie stone-still in a state resembling a coma, sometimes remaining flat on the floor for hours at a time. Some participants call the experience being "slain in the Spirit." Others simply refer to receiving the touch of God. Regardless of what they call it, these people are putting the "roll" back in "holy roller." (Rabey 1998, 4–5)

Although religious revivals have been said to be "as American as baseball, blues music and the stars and stripes" (McClymond 2007, xvii), they inevitably stir up controversy as well as revive faith. The Azusa Street Revival that occurred in Los Angeles between 1906 and 1909, now commonly credited as the birthplace of Pentecostalism, had followers and detractors, as did the Pensacola Outpouring some ninety years later. In both cases, many people attributed spiritual and social transformations to these events while others were put off by the turbid emotionalism they saw at these revival meetings.

The Assemblies of God (AG), a Pentecostal denomination, was founded in Hot Springs, Arkansas, in 1914 by men and women whose lives had been changed by the Azusa Street Revival. By the 1990s membership had reached a plateau and the early Pentecostal fervor had cooled. As the century came to a close, however, another revival known as the Pensacola Outpouring, which broke out on Father's Day in 1995 at an Assembly of God church in Pensacola, Florida, offered hope for those seeking a new Pentecost like the one reported in the biblical book of Acts. In this account, Jesus's believers, who had gathered on the Jewish feast of Pentecost following his resurrection from the dead and ascension into heaven, experienced "tongues of fire" and began to "speak in other tongues." Although traditional Christians came to regard this event as the birth of Christianity, Pentecostals emphasize their *interpretation* of this biblical experience over simply remembering the historic event. Just as onlookers apparently were drawn to the first Christian Pentecost by unusual somatic manifestations, the faithful, the curious, and the media alike were drawn to the Pensacola revival. For the next few years the experience described succinctly in the epigraph above were reported (and repeated) in scores of AG churches around the country.

The Assemblies of God at the Crossroads: Charisma and Institutional Dilemmas (Poloma 1989; hereafter referred to as *Crossroads*) provided a sociological assessment of the AG through the lens of Max Weber's thesis concerning the inevitable routinization of charismatic experiences. According to Weber, spiritual experiences are at the root of the origin of new religions; these experiences often morph into religious doctrine that gives meaning to the original experiences, and into religious rituals that commemorate them. In this process of routinization, the actual spiritual experiences of the visionary founders and early followers are eclipsed by religious institutional developments that focus on institutionalized beliefs and practices. While making room for angelic rumors about revitalization through accounts of historic revival experiences, the cold sociological facts pointed to the AG being on a journey from its early "charismatic moment" toward a routinization similar to that experienced by countless other sects and denominations in modern history.

When *Crossroads* first appeared in print in 1989, there was little evidence of pentecostal revitalization in the AG, in other Pentecostal denominations, or in the so-called charismatic movement or "second wave" during which mainline Christian denominations (commonly referred to as charismatics or neo-pentecostals) experienced revivals in the 1960s and 1970s. The routinization of charisma within American pentecostalism[1] seemed to be taking its predicted course. However, a third wave of the movement began to form on the West Coast of the United States even as the second wave crested—though most Americans (even Pentecostals and the neo-pentecostals of the second wave) were generally unaware of it. The boundaries between pentecostal and non-pentecostal began to blur with the coming of this so-called third wave, which developed out of the remnants of the "Jesus (People)" movement. The Jesus movement can be traced to 1967 and a Christian mission in San Francisco's Haight-Ashbury District. Historian, author, and documentary filmmaker David Di Sabatino (1999, 34) described the emerging movement (labeled the "Jesus movement" by *Look* magazine in 1971) as "the independent collection of evangelical hippie pioneers [called] 'street Christians' and 'psychedelic evangelists' only later to be dubbed either 'Jesus freaks' or 'Jesus people.'" It was the beginning of an underground movement that took a stream of pentecostalism out of its staid churches and presented it with a fresh face throughout the globe. Through its religious music festivals, Jesus marches, hippie Christian churches, coffeehouses, and communes, the Jesus movement sowed seeds for the "third wave" of the pentecostal movement (Wagner 2002).

The third wave could be seen dimly and from a distance in the early 1980s as it brought into being numerous independent pentecostal churches and parachurch ministries. "Relational networks" rather than denominational affiliation became the modus operandi, and fresh experiences of the Holy Spirit rather than doctrine was the goal. Elements of pentecostal belief and practice, including a focus on experiences of the supernatural (divine healing, prophesy, miracles, and speaking in tongues), continued to filter into yet other streams of Christianity. This process involved not only an "evangelicalization of Pentecostalism" but also a "pentecostalization of evangelicalism," as mystery and miracles filtered into evangelical Christianity's rational belief system (McGee 2005, 40–41).

In the midst of the diffusion of pentecostalisms, the AG remains a classical Pentecostal denomination with roots that can be traced to Azusa Street Revival of the early twentieth century. While the AG has both impacted and been impacted by post–Azusa Street revivals, generally it has been resistant to the contemporary renewals and revivals, which have often spawned new rival pentecostal streams. As the second-largest single Pentecostal denomination (the black Church of God in Christ is the largest), the AG has its own history and has developed its own structure as a "cooperative fellowship" that spans the globe.

What Is Pentecostalism?

As already suggested, there is no single "Pentecostalism" but rather many "pentecostalisms" found under a single umbrella. In this work we use "pentecostal" as an inclusive term to refer to any group under this broad covering, and "Pentecostal" to designate historic denominations, including the AG. Pentecostalism itself is covered by a larger umbrella known as evangelicalism. Of the relationship between pentecostalism and evangelicalism it is safe to say that although nearly all pentecostals would consider themselves to be evangelical, only a minority of evangelicals would consider themselves to be pentecostal. Here we use sociologist James Davidson Hunter's (1987, 3; see also Hunter 1983) succinct definition of evangelicalism as "the North American expression of theologically conservative Protestantism." It embraces a wide variety of religious traditions, including Holiness (e.g., Wesleyan Methodism), Reformed (e.g., conservative Presbyterian), Baptist, and the growing number of "independent," "non-denominational," "inter-denominational," "intra-denominational," and other congregations who refuse to identify with historic Protestantism. It also includes some Anglican, Catholic, and Orthodox believers who identify with evangelicalism's conservative Christian orthodoxy. Although many self-identified fundamentalists also identify as evangelicals, few evangelicals identify with the extreme doctrinal conservatism that fundamentalism historically has represented. Evangelicals are commonly identified in opinion polls by a question about whether the respondent is a "born-again" Christian.

The pentecostal movement was birthed in the larger evangelical movement and continues to reflect evangelicalism's commonalities and internal distinctions. A significant marker for both groups is a salvation experience known as being "born again" or "getting saved." A cognitive profession of faith that Jesus Christ is savior and repentance from sin are pivotal, and being "born again" is believed to bring with it a relationship of union with God ("Jesus has come into my heart" is a common refrain). To this first blessing of being "born again," pentecostals have added another, namely "baptism in the Holy Spirit," an experience that opens the door for the so-called "spiritual gifts" or charismata, including speaking in tongues (glossolalia), "word gifts" of prophecy, extraordinary knowledge and wisdom, miraculous healing, and miracles as reported in the biblical book of Acts. Historically pentecostals have always regarded Spirit baptism and the charismata as equipping or empowering them for evangelistic outreach.

The pentecostal and evangelical umbrellas are best distinguished from one another by comparing their worldviews. Evangelicalism is in many ways a Protestant cognitive response to post-Enlightenment thought, which increasingly has debunked traditional religious faith. Belief and profession of belief open the doors to salvation from sin and the reward of heaven, whether or not any special experience accompanies this evangelical profession. Pentecostals would not debate the importance of a modernist interpretation of the "first blessing" of salvation, but the "second blessing" of Spirit baptism reflects a decidedly non-modern perspective, with expectations of magic, mystery, and miracle that match or even exceed premodern biblical accounts.

Pentecostalism emerged from a diverse American Protestant religious mosaic, so it is not surprising that historical accounts of its rise emphasize different evangelical roots while acknowledging a common debt to the Azusa Street Revival. Some historians have noted that not all early Pentecostal communities were torched by the Los Angeles event. (India, for example, had its own revival that apparently cannot be traced to Azusa Street.) Having acknowledged that caveat, scholars would concur that directly or indirectly the Azusa Street Revival marked the beginning of pentecostalism as it has come to be known. Whether this revival was planted and nurtured in Wesleyan (cf. Synan 1971/1997) or Reformed soil (cf. Blumhofer 1993), or whether it sprung from a "black oral root" transmitted by the African American revival leader William Joseph Seymour (cf. Hollenweger 1997), what defines the pentecostal movement is not doctrine but a shared non-modern or primitive worldview that coexists with common assumptions about modern pragmatism. The "genius" of pentecostalism, according to pentecostal historian Grant Wacker (2001, 10) "lay in its ability to hold two seemingly incompatible impulses in productive tension." Wacker labels these impulses as "primitive" and "pragmatic," the former reflecting premodernity and the latter, modernity.

Although many Pentecostals contend that there is no human founder of pentecostalism, leaders and scholars alike have traditionally accorded the honor to Charles Fox Parham (1873–1929). It was Parham who formulated classical pentecostal theology in Topeka, Kansas, in 1901 with "basic tenets that later defined the movement" (Goff 2002, 955). These tenets included "evangelical-style conversion, sanctification, divine healing, premillennialism, and the eschatological return of Holy Spirit power evidenced by glossolalia." While Parham undisputedly laid the foundations for pentecostal theology, it was William Joseph Seymour (1870–1922) who led the Azusa Street Revival. The crucial role of Seymour, the son of slaves who spearheaded the revival that sowed pentecostal seeds around the world, is increasingly emphasized by both white and African American Pentecostals. Seymour "clearly had the confidence of the African-American, Wesleyan-Holiness community," notes Pentecostal historian Cecil M. Robeck (2002, 1055), "when he began studying with Parham in 1905."

In 1906 Seymour received an invitation "from the colored people of the City of Los Angeles" to take the pastorate of a small Holiness mission there. Although Parham had defied local Jim Crow laws in allowing Seymour to study with him at a small bible college, he advised Seymour not to go to Los Angeles and later became a staunch and vocal critic of Seymour's racially integrated revival. While Parham undisputedly laid the groundwork for a pentecostal theology, Seymour was the visionary whose "mission" was to found a church composed of members of all races. It was in pursuit of that dream that the famed revival erupted in 1906.

Despite its integrated beginnings, segregation soon took its toll on the fledgling countercultural pentecostal movement. To use Wacker's terms, "pragmatism" began its ascent as criticism mounted against the revival's "primitive" experiences. In the area of racial integration, the pragmatic clearly trumped the primitive in the Assemblies of God. For much of its history, the AG would be a segregated white pentecostal denomination, a "sister congregation" to the black Church of God in Christ (COGIC), where any African Americans seeking ties with the AG would be directed.

What Is the Assemblies of God?

The Assemblies of God is arguably the best-known of the Pentecostal denominations that developed from the Azusa Street Revival. The early founders of the AG were initially resistant to starting a new denomination and to developing any kind of doctrinal statement, but the modern pragmatic forces of institutionalization soon came into play. When they gathered in 1914, this "cooperative fellowship" stood firm that the AG would have no formal creed. By the time of their next meeting in 1916 they found it necessary to produce a statement of faith that began to regulate both religious experience and doctrinal beliefs—the primitive and the pragmatic—in this nascent denomination.

There is increasing evidence that racism was also a significant factor in the founding of the AG. As already noted, Pentecostalism had been successfully introduced to the COGIC through Seymour and the Azusa Street Revival, where whites were accepted into full fellowship. When the need for ordination was recognized by emerging white leaders (in part to secure discounts on the railroads, a mode of transportation vital to the spread of the Pentecostal message), it was sought from black bishops. These newly ordained white leaders were given permission to issue ministerial credentials to other white ministers under the auspices of the COGIC. The lure of cultural racism, however, proved stronger than the extended hand of fellowship offered by the COGIC.

It was not until 1994, long after the cultural and legal tides had clearly shifted away from racial segregation, that the AG would disavow its racist past in a reconciliatory event known as the "Miracle of Memphis" (Newman 2007). Accounts of the founding of the AG, however, have commonly been silent on the issue of racism, focusing instead on the struggles over doctrine.

Those at the 1914 meeting of the AG in Hot Springs, Arkansas, voiced a strong resistance to the development of a creedal statement, but a Oneness "heresy"—denying the triune godhead of three persons in one God—developed among its ranks between 1914 and 1916 and forced the adoption of a statement of faith that affirmed a triune God of Father, Son, and Holy Spirit (Bernard 2007). The 1916 founding pioneers adopted and approved a list of sixteen beliefs for the fledgling denomination that remains virtually unchanged. Known as the Statement of Fundamental Truths, the document reiterated the basic tenets of the fundamentalists while adding two important articles, namely, "healing by the atonement" and tongues as "initial evidence" of Spirit baptism. The belief in divine healing is not distinctively Pentecostal, having been promoted by other sect-like groups since the nineteenth-century Wesleyan Holiness movement. The doctrine of speaking in tongues as "initial evidence," however, is distinctively Pentecostal and has been embraced to varying degrees by most pentecostal groups in North America (McGee 2002; Wacker 2001). At its core, however, the AG Statement of Fundamental Truths is basically a fundamentalist-dispensationalist creedal statement, with "initial evidence" added to the other largely eschatological concerns. With the adoption of a formal creed, the AG would begin the trek from amorphous revival movement to international organization.

The key terminology in distinguishing local congregations from the national organizations, and the national cooperative fellowship from the global one, is consistent and straightforward. The national organizations, including that of the United States, are known as the "Assemblies of God"—in the case of North America, the Assemblies of God, USA. Congregations affiliated with the larger national organization are known simply as an "Assembly of God"—traditionally with nomenclature such as First Assembly of God, Evangel Assembly of God, or Citywide Assembly of God. As we will see, increasingly such traditional denominational designations (especially in Eurocentric and often in multicultural congregations) are being replaced with more generic church names such as Community Church, Family of Believers, or Happy Days Center. The Assemblies of God, USA, and other AG national organizations are part of a global cooperative organization known as the World Assemblies of God Fellowship.

World Assemblies of God Fellowship

The World Assemblies of God Fellowship is a loose alliance of independent national fellowships, one of which is the Assemblies of God, USA.[2] It is reportedly the world's largest Pentecostal denomination, with over 60 million adherents and some 312,000 churches located in more than two hundred countries and territories. The World AG Fellowship is not a governing body; rather, it operates within a framework of consultation and cooperation, especially in missionary work and world relief projects. Its organizational work is carried out by an Executive Council consisting of some twenty members representing different regions of the world. This book makes no attempt to explore differences and similarities among members of the World AG Fellowship or to describe the historic role that American missionary work has played and continues to play in pentecostal globalization. Denominational leaders are careful to designate whether they are talking about the Assemblies of God, USA, or the World AG—a designation that was muted during the years of the 1989 study—as the World AG increasingly has found a voice of its own. Our focus here is on the 2.9 million reported members of the Assemblies of God, USA, referred to hereafter as simply the "Assemblies of God."

The Assemblies of God Today

The Assemblies of God is a classical Pentecostal denomination with roots that are commonly traced back to the "first wave" of the Azusa Street Revival of 1906–9 in Los Angeles. Believers gathered in 1914, not with the intent to form a new denomination or develop a set of doctrines, but rather to come together as a cooperative fellowship. While the Assemblies of God would increase in size and influence to become the largest white American Pentecostal denomination (and the ninth largest denomination in the United States based on self-reported membership), the largely African American Church of God in Christ (with whom many white Pentecostals had at least a loose affiliation until 1914) would become *the largest* American Pentecostal denomination (and fifth largest denomination in the United States based on self-reported membership).

The AG is organized under the General Council of the Assemblies of God, with a reported 2,899,702 members and regular (non-member) adherents. The American AG has become more ethnically diverse as whites of European heritage continue to decrease in proportion to other ethnic groups, especially Hispanics. Given the AG's insistence that it is a "cooperative fellowship" rather than a denomination, local congregations take pride in their independence and self-government, which give them considerable freedom from the national body in electing their own pastors and managing their own affairs. In fact, it is not unusual to find congregants who do not even know that their church is a member of the AG. Not surprisingly, appreciable differences are found among American congregations. The General Council's national headquarters are in Springfield, Missouri, where the administration building, Gospel Publishing House, Assemblies of God Theological Seminary, Central Bible College, and Evangel University are located.

The judicatory offices in Springfield can be said to represent the pragmatic, institutional, contractual, and modern face of the AG, which we will explore in early chapters of this book. Its "core values" revolve around evangelism, proclaiming "at home and abroad, by word and deed Jesus as Savior, Baptizer in the Holy Spirit, Healer, and Soon Coming King." As facilitators of this central value, other values include a mission to "strategically invest in the next generation," to "vigorously plant new churches," and to "skillfully resource our Fellowship" (www.ag.org; accessed on October 5, 2009). The judicatory is responsible for organizing the religious work that serves the denomination (Roozen and Nieman 2005). Although congregations differ in the extent to which they are open to the public expression of glossolalia, testimonies of healing and miracles, and prophecy, they typically allow for some degree of charismatic ("primal") expression and emphasize relational covenant over bureaucratic contract. In this book, AG congregants provide a portrait of lived religion as found in the congregations, one that complements the assessment of the judicatory provided by the pastors. It is only in taking these two components together—the primarily pragmatic judicatory and the more primitive facets of congregational life and the spirituality of its members—that the Assemblies of God can be understood and assessed as one of the leading denominations on the American religious scene.

Revival and the Assemblies of God

As we have seen, the Assemblies of God was birthed out of a major American revival. Revival remains a viable force in contemporary American religious movements. Throughout history, local, regional, and international renewals and revivals have intermittently flooded parched spiritual lands with their "rains," "rivers," and "waves" (all commonly used metaphors in the movement). While the AG itself traces its roots to a revival, subsequent revivals have been met with general indifference, words of caution, and sometimes hostility by AG leaders. Though direct experience of the divine is valued within pentecostalism, it is also challenging from an institutional standpoint because it keeps significant power in the hands of individuals rather than with religious leaders and established doctrine. Thus, as we will see, some pastors and denominational leaders find it difficult to accept ongoing revival and experience of the divine among AG congregants even though they say this is needed.

In 1992, for example, a so-called "Laughing Revival" ignited by South African evangelist Rodney Howard-Browne sparked controversy in a large AG congregation in Lakeland, Florida. Although "holy laughter" (spontaneous, uncontrollable laughter spreading through congregational gatherings during worship, messages from the pulpit, and times of prayer) was known by scholars to be part of many earlier revivals, it had seemingly long ago disappeared from Pentecostal services (Poloma 1998a; Taves 1999). Holy laughter became another pawn in the struggle between primitivism and pragmatism, developing as a point of contention between those who promoted the revivals of the 1990s and those who opposed them. The Laughing Revival was a precursor to scores of other revivals during the 1990s, the best-known being the "Toronto Blessing" (1994–2004), with its epicenter at the Toronto Airport Christian Fellowship (Poloma 1997, 1998a, 1998b, 2003, 2006b) and the "Pensacola (Florida) Outpouring" (1995–2000) at Brownsville Assembly of God (Rabey 1998; Poloma 2006a). Major revivals were also experienced in AG churches from Redding, California (Bethel Assembly of God),[3] to Grand Rapids, Michigan (First Assembly of God),[4] as well as Lakeland, Florida (Carpenter's Home Church).[5]

It was during this time of inter-pentecostal and non-denominational revivals that we began to rethink Poloma's thesis on pentecostal routinization in light of the periodic waves of revival observed in the twentieth century, and to collect empirical data that would allow us to explore the revitalization process within the AG.

Sources of Empirical Data

Our research methodology employs both qualitative and quantitative techniques, including participant observation, church Websites, open-ended interviews, and two major surveys. The different techniques have provided data that permit us not only to describe AG beliefs and practices but to assess where the denomination has been and where it may be headed. Working in tandem, these different data-gathering techniques have provided a rich story of the AG as it moved into the twenty-first century.

Qualitative Data

Although participant observation and open-ended interviews are commonly regarded as "soft data" (in contrast to "hard data" that appears more objective and is amenable to statistical analysis), observation and interviews were essential for getting a pulse on the AG. Poloma conducted at least one face-to-face unstructured interview with each of the pastors, as well as some associate pastors, of the non-Hispanic congregations included in this study. Each pastor was provided an opportunity to respond to the statistical results of the congregational survey for his church, and then to the profile presented in the following chapter. Other emails and telephone calls were exchanged as appropriate. Fernando Tamara, founding pastor of a Latino church and a graduate student at Vanguard University, interviewed the pastors of the six Hispanic congregations included in the study.

Already familiar with AG congregations from her earlier research, Poloma visited each congregation on at least one occasion to compare the contemporary Sunday rituals she observed with those she studied over twenty years ago. She attended a Sunday service at each local church periodically to follow developments as the quantitative data was being processed and the manuscript written. We also followed the developments of all of the churches by checking Websites (where available) periodically. Insights from the qualitative data provided an important backdrop for interpreting the so-called "hard data."

During the process of writing up these findings, Poloma and Green became involved in the Flame of Love Project (www.godlyloveproject.org), a study of "Godly Love" in the pentecostal tradition. "Godly Love" is a concept we will be using and refining throughout the book, employing it to discuss the revitalization process in the AG. We define it as a "dynamic interaction between divine and human love that enlivens and expands benevolence" (Lee and Poloma 2009a). In other words, it is about what has long been known as the Great Commandment found in Jesus's reply to an expert of the law: "Love the Lord your God with all your heart and with all your soul and with all your mind. This is the first and greatest commandment. And the second is like it. Love your neighbor as yourself" (Matt. 22:17–10 [NIV]). Godly Love essentially looks at how people deal with one another based on perceived love from God, which spurs them to act well in the world. An emphasis on Godly Love, although by no means the sole property of pentecostalism, may be particularly strong in the midst of revivals and revitalization (for example, the love demonstrated between African Americans and Euro-Americans as reported during the Azusa Street Revival).

As part of the Flame of Love Project, Poloma and another collaborator (Matthew Lee) conducted open-ended interviews with 116 respondents recognized by their respective communities as exemplars of Godly Love. Interviewees, including many current and former members of the AG, were encouraged to share narratives of their spiritual journeys in their own words. Some of these stories are used in this book to flesh out the bare statistical bones of survey research and illustrate experiences of Spirit baptism, glossolalia, prophecy, healing, and other unique pentecostal experiences.

Quantitative Data

As much as possible we seek to report a social-scientific narrative of the AG rather than a straightforward statistical research report. We use historical references, select theoretical references, findings from other pertinent studies, and the qualitative data to frame our narrative. We regard the statistics as a kind of skeletal frame that supports the narrative, permitting us to go back and forth from "soft" to "hard" data. They also permit us to make generalizations beyond those warranted from anecdotal data. The statistics come from two primary sources: a pastoral survey and congregational surveys.

Pastoral Survey

Poloma used an invitation to join the multilayered Organizing Religious Work (ORW) project as a sociological voice, complementing the voices of an AG historian and a missiologist, to collect new pastoral data on AG pastors (Roozen and Nieman 2005). The survey focused on questions that reflected the dilemmas presented by the intersection of charisma and institutionalization, discussed earlier in *Crossroads.* With resources provided by the ORW project, a survey was mailed to a random sample of American AG pastors in 1999. The survey brought responses from 447 AG pastors, with a response rate of 37 percent, and served as the basis for an essay published in David A. Roozen and James R. Nieman's edited volume on theology and denominational structures (Poloma 2005). Questions used on the survey and statistics undergirding the reported findings presented in chapters 3 and 4 can be found in appendix A.

Congregational Surveys

The pastoral survey was complemented with congregational surveys collected at twenty-one AG churches across the country, made possible through a generous grant from the Louisville Institute, a Lilly Endowment–funded program based at Louisville Seminary. We purposively selected twenty-one congregations that reflected the diversity within the AG to conduct a survey that tapped into the worldview, beliefs, and practices of its members.[6] Poloma administered the survey to the English-speaking churches, thirteen of which were primarily Euro-American, one African (Ghana), and another Caribbean. As noted, Fernando Tamara, a Hispanic pastor and graduate student, conducted the six surveys of the Hispanic congregations, all in Southern California. The survey responses were processed by the Bliss Institute at the University of Akron.

The surveys netted responses from 1,827 AG constituents. Surveys were conducted after the Sunday morning service, in most cases before the congregation was formally dismissed. Fifty-eight percent of the respondents were female, and the average age was forty-six. Sixty-five percent of respondents were born in the United States, with the remaining 35 percent coming largely from Mexico, Central America, the Caribbean, and Africa. Seventy percent self-identified as "white," 17 percent as "Hispanic," 8 percent as "black," 4 percent as "Asian," and 1 percent as "other," reflecting the pattern of diversity found in nationwide statistics for the denomination. The average respondent had at least some college or vocational training beyond high school, with 38 percent reporting a college degree, 18 percent of whom had pursued graduate studies. The majority of the respondents (60 percent) were married at the time of the interview; 8 percent were divorced or separated, 10 percent were widowed, and the remaining 22 percent had never been married. The questions asked in the survey were used to create the scales found in appendix B.

Overview of the Book

This book seeks to present a broad narrative, complete with our statistical findings, of a prototype of Pentecostalism and the issues facing this American-born and -bred approach to Christianity that has become a global force. At its core the AG is an historic Pentecostal denomination, but one that—whether it has embraced them or not—has been influenced by subsequent pentecostal renewals and revivals as well as by the countervailing force of evangelical Protestantism. Although it would be a mistake to see AG revitalization and evangelicalization as one-way processes, this book focuses on the effects these two seemingly countervailing forces have had on the AG in the United States.

Central to the revitalizing process is Godly Love, a dynamic that is rooted in perceived experiences of the divine that deepen a person's love for God and in turn empower acts of benevolence (see Lee and Poloma 2009a). Godly Love begins with knowing the love of God and responding to that experience with acts of love and compassion. One of the interviews for the Flame of Love Project was conducted with Heidi Baker, a well-known American pentecostal missionary to Mozambique and frequent revival conference speaker who holds both a bachelor's and master's degree from an AG university. Perhaps more than any other single exemplar in the Flame of Love Study, Heidi personifies our model of Godly Love. In calling others to be "laid-down lovers," Baker (2008, 146) writes: "God has to move on the inside of us. We have to feel His heart before we ever have anything to offer anyone else. Then, when we have rested our heads against His chest, like John the Beloved, we can move and go out to others according to His heartbeat. . . . It is all about this passion; it is all about where He is. All I care about is union with Him and embracing the one in front of me." Our thesis about pentecostal revitalization centers on the power of love—experiences of divine love, the intersect of divine love and human love, and benevolent service.

Chapter 1 introduces the twenty-one congregations we surveyed, placing them within four major types of American AG congregations: traditional, evangelical AG, renewalist, and alternative. We developed the four-fold typology as a framework for selecting the congregations to be surveyed, as well as a means to present the profiles of the congregations developed through observation, interviews with pastors, historical accounts, and select survey questions. The profiles are a heuristic device that illustrates the similarities and differences among congregations included in the study. The profiles allowed us to highlight the dynamic nature of congregations that cannot be captured through a one-time survey. A handmaiden to our major thesis on charismatic routinization and revitalization through Godly Love, the congregational profiles provide a panoramic and dynamic backdrop for the survey findings presented in subsequent chapters.

Chapter 2 outlines the major theoretical guideposts used to frame the presentation of our empirical data. Sociologist Thomas O'Dea's theory concerning the development of charisma and his positing of five institutional dilemmas to its maintenance is introduced. This thesis, which guided the presentation of survey data in *Crossroads,* is drawn upon in chapters 3 and 4, which present the results of the pastoral survey. The concept of Godly Love is developed further to guide the analysis of the congregational survey presented in chapters 5 through 8. We use the concept of Godly Love to assess the intersection between religious experiences of the divine and human works of benevolence. The dynamic theory of Godly Love helps to account for the revitalization process that has persisted in Pentecostalism for more than a century.

In chapter 3 we examine the first two of O'Dea's dilemmas to assess the state of Pentecostal identity and charismatic experiences as reflected in the pastoral survey. Our presentation suggests that pastors are generally of one mind regarding the *need* for ongoing revival, but they have been unwilling to accept it when it appears. Most pastors seem to prefer the safety of doctrine to the unpredictability of the sort of revivals that gave birth to Pentecostalism.

Chapter 4 considers the relationship between structural developments and a free-flowing charisma. As social psychologists from William James to Abraham Maslow have long recognized, and as Poloma's 1989 study of the AG bore out, organized religion is wary of religious experiences. Whatever else they are, religious experiences are institutionally dangerous. Still using the pastoral data set, chapter 4 considers the remaining three O'Dea dilemmas to assess AG structural form as it relates to the flow of charisma. It concludes that "the mystical is more than a memory," but whether the AG can continue to surf the tension between charisma and structure is open to further assessment.

Our use of the congregational data begins in chapter 5 to present a discussion of Pentecostal spiritual transformation with a focus on Spirit baptism and speaking/praying in tongues. In the Assemblies of God, Spirit baptism *with the initial physical evidence of speaking in tongues*, is regarded as the key transformative experience and is central to Pentecostal identity. Scholarly research on glossolalia and AG congregational data are used to explore the meaning and practice of speaking in tongues for congregants and its relationship to other embodied religious experiences found in revivals. Of particular significance is the relationship of embodied experiences, including glossolalia, and the experience of Godly Love.

Chapter 6 continues to explore empirically the interrelationship between vertical God–human interaction and the inter-human response (i.e., benevolence) with a focus on divine healing. Following a general discussion of spiritual healing and Pentecostalism's place in it, we use the congregational survey data to test the relationship between divine healing and the charismata. We present a holistic model of healing to frame the survey responses—one in which a two-way collaborative relationship with God (especially as experienced through prophecy) is central for understanding the practice of divine healing, including having the gift of healing others.

Chapter 7 explores answers to questions raised by the late sociologist Philip Rieff about whether charisma exists in contemporary society, by pentecostal theologian Kimberly Alexander's concern about "almost Pentecostals" in American Pentecostalism, and by philosopher Rolf Johnson's thesis on the three faces of love, especially "appreciation-love." The focus of the chapter is the relationship between a "love of law" (as reflected in strong agreement with Pentecostal doctrines, the practice of ritual prescriptions, and avoidance of moral taboos) and the "law of love" (as measured by works of compassion, evangelism, concern for the poor, and care-love). It appears that for many believers *love is the law* that sows benevolence toward others. There is no evidence that restoring old legal traditions would enhance charisma or benevolence in the AG, but there is evidence that more emphasis on the charism of prophecy might further the practice of other charismata and benevolence.

Chapter 8 continues to explore the effects of charisma on benevolence as reflected through the prism of religious values and public affairs. We review the impact of religious experience and traditional religiosity on public affairs, including activities such as charity and political action. Although cultural issues have dominated the politics of the Assemblies of God laity in recent times, there is evidence that benevolence enlivened by religious experience of the divine does matter in accounting for differences in both attitudes and behavior.

The concluding chapter, coauthored with Matthew T. Lee,[7] provides a synthesis of the book's argument and looks to the future. The institutionalization and routinization of charisma as presented through the lenses of the pastoral data are integrated with the dynamic pentecostal experiences and their restrictive interdicts as portrayed through the congregational data. Adopting and adapting a theoretical model of Godly Love, in conjunction with Johnson's typology of the faces of love, shows that the contractual nature of the denomination (described in chapters 3 and 4) complements the covenantal relations of congregational life (presented in chapters 5 through 8).

In this work we provide a social-scientific description of the Assemblies of God in the early twenty-first century that draws from a variety of empirical sources, presenting them within a theoretical framework that integrates the thesis of pentecostal routinization and revival, with an emphasis on the experience of Godly Love as a key motivator for revivalist impulses within the movement. This description unfolds chapter by chapter, with supporting theories, data, and interpretations added when appropriate, all working together to reveal both the pragmatic and primitive faces of the AG. Although we lack a crystal ball to predict the future of American denominationalism, the AG continues to be a success story in an age of shrinking denominational affiliation in large part due to the interplay of routinization and revival. The AG still stands at a crossroads, but the alternative roads may be clearer than in the immediate past.

1

Congregational Overview

> The first thing you will likely notice is that our facility is rather large, but you will be met immediately by greeters at the doors who can point you to the right direction. As you enter the church lobby you will also see a lot of younger people, a lot of older people, and a lot of people in between like me. You will also notice that some like to dress up for church and others like to come casual. We have it all—so come as you are! (www.centralassembly.org; accessed on February 24, 2009)

The above epigraph was penned by Pastor James T. (Jim) Bradford of Central Assembly of God in Springfield, Missouri, one of the twenty-one congregations included in our study. Bradford has since relocated to the nearby U.S. Headquarters of the AG, where he serves as General Secretary and a member of the denomination's Executive Presbytery. If Springfield is (as some have affectionately and humorously called it) "Rome on the Ozarks," Central Assembly has been the AG's St. Peter's Basilica. But as we will see, Central Assembly has been in transition, providing an excellent illustration of what sociologist Malcolm Gold (2003) has called a "hybrid church," a synthesis between traditional Pentecostal beliefs and practices and those of the wider evangelical movement. Bradford left his mark on Central Assembly, just as he left his imprint on another congregation in our study, Newport Mesa Church (NMC) in Costa Mesa, California. As Gold's work reminds us, congregations do not stand still and our static typologies can be illusive. Central Assembly can serve as a prototype, however, of the most common type of AG congregation, which we call "evangelical AG." While remaining loyally Pentecostal and committed to the Assemblies of God, evangelical AG congregations have moved or are moving (in varying degrees) away from the unique experiences that were once important markers of Pentecostal identity. "Traditional" congregations, on the other hand, exhibit a strong commitment to the AG (or at least to being Pentecostal) while retaining wider and more intense experiences of *charismata*, or gifts of the Holy Spirit (especially "baptism in the Spirit" and the paranormal experience of glossolalia, as well as those of healing, miracles, and prophecy).

Central Assembly is an historical landmark, so to speak—a largely white congregation that traces its history to the earliest days of Pentecostalism. It is a church that reflects well the crossroads between charismatic experience and institutional routinization. Although Central represents perhaps the most common type of AG congregation, its distinct identity is colored by its unique history, as well as its emergence as a twenty-first-century megachurch with strong ties to the denominational leadership. (Three of its former pastors have become General Superintendents of the denomination.) Although it is but one AG church among the thousands that dot the American landscape, in many ways it is prototypical of the ongoing transformation of the denomination.

Pentecost Comes to Springfield

> It was the latter part of May in the Spring of 1907. The rain was falling on the trees in front of our white clapboarded farm house on Division Street, out beyond the city limits of Springfield, Missouri. My sister, Hazel (age 10), and I (age 7) were playing on the front porch when I heard a sound of wagon wheels coming up the road. We were expecting a visit from my Aunt Rachel Sizelove, who had been to the Azusa Street meetings in Los Angeles, California. Hazel and I ran through the front door into the farm house, "Mama, Mama, she's here! She's here!" (Corum and Bakewell 1983, 1).

It was later during that visit, on June 1, 1907, that Lillie Harper Corum was baptized in the Spirit in her living room while praying with her sister, Rachel Sizelove—an event Central Assembly of God celebrates as its birth date. Sizelove brought with her the power of the Holy Spirit that she had experienced at the famed Azusa Street Revival (1906–9) in Los Angeles. Reinforcements from the Azusa Street Revival would come and go in Springfield over the years that followed, increasing the number of believers who eventually would be counted among AG adherents. Sizelove would return to Springfield in 1913 to preach and rekindle the faith of this small band of followers. By this time the little church had a young pastor, Bennett Lawrence, who would represent it at the first gathering of the Assemblies of God in Hot Springs, Arkansas, in 1914. Within two years Brother Lawrence would break with the AG to join the schismatic "Jesus only movement," but the church that became Central Assembly of God remained with the General Council and the emerging AG denomination.

Fred Corum, a descendent of Lillie Harper Corum, recounts in *Sparkling Fountain* (Corum and Bakewell, 1983, 249) how "the foundation stones were hewn and laid" for Central Assembly by ordinary folk, with his mother playing a central role:

> We were just laymen, beholding the hand of God as the fountain began to bubble forth. Mother was the first pastor of Central Assembly. We just called it the Pentecostal Church then. Preachers would come through and stay at our home. As we look back, we believe that at times we have entertained angels unaware. God blessed us with the miraculous. Mother couldn't preach. She was only an exhorter. She would get up and say, "Glory to God! Hallelujuh! [*sic*] I'm so glad I'm saved, sanctified, and filled with the Holy Ghost." And then they would have testimonies and sing and sing.

By the time Poloma first encountered Central Assembly of God in the 1980s, the congregation had grown into an unofficial flagship for the denomination. In terms of the typology we are presenting, Central Assembly of a generation ago would have fit what we are labeling "traditional Pentecostal," higher than average on AG identity and on expressions of the supernatural, especially speaking in tongues or glossolalia. There were signs, however, both in this congregation and in the larger denomination, that the "routinization of charisma," in which charisma succumbs to institutional forces, was gaining ground in the last half of the twentieth century. The early "charismatic moment" in which the Pentecost came to Springfield is now part of history, and doctrine, set rituals, and institutional programs threaten to eclipse the felt movement of the Spirit. On Poloma's visits to Springfield in the 1980s to gather data for *Crossroads*, she observed that Central was the church home of many of the denominational leaders. Although culturally Pentecostal, the church seemed stalled in once meaningful rituals of an earlier era and lacked the effervescence of many emerging neo-pentecostal groups. When she revisited the congregation two decades later for the present study, there were ample signs of cultural adaptations that made the church more appealing and more culturally relevant to a new generation of young members, with outreach programs that served to attract the churched and unchurched alike. It has adapted further to the larger Springfield culture with its extensive outreach to the community in benevolent ministries, a move that has come to be known as "progressive Pentecostalism" (see Miller and Yamamori 2007).

The Sunday that Poloma arrived at Central to conduct our survey was "Small Group Celebration Sunday." The church lobby was lined with several dozen booths reflecting the diversity of the congregation's groups, from those focusing on hobbies or sports to more traditional Bible study. As promised in the epigraph, greeters were there to welcome and direct new visitors. At the time Pastor Bradford had reported that approximately half of regular attendees were also church members, a figure that reflects the relaxed attitude that the AG has toward formally joining a congregation. Our survey figures support Bradford's report, with 66 percent of the congregation indicating that they had become members, while 32 percent were regular attendees but not members. The overwhelming majority of the congregational survey respondents (96 percent) were non-Hispanic whites, 2 percent were Asian, and 2 percent Hispanic. It is worth noting that Central is but one of approximately fifty AG churches within a twenty-mile radius, with some thirty inside Springfield proper. Since Bradford had arrived as pastor in late 2003, the congregation had reportedly increased in size by more than 50 percent.

Although a generation ago Central Assembly would clearly have been considered a traditional AG congregation, high on both Pentecostal experiences and Pentecostal identity, our evidence suggests that the congregation has slowly been shifting toward the type we are calling "evangelical AG." According to results from the congregational survey, Central remains higher than average with regard to the importance placed on Pentecostal identity, but slightly lower than average on distinctly Pentecostal experiences. A slight majority (52 percent) of the respondents indicated that it was extremely important to them that their church had a strong Pentecostal identity, but only 24 percent reported that it was extremely important for them "to walk in the supernatural." Although a clear majority of the respondents reported praying in tongues at least on occasion (89 percent), only 37 percent were regular users of glossolalia who prayed in tongues "most days" or more.

Bradford is personally committed to the ministry of the Holy Spirit that has been a distinctive feature of the AG. In a recent online interview with Dr. George Wood, General Superintendent of the AG, on the occasion of the announcement of Bradford's appointment as General Secretary for the denomination, Bradford shared his sense of divine calling into ministry and his experience of divine guidance throughout the major changes in his ministerial career. When asked about the focus on the "person and ministry of the Holy Spirit," Bradford (who holds a Ph.D. in aerospace engineering, but no bible college or seminary degrees) noted how he may be even more dependent on the Spirit than some because he has "not had the training in ministry that others have been privileged of doing. That made me a little extra desperate—for whatever progress I have had in ministry, I have had to lean on the Holy Spirit." Bradford elaborated about the Holy Spirit:

> He is not old fashioned—the Holy Spirit is not archaic. I don't think that we need to relate the Holy Spirit to stylistic subcultures of 40 or 50 years ago because the culture is different, but yet the tangible evidential power is not—and we need to keep giving place to this in new wineskins.[1]

As we will see, these "new wineskins," as mirrored in the congregational diversity found in our sample of churches, come in various sizes and shapes, colored by ethnicity and region, sometimes with unusual missions, and most importantly, with significant differences in what it means to be Pentecostal. All evangelical Christians would profess the Holy Spirit to be the third person of a triune Godhead, but they differ from pentecostals in the degree to which affect plays a role in this doctrinal confession. While evangelicals and pentecostals are united in their cognitive profession of an unwavering belief in the Holy Spirit, historically Pentecostals have been more likely to expect affective or primal experiences to accompany the work of the Spirit. Contemporary AG congregations represented by the four-fold typology differ widely in their openness to overt emotional responses and somatic manifestations commonly found in the "stylistic subcultures" of a half century ago.

Overview and Typology of AG Congregations

When *Crossroads* was published in 1989, it was accurate to describe the Assemblies of God as a largely white, working-class denomination with most of its churches having fewer than one hundred members. By 2006, the Assemblies of God, USA, numbered 12,311 American congregations, including more than one hundred megachurches scattered around the country, and numerous suburban churches with memberships of several hundred members, as well as small urban and rural congregations representing a wide array of ethnic groups and social classes.[2] The average size of an AG congregation as reported in 2006 was 132 members (230 when including regular adherents who are non-members). Yet there are scores of congregations—including Central Assembly—with a thousand or more adherents, the largest of which is Phoenix First Assembly of God in Arizona, with an average Sunday attendance of 9,500.

Perhaps even more important than the increase in size of the AG denomination and its congregations are changes in its ethnic and racial composition. In 2006 less than 70 percent of AG churches were predominantly white congregations; increasingly, AG congregations, especially large ones, are multicultural. Ethnic congregations are also on the rise, with AG churches that identify as Hispanic (18 percent), Asian or Pacific Islander (3.8 percent), African American (2.5 percent), Native American (1.5 percent), or "other" (4.7 percent). Although for decades African American Pentecostals were excluded from the AG and encouraged to join its "sister church," the Church of God in Christ (COGIC), efforts are now made to woo persons of color into the denomination (Rodgers 2008). At the fifty-second General Council in 2007, Zollie L. Smith, Jr., was elected to serve as Executive Director of Assemblies of God U.S. Missions, becoming the first African American member of the six-man Executive Presbytery.

Ethnic churches, on the other hand, could always be found within the AG, though until recently they had a low profile in the denomination.[3] The fifty-first General Council, held in Denver, Colorado, in 2005, seemed to mark a watershed in this regard. Of the event that celebrated the cultural diversity found in the AG, John W. Kennedy (2005, 6) wrote:

> The Assemblies of God provided an unprecedented high-profile forum for diversity last month at its biennial General Council, featuring various ethnic and foreign language leaders at a U.S. Missions Intercultural Ministries luncheon followed by a two-and-a-half-hour service at the Colorado Convention Center. The August 5 activities provided a significant and joyous unification of culturally and linguistically distinct elements within the Fellowship that never had gathered in one spot before. General Superintendent Thomas E. Trask said ethnic minorities are a unique contribution to the Fellowship that will enable the Assemblies of God to reach the entire nation with the gospel.

Although it has long been noted that without the steady growth of its ethnic churches the AG would be declining in membership, until the past decade or so the majority Anglo constituency seemed oblivious to their presence (see Tinlin and Blumhofer 1991).

As significant as increasing church size and ethnic/racial diversification are, other changes are afoot that may be even more telling about the Assemblies of God in the twenty-first century. These markers suggest ongoing erosion of the decidedly Pentecostal identity that has characterized the AG since its inception in 1914. Political scientist Eric Patterson, for example, has noted a decline in the emphasis on Spirit baptism and its attendant charismata (the paranormal "gifts of the Holy Spirit") in AG congregations.[4] According to Patterson (2007, 207), "It is simply impossible to be Pentecostal without the charismata, and yet classical Pentecostal denominations seem to have handed off their gift to the younger movements such as the Vineyard and non-denominational charismatic churches." Patterson's observation resonates with our own findings, but a review of the 2006 statistics suggests an important modifier.

While English-speaking congregations in the United States may be experiencing a dilution of Pentecostal identity, this may not be the case for most Latino congregations (and probably not for many other non–English-language churches either). In reporting on the number of Spirit baptisms by English-language and non–English-language districts, for example, most categories show a clear decline between 2005 and 2006. Overall the Great Lakes region reported a *decrease* of 43 percent; the Gulf Region of 29 percent; and the Northwest of 16 percent. However, the non–English-language districts reported an 80.5 percent *increase* in Spirit baptisms, with the Spanish-language district reporting a 100 percent increase. The Southwest Region (which also includes many Hispanic congregations) showed a sizable increase of 37 percent.

Reflecting Patterson's concern about the general decline in a distinct Pentecostal identity, our four-fold typology of AG congregations is created from two variables found in our congregational survey—one measuring the importance of "Pentecostal identity," and another, the importance of "walking in the supernatural." Thirty-seven percent of the total sample responded that "a strong Pentecostal identity" was extremely important, with individual congregational scores on this response ranging from 12 percent to 64 percent. Twenty-seven percent of the respondents "strongly agreed" that "walking in the supernatural" was "very important," with particular congregational scores ranging from 10 percent to 66 percent. Those we labeled "traditional" churches scored above the mean or average on both Pentecostal identity and the supernatural; those (including Central Assembly of God) that were above the mean on Pentecostal identity but below it on the supernatural we termed "evangelical AG" churches; churches high on the supernatural experiences but low on Pentecostal identity we called "renewalist" or "charismatic" churches; and finally, those congregations low on both dimensions we categorized as "alternative" churches, an innovative category that includes "seeker-sensitive" and "emerging" churches. The labels "traditional," "evangelical AG," "renewalist," and "alternative" reflect the differences that any observant visitor would soon note in visiting AG churches around the country. A caveat is in order: significant variance exists within each of these ideal typical categories, with some churches being more (or less) "traditional," "evangelical," "renewalist," or "alternative" than others. This is especially important to keep in mind as we provide profiles of select congregations. It is also important to remember, as we have already seen with Central Assembly, that congregations are not static; they can and do shift from one cell in the typology to another.

Traditional English-Language Churches

Traditionalists are not only proud to be part of the Assemblies of God, with church signs and symbols openly proclaiming this affiliation (including Websites that contain information about the AG), they also allow room for distinctly Pentecostal exuberance, teaching, and experience within their rituals. These rituals have a unique acoustical feel, with occasional messages in tongues (glossolalia) followed by a prophetic interpretation; persistent altar calls (often with "tarrying" or waiting expectantly in God's presence); loud, fervent prayer for special needs; shouts of praise that can be heard from the parking lot; and opportunities for testimonies that model experiences and expectations. The services of traditional congregations often are less bound by time constraints—particularly the Sunday or Wednesday evening services, which increasingly have been abandoned by other types of congregations. In traditional ethnic churches the sense of community is strong, and it is not unusual for many members to spend all of Sunday together in prayer, including Sunday morning and evening services, Sunday school, and fellowship.

Traditional congregations are the most likely of the four types of AG churches to uphold many of the moral taboos brought into early Pentecostalism from the Wesleyan Holiness movement that sought to revive Methodism after the Civil War. They are least likely to approve of the use of alcohol or tobacco under any circumstances, or to approve of gambling (even the lottery), social dancing, or even (for some older Pentecostals) going to movies. Their adherents are more likely not only to be glossolalic but also to profess that "speaking in tongues" is the "initial physical evidence of Spirit baptism," a core doctrine of the AG. It is significant that all of the Latino and other ethnic churches (one Ghanaian and one Caribbean) included in our survey registered higher than Anglo churches on valuing a strong Pentecostal identity, with congregants who also reported high scores on "walking in the supernatural." We present below a profile of First Assembly of God in Akron, Ohio, to illustrate one variant of a traditional congregation.

Akron First Assembly of God (Akron, Ohio)

Like Central Assembly in Springfield, Missouri, First Assembly in Akron, Ohio, has roots that can be traced to the beginning of the denomination. The congregation now known as First Assembly of God (Akron) was founded in the 1890s by Christian Missionary Alliance pastor C. M. McKinney. McKinney became a charter member of the AG, and his congregation was incorporated as an AG church in 1917. While research was underway for *Crossroads,* First Assembly was led by Pastor Eugene Meador, a second-generation Pentecostal who came to the congregation in 1970 and served as its pastor for the next thirty-one years. Kent Jarvis, who, like Eugene Meador, was raised in the AG ("fourth generation on one side and third generation on the other"), became its new pastor in 2001.

Given Meador's long tenure, it is probably not surprising that there were a few bumps on the road to transition. There has been a turnover of membership, as a number of older members left ("Many of them moved away," says Jarvis), but younger families have taken their place. Under Pastor Jarvis's leadership, some cultural changes have been made, but the congregation has retained its traditional content—high on both Pentecostal identity and experience. Almost all of the 250 regular attendees are white, mostly lower middle to middle class, and many have been raised in the denomination. A section from the field notes Poloma took on the day she administered the survey to the congregation speaks to Jarvis's openness to the unexpected—even when the scheduled events seemed already set in place for this Sunday service—that fans the flame of pentecostal experiences:

> The service began with music as usual. Approximately 30 persons were in the choir; a guitarist and a drummer were there to supplement the traditional piano, once the only musical instrument used at First AG. It was interesting to note how the choir robes had been abandoned in favor of street clothes—especially after the controversy that the wearing of choir robes had caused a generation ago (they were seen as too liturgical). Music selections could be seen on a large overhead screen, replacing most of the old hymns found in the hymnal with contemporary Christian songs. What did strike me is that while the same songs are used here as in the Vineyard

> and other neo-pentecostal congregations there is a noticeable difference. Most neo-pentecostal and charismatic services that customarily have a half hour or more of worship in song regard "worship" as an uninterrupted flow of music that allows the worshiper a place and space to enter into the divine presence. The AG tradition has customarily used the minister and the music leader to enthusiastically interject his (or her) thoughts to direct the worshipers. This custom is still in place at First Assembly.
>
> At one point worship time was interrupted by a woman in the choir who spoke out in tongues (and provided the interpretation of the message as one of God's love), while another woman (also in the choir) gave another generic prophetic message about God's deep love for the people gathered. Pastor Jarvis arose as a man from the congregation approached him. Jarvis then came up to the platform (he had been sitting in the first row with his wife) and said, "Brother Jim has just received a word that God wants to set people free this Sunday. I am interpreting this promise of 'freedom' very generally—it might be an illness, being depressed, not being able to forgive—anything that is keeping you from being free in Jesus Christ. I believe we must stop to hear this word of God. Keep standing in your place, kneel, come up to the altar—do whatever will help you to receive this word. We have a very full agenda for this morning's service, but we must honor the word that God has spoken to us."
>
> The next half hour (there had been nearly a half hour of worship music already) turned into a revival-type altar service, where people "tarried" in prayer. About 50 congregants went up to the altar for prayer, where they were met by Jarvis, his wife, visiting missionaries, and some elders. Several were slain in the spirit. The rest of the congregation seemed to be worshiping quietly in the pews as the music continued to play without interruption.

It has been our observation that most traditional white AG congregations have not been able to retain the openness to the unexpected during a Sunday morning service that was on display at First Assembly during the morning of Poloma's visit. Many formerly traditional congregations have shifted into the evangelical AG mode in which the charismata diminish in importance. Traditional Anglo congregations tend to be small in size, and they retain traditional AG practices that may be out of sync with a culture that prefers a Sunday service with a predictable program that lasts no more than one and a half hours. While older members may remain in these small, traditional churches, their families may have moved on to more culturally adapted congregations that, advertently or inadvertently, have pushed the charismata off of the center stage in Sunday services. Where traditional churches seem to predominate is among ethnic minorities, especially Hispanic congregations, which have experienced a 31 percent increase in the past dozen years or so and which represent two-thirds of overall growth in the denomination (Kennedy 2005, 7).

Traditional Non-English-Language Congregations

Hispanic Congregations

While many traditional Anglo churches of a generation ago have shifted into other congregational types, ethnic churches in our sample appear to have retained more traditional Pentecostal rituals and practices, albeit ones that have been adapted to specific ethnicities. Six Hispanic congregations were included in our sample. Although these six churches—all located in Southern California, with some belonging to the Southern California District and others to the Southern Pacific Latin American District (SPLAD)—can hardly be considered representative of all Latino/Hispanic AG congregations, it is striking that all of them are traditional. The scores of all six congregations showed that congregants tended to be high on Pentecostal identity and Pentecostal experience. These congregations differed in country of origin, in whether they used only Spanish or were bilingual, in dress norms, and in worship rituals, yet they were united in their Pentecostalism.[5]

Roca Firme, a Mexican American congregation belonging to the Southern California District, averages around seventy-five people at a Sunday service. Church services are generally formal, noted Fernando Tamara, our research collaborator for the Hispanic part of the study, who is also an AG pastor. "They are very formal—so formal that everybody gets in their best outfit (the best shirt and pants) to go to church." Tamara continues:

> We feel that we have to bring the best to God. To do otherwise is an offense to God. We were perplexed when a white pastor (who owns the building where we worship) would come to preach in a t-shirt. My church members would come to me and say, "Pastor, you have got to go and exhort this pastor. He has to wear a tie. Doesn't he understand that we always give our best to God—shoes shined, everything needs to be clean." In some families, the women are expected to come to church in dresses—not skirts but dresses. Women may wear pants, but there is the belief that women who wear pants are provoking men's lust and they are stigmatized. If a woman wears pants, she is categorized as an immature person or someone who doesn't know the Bible.

Even as Tamara generalizes about Hispanic congregations, he is careful to emphasize that "every church is different."

Pastor Tamara's own congregants are from Mexico, Guatemala, and Peru. As with many other Hispanic congregations, he blends English and Spanish in prayer and worship. The music choice is usually a jazz, soft rock, or basic rock sound, and Tamara sometimes translates English songs into Spanish. Although he conducts regular altar calls, he does not call people to come to the altar and "repent." He prefers to use language like "come and be humble" that encourages congregants to respond to the message he has preached during the service, rather than limiting this ritual to soul-saving. Tamara gave the example of a sermon he recently delivered on Jesus's temptation in the desert, which led to the question "How many times have we resisted the Spirit?" and then urged people to "come and be humble" as they approach the altar in response.

Tamara says he tries to resist the lure to shorten church services at the expense of traditional rituals such as testimonies, individual prayer with congregants, and altar calls. He laments what he sees as the Hispanic trend to "imitate the Anglo churches in this way" (with shorter Sunday services). "These pastors say you can do your testimonies at a prayer vigil, a small group, in your home," explains Tamara, "but not on Sunday mornings. They say it takes too much time." At the same time Tamara knows that life is tough in California: "For an immigrant to live, he is going to have to have two jobs just to pay his bills. So they are looking for a church that preaches the Word—but "don't extend the program, pastor—because if you do, I am going to have to find another church." He is saddened by the fact that "everyone wants to purchase a house," but they are unwilling to come to church as they once did as "they fasted for and prayed for days." Tamara, himself an immigrant from Peru, describes the changes that he has witnessed in Hispanic AG churches as follows:

> When I got here in 1993, I remember visiting so many churches, and they were all incorporating testimonies and altar calls, but now—I don't want to say that the Hispanic church has assimilated to the Anglo church, but in most churches they are very concerned with time. I ask them, "Why are you limiting your services and the power of the Spirit?" And they say, "People don't like to stay in the church; they are looking for churches that are very precise in their sermons, and that's that. If all happens in an hour or an hour and a half, that's fine."

Perhaps this trend away from the free flow of old traditional churches, where congregants were willing to "tarry" for the divine presence, is inevitable for Hispanics as it seems to have become for Anglo congregations. Our survey responses suggest that this transition is not yet a fait accompli, however, as Latino AG congregations still appear to lean toward traditional norms and rituals. As Arlene Sánchez-Walsh and Eric Dean Patterson (2007, 79) remind us, "Latino Pentecostalism has been the nexus of Pentecostal spiritual experience and Latino ethnic and community identity. . . . There is no single Latino community nor is there a single Pentecostal identity." Given the important role that Hispanics are playing in the growth of the AG, they are of crucial importance to the denomination's future.

Jesus Power Assembly of God (Columbus, Ohio)

Jesus Power is a newly established African immigrant congregation with a story that is alive with the types of extraordinary happenings and serendipitous events that are the hallmark of Pentecostalism's early history. Unlike many AG church Websites, which minimize distinctly Pentecostal qualities, Jesus Power's boldly proclaims its AG affiliation together with the "nonnegotiable tenets of faith that all Assemblies of God churches adhere to" as found in the Statement of Fundamental Truths (www.ghanalounge.com/jesus-power; accessed on February 28, 2009). Its vision is bold and simply stated: "To be a community of Spirit-filled (anointed) witnesses taking nations for Christ, preaching the Good News, comforting the broken-hearted and setting captives free." It is not unusual for congregants to arrive early on Sunday morning to offer prayers for the service, to attend Sunday school, followed by participation in a worship service that often lasts three hours (or more), and then return that evening for more prayer and worship. The congregation also hosts regular extended revivals where congregants "tarry" in prayer to renew their Pentecostal fervor. Like the other ethnic congregations in our sample, Jesus Power is high on both Pentecostal identity and experiences.

In 1986, when Pastor Bismark Osei Akomeah worked as a tailor and served as an active member of Emmanuel Assemblies of God Church in Ghana, God "called" him into ministry as an evangelist and a church planter. In 1999 God again spoke to Akomeah, this time to move his family to the United States. In a story reminiscent of early U.S. Pentecostal ministers, this was a reverse mission journey, from Africa to the United States. In 2001, after living in Houston for two years, God spoke another word of direction—this time a call to Columbus, Ohio (a city that Akomeah did not know existed), to plant a church that would reach the African community there. He and his family arrived in Columbus on June 15, 2001, and two days later they started a church in the basement of their apartment building. In September of that year, thirty new people joined them in their new temporary house of worship; on December 17, the fledgling church was "inaugurated" into the Assemblies of God. By its first-year anniversary $75,000 had been raised, allowing them to acquire property—valued at $600,000—with a building to hold church services and outreach for the immigrant community.

Jesus Power has approximately 700 members and is growing. In an interview, Pastor Bismark said that he has been asked to speak at conferences where ministers want to know about his plan for church planting. His response: "I don't have a plan; God has the plan. You have to pray. Too many pastors don't spend enough time in prayer." Since its founding, Jesus Power Assembly has planted five churches, including Swahili and French congregations in Columbus and African congregations in Cincinnati and Atlanta. In 2005 the Ohio District Council of Assemblies of God Church ordained Pastor Bismark Osei Akomeah as a minister in the denomination.

Evangelical AG Congregations

Evangelical AG congregations are less overtly Pentecostal than traditional congregations. Despite the occasional AG sign out front, the basic Pentecostal format of the service, and a list of the sixteen AG doctrinal statements on the church Website, the paucity of pentecostal experiences during the Sunday morning service may leave an astute visitor wondering whether the church is in fact Pentecostal. On more than one occasion while visiting different evangelical AG churches, Poloma would find herself talking with an adherent who didn't know the church was Assemblies of God—or what it meant to be Pentecostal. With religious services that are subdued, programmed, and focused on a sermon, the gatherings seem more like generic evangelical services than those in a traditional Assembly of God congregation, with their customary exuberant prayer and worship. Like many other Protestant churches, evangelical AG churches are increasingly likely to include contemporary music and to use audio-visuals instead of a hymnbook in their services. Sermons tend to be timely lessons rather than the "old-fashioned" cadenced preaching on biblical themes that once characterized Pentecostalism. While traditional churches tend to retain the Sunday night revival service with personal testimonies and other pentecostal practices, many (if not most) evangelical churches have canceled Sunday night services. Although we have only soft indicators rather than hard data to support this observation, it seems that if there is a "typical" Anglo AG congregation, it is of the evangelical strain.

We began this chapter with a congregational sketch of Springfield's Central Assembly as a prototype of this category. Central, however, differs from most evangelical AG congregations in very significant ways, including its size, location, and relationship to the AG judicatory. We have selected one other evangelical congregation that is closer in size to the average AG church of 230 members. While such churches go largely unnoticed by the local media and the denomination itself, their ongoing support and open identification with Pentecostalism makes them a significant force for the future of the AG. Representing this category is Celebration Church of Akron, Ohio, a congregation that at one time would have been classified as traditional AG, but like Central Assembly has been impacted by the seemingly irresistible cultural pull toward evangelical Christianity. Although there are differences among evangelical AG congregations, they seem bound together by a hybridization process that leaves many of them nearly indistinguishable in practice and belief from non-Pentecostal evangelical congregations that focus on biblical orthodoxy and moral conservatism.

Celebration Church (Akron, Ohio)

Known until recently as Evangel Temple, Celebration Church was founded by Dr. Richard D. Dobbins, who served as its pastor for twenty years. He stepped aside in order to devote all of his efforts to the development of Emerge Ministries, a Christian counseling practice he began while still serving as pastor. During a time when Pentecostals eschewed both education and psychological counseling, Dobbins pioneered a radical change in the AG by earning a Ph.D. in clinical psychology while serving as an AG pastor and by promoting counseling as well as prayer for mental health and healing. In light of Dobbins's work and his eventual recognition by the larger denomination, it is not surprising that Evangel Temple was commonly perceived at the time of the *Crossroads* research as a congregation for the denomination's more progressive thinkers on a path away from traditional Pentecostalism. The composition of the congregation continued to change in the years that followed, reflecting changes in the surrounding community. The recent name change to the more contemporary Celebration Church occurred under the present senior pastor, Jeff Wade. Wade, the son of an AG pastor and a graduate of an AG college, became senior pastor in 2003. His wife, Lois, also an ordained AG minister and the daughter of an AG minister, serves as

Christian Education Director for the church.[6] Celebration Church's affiliation with the AG continues to be readily recognizable from links to other AG sites on its homepage, and from its listing of the "16 Fundamental Truths" on its Website (www.ccakron.org; accessed on March 7, 2010). Its comparatively strong ties to the AG were confirmed by the 44 percent of respondents who agreed that having a "strong Pentecostal identity" was extremely important to them, while its reserve about extensive use of the charismata is reflected by the only 10 percent who reported that it was extremely important for them to "walk in the supernatural." Unlike AG churches of a generation ago, Celebration Church joins the increasing number of congregations that reach out to the larger community. Celebration Church is involved in its struggling local neighborhood in ways that go beyond typical church ministries supported by AG congregations. Outreach programs include partnership with a local public high school, particularly with the school's fine arts program, and a ministry to help families in the larger community who are in need.

Renewalist (Charismatic) Congregations

Renewalist AG churches are not nearly as prevalent as evangelical and traditional congregations, but they do sprinkle the AG landscape. Just as traditional churches are prone to shift into the evangelical AG category of our four-fold typology, renewalist or revival churches seem to slide easily into the non-charismatic "alternative" category—or to leave the denomination for one of the neo-pentecostal networks, where they find others who are pushing the charismatic envelope toward more of the supernatural.[7]

Renewalist (revival/charismatic) congregations are less interested in Pentecostal identity than they are in pentecostal experience and empowerment. They offer effervescent worship and prayer, and often bring in non-AG revivalists to conduct conferences or visit revival sites to keep the fire burning. Although they share with evangelical AG congregations much of the same contemporary Christian music with loud percussion instruments (rather than the more traditional hymnbook and a piano), they are less likely to have soloists or a featured "worship leader." The worship director/minister is more likely to have been trained with an ear for the emergence of a liminal state of consciousness within the worship gathering and to work with it rather than to direct it. Dress is casual and the ambiance of the worship site is familiar. The goal is for the congregation to enter together into the felt presence of God. A newcomer might be likely to be welcomed with coffee and donuts complemented by a greeter passing out bulletins. Meetings can be held in an old warehouse, an abandoned theater, or a church structure, but usually with no sign of AG affiliation either inside or outside the building.

The charismata, should any develop, are permitted to flow during congregational worship, rather than being relegated to private use or limited to home fellowships. Prophecies are spoken colloquially, as personal words from God that affirm divine love for those gathered and the felt divine presence, rather than through a dramatic utterance in tongues (glossolalia) followed by a fervent "interpretation." Prayers for healing and special needs may be offered after the service by lay church women and men serving on prayer teams, rather than being limited to the pastor and male elders. Testimonies of divine activity are welcome during the service. Occasionally, revival conferences are sponsored in larger congregations or members seek parachurch meetings outside the congregation for spiritual revitalization. Physical manifestations, including falling down under the power of the Spirit, shaking and jerking, laughing and weeping, can be found in greater or lesser degrees, especially in special revival services. Worship focuses on experiencing the felt presence of God—a divine presence that is thought to empower believers through the charismata of "signs and wonders" to evangelize and to bless a larger world.

Three congregations from our sample originally fell into the renewalist category, all of them low on Pentecostal identification but high on supernatural experience. At the time of this writing, only one clearly remains in this category. The Father's House, a church planted in the mid-1990s by Pastor Mike Guarnieri in a working-class community outside of Akron, Ohio, is the best example of a renewal or charismatic church in our sample.

The Father's House (Norton, Ohio)

Pastor Mike Guarnieri describes his congregation on his MySpace blog as follows: "We are a church that values the presence of God and are in continual pursuit of revival and renewal. We desire to win the lost, disciple new converts, train leaders and release five-fold ministers to gather the harvest; all in an atmosphere of the Father's love" (www.myspace.com/thefathershouseohio; accessed March 7, 2010). Guarnieri was raised a nominal Catholic ("we went to church once a year—maybe") but was "led to the Lord" by a disciple of Watchman Nee, a controversial but influential native Chinese preacher of the 1920s, in an independent church at the age of fifteen. He pastored two other independent churches before planting The Father's House in 1996 and joining the AG in 1998. Guarnieri explained in a personal interview:

> I had been an independent pastor for so many years that I was looking for connection. I had seen how quickly good things in an independent church can get corrupted. At that point in my life I told our church leaders, "You want to be part of something bigger, with a longer history, that is established, yet that allows us to be ourselves."

Guarnieri has been satisfied with his affiliation with the AG, as he reports: "Not once has anyone told me that they don't like what I am doing—that I should be doing something differently. They even asked me to speak at a pastor's meeting on revival." Despite this affirmation, the AG and The Father's House seem to travel different paths that only occasionally cross.

The revival at the Toronto Airport Christian Fellowship (TACF) had begun nearly seven years before Guarnieri's first visit; he was initially put off by some of the reports about the strange manifestations that commonly took place at TACF. It was not until the fall of 2000 that Guarnieri visited this epicenter of this 1990s revival: "Despite years of fruitful ministry," he wrote, "there was a hunger in our hearts for more than 'church as usual.' We wanted to experience MORE of God" (Guarnieri 2008, n.p.). Guarnieri reported how he was "worked over by God" during his first week at TACF and then described what happened upon his return as follows:

> After I repented, He let me up off the floor. I was a new man! We went home from Toronto with a new zeal, waiting to see what God was going to do, and we were not disappointed. . . . [It] was like a mini TACF conference. As we prayed for our church members, the floor became strewn with people, all enraptured by the presence of the living God. All the same reactions that we had seen in Toronto were happening right here in our home church. The most amazing thing to us was that none of our members had ever been to Toronto; so they were not imitating anything they had seen before. They were simply responding to a dramatic increase in His mighty presence. Our church, The Father's House, has been in renewal ever since.

The following field notes by Poloma from January 2008 describe a repeat visit to this unusual congregation, where Guarnieri believes the "river of revival is still flowing":

> As I drove into the parking lot of this once-supermarket on a cold winter morning, I noticed more cars than when I last visited two years ago. Once inside the building I noted simple renovations that had been made,

including to the worship area, with a simple platform at the front, racks of clothes lining one wall and bags of groceries another. Outside the one-room sanctuary, offices and classrooms had been constructed for Sunday school use. I knew from the church Website (http://fathershouseohio.com) that The Father's House had established a "Love Center," but I was struck by how the ministry was blended into the worship area.

The Love Center has a link on the church's site that included a YouTube video and a warm invitation: "Are you troubled by stress, financial worries, loneliness, divorce, bankruptcy and unemployment? Come visit us." Looking around this Sunday morning at the congregation of some one hundred fifty persons gathered for worship, I wondered how many of this working class congregation had suffered hardships listed on the Website. I recalled the invitation on the site, "Come enjoy a hot meal with friends, pick up free groceries for your family and hear a talk addressing life's problems. Come as you are—you'll be loved." The sanctuary, like the Website, had a somewhat different feel. As the service began, there were indications that my preliminary assessment of a turnover of members might be correct.

Pastor Mike Guarnieri led worship as he customarily does, but he stopped the worship music just when the congregation seemed to have entered into a liminal space. His affirmative dialogue with the congregation that followed indicated that many of them were new to charismatic worship: "Did you like what you felt? It was the presence of God. Did you mind going a bit longer in worship this morning? We are going to spend more time in this kind of worship in Sundays to come." Clearly he was teaching the congregation about charismatic worship. The sermon was a simple one—at times I wasn't sure where it was headed (Guarnieri admitted to his congregation that he wasn't sure either; he was preaching without notes). He did capture their attention with his use of an orange as a prop to illustrate the Trinity—Jesus is the skin, underneath the skin is the Father, and the juice (which Guarnieri drank during the sermon) was the Holy Spirit. Pastor Mike then asked if anyone wanted to be baptized in the Holy Spirit, noting that the outreach and the ministry of the church was increasing and all of them needed the power of the Spirit to continue this important work. To my surprise (and further indication that the congregation had many newcomers), some 50 people came forward to be baptized in the Spirit. Pastor Mike slowly made his way through the group, praying quietly in tongues, asking some of them whether they had not received the baptism before (most seemingly had not), and encouraging them as they began to speak haltingly in their new "prayer language." Standing at the back of the room I could hear a small chorus of tongues erupt, then the sound of laughter; I could see some dancing and others fall to the floor under the power of the Spirit.

Although I have seen many calls for Spirit baptism over the years, most have involved the response of fewer people, more "tarrying," more coaching, and fewer external manifestations. Guarnieri moved quietly but surely through the group like a man who sensed he had an inner strength and power. The focus was not on being baptized in the Spirit "with physical evidence of speaking in tongues," as AG doctrine states, but rather on the importance of Spirit empowerment for the ministry already underway at the church.[8] As links on the church Website suggest, the congregation and its pastor seem to have only weak ties with the AG and stronger ties with neo-pentecostal revivalist and prophetic ministries outside the denomination.

Given the apparent turnover of members since the congregational survey, it remains unclear whether 25 percent of the present congregation would still say that a very strong Pentecostal identity is important to them, or that 60 percent would claim that it is extremely important for them to "walk in the supernatural." What does seem certain is that under the leadership of Pastor Mike Guarnieri the church remains one where his walk in the supernatural matches his talk about the importance of revival: "I believe that when a local church responds properly to revival, it will cause the local church to survive and thrive. I am now starting my 30th year in full-time ministry. I am more passionate than ever and more excited to see the River flow wherever I go" (Guarnieri 2008, n.p.).

Alternative Congregations

Alternative AG churches tend to eschew labels, but many can be subsumed under nomenclature known to scholars of contemporary Christianity, including "seeker sensitive" (c.f. Sargeant 2000) and "emergent" churches (c.f. Gibbs and Bolger 2005), that reflect postmodernism's strong resistance to labels and old ways of "doing church." These churches commonly remain under the evangelical umbrella, but they typically develop a wide variety of policies and practices to meet the expressed needs of the unchurched. They often gather in non-church locations (coffee shops, old movie theaters, or homes), deliberately downplay their AG affiliation, avoid the display of common Christian symbols, and are more likely to post "common values" than creedal statements on their Websites. Earl Creps (2007), an AG minister and scholar of postmodern Christianity, has explored the emerging subcultures of young Pentecostal leaders, some of whom will eventually be in positions of leadership within the denomination.[9] In researching how these young leaders understand their Pentecostal identity, he identified "three voices": "loyalist," "post-distinctive," and "post-modern." The loyalist young leaders align with what we have called "AG evangelicals"; they have searched and weighed the issues and have decided in favor of a path more closely aligned with evangelical doctrine than with experiences of the charismata. The post-distinctive AG leaders, on the other hand, recognize the dangers posed by the ongoing evangelicalization of Pentecostalism and "the 'routinization of the charismata,' the tendency to reduce spontaneous religious experience to a predictable template that is more easily controlled" (Creps 2007, 33). With their emphasis on religious experience, these young post-distinctive leaders may eventually pastor either traditional or renewalist congregations (depending on the strength of their affiliation with the AG judicatory), where experiencing the charismata is normative. The post-denominational group shares some traits with the other two groups, but differs in its rejection of "the idea of being formally affiliated with a judicatory structure" (p. 36), and is most likely to be "emigrating to a non-denominational status" (p. 37). It is this last group that most resembles what we have labeled "alternative congregations." We have chosen to profile Newport Mesa Church of Costa Mesa, California, as an example of an alternative church that scores low on both Pentecostal identity and charismatic experience.

Newport Mesa Church (Costa Mesa, California)

As the band plays secular-sounding music, worshipers may sit quietly around tables with soft drinks and coffee. The announcements are playful, making use of the latest audio-visual equipment and witty exchange between the pastor and the congregation. As in other non-traditional congregations, sermons tend to be taught, not "preached," on topics of general life interests and concerns. Videos, multimedia presentations, and, on occasion, skits and drama are used to complement the minister's spoken word. Although Newport Mesa Church (NMC) fits descriptions of what are commonly known as "seeker churches," NMC prefers the term "journey-oriented church" to describe its loosely affiliated, purpose-driven congregation with innovative new rituals. Whether "seeker" or "journey-oriented," NMC represents what religion scholar Donald Miller (1997) has called "new paradigm churches," congregations that are "reconstructing the organizational character of institutional religion."

Members of seeker churches, like their pastors, are unlikely to report that a Pentecostal identity is very important to them. NMC congregants who responded to the survey were less than a third as likely as the average AG survey respondent to say that a strong Pentecostal identity was extremely important (11 percent of NMC, as compared with 37 percent of all respondents). Nor are they likely to say that experiences of the "supernatural" (e.g., glossolalia, healing, and prophecy) are central to their spirituality (11 percent of NMC, as compared with 27 percent of the total sample). Instead of patterning itself after old models that seem culturally obsolete to many, seeker churches utilize appropriate arts and technology to create a relaxed and welcoming atmosphere to draw in the unchurched. Although a somewhat more formal and subdued early Sunday service may be available for congregants, the pastor's relaxed style and innovative spirit typically keeps even this gathering from reverting to a fixed format.

Newport Mesa Church, once a flagship for AG churches in Southern California, has increasingly distanced itself from both the denomination and distinctly pentecostal practices. Its Website (www.newportmesa.org; accessed on March 5, 2009) promises, "If you've ever been bored with 'church music,' we don't think you'll run into that here," and informs prospective visitors that NMC provides regular biblical messages "surrounded by special music, dance, drama, and creative video capturing our attention and communicating the same concepts in a new format." Pastor Scott Rachels, who had never served as a minister in an AG church before coming to NMC, has transformed this successful AG evangelical church to a seeker church with 1,500 members. Rachels shared at length why he became disappointed in the AG church of his childhood, particularly what he perceived (and he emphasized repeatedly that this was just his perception) to be its elitist attitude: "It was as if we were saying, 'we have something you don't.' Although unspoken, there was a distinct awareness of us (Pentecostals) versus them (evangelicals)." Rachels continued, "I grew up in the Assemblies thinking it was an island unto itself who had a God unto itself." While still in college he got a job with one of Southern California's megachurches, followed by a position in a Baptist church in the Bay Area, before returning to another megachurch in Southern California, where "a postmodern minority" asked him to serve as the congregation's youth pastor. It was somewhat of a surprise to him when he was invited to pastor NMC with its rich AG heritage. Rachels believes that both he and the congregation have changed under his pastorate.

He noted repeatedly and passionately his commitment to meet people where they are in their journeys, in contrast to those churches that "tend to cater toward a more established crowd." He has sought to use what he regards as "the language of the people"—a language that reflects the everyday culture—in a church where "the lesbian and the drug addict can come to discover the mercy of Jesus alongside the mature follower of Jesus. All are welcome to our fellowship and invited to enter the kingdom of God."

Differentiations within the Typology: Diversity and Departure

We have sought here to describe the differences among AG congregations based on the importance of Pentecostal identity and openness to the paranormal gifts of the Holy Spirit (charismata). As can be gleaned from the congregational sketches, a good deal of diversity exists within each cell of our four-fold typology. Such diversity is readily evident within the traditional quadrant, not just between the Latino and Anglo congregations but also within the Hispanic AG community. Cultural diversity will undoubtedly be an even more important factor in describing the AG in the future, as ethnic churches and congregants continue to grow in number and in proportion to Anglo communities. Furthermore, emergent multi-ethnic congregations potentially present additional nuances to the typology that are not yet evident.

What we have highlighted in this typology is the departure from the norm of high Pentecostal identification coupled with unique pentecostal religious experiences that once characterized the AG. Traditional congregations come closest to the norm, and they are arguably best represented by ethnic congregations. The other congregational types are all departures from the once commonly found traditional type. It would appear, based on statistics and interpretations from the pastoral and congregational surveys, that evangelical AG congregations are most in line with the direction in which the AG is moving, at least in the case of Anglo congregations and perhaps multi-ethnic ones. Renewalist congregations are possibly the most readily destabilized within the AG. As we will see, there is little evidence that AG pastors (or many of their congregants) are interested in cooperation with charismatic or neo-pentecostal churches and ministries, yet these are the very places where renewal and revival is actively pursued and modeled. Renewalist congregations tend either to leave the AG to align with neo-pentecostalism or to slide into the evangelical AG or alternative quadrant of the typology. Alternative congregations, as we have seen, represent the greatest departure from the once taken-for-granted norm of a high degree of Pentecostal identity coupled with the lived experience of walking in the supernatural.

Yet another source of diversity appears to have developed within the last generation that transcends the four cells of this typology; namely, a greater concern for social outreach into the community. We have mentioned some examples of this shift, which has been called "progressive Pentecostalism," in the congregational sketches, and it can be found to some degree in all of the congregational types. Donald E. Miller and Tetsunao Yamamori (2007, 3–4) describe progressive Pentecostalism as follows:

> Viewed positively, we define Progressive Pentecostals as Christians who claim to be inspired by the Holy Spirit and the life of Jesus and seek to holistically address the spiritual, physical, and social needs of people in their community. Typically they are distinguished by their warm and expressive worship, their focus on lay-oriented ministry, their compassionate service to others, and their attention, both as individuals and as a worshiping community, to what they perceive to be the leading of the Holy Spirit.

The term "progressive Pentecostal" might have been an oxymoron only a generation ago, but more churches are working at becoming an integral part of their communities with ministries of benevolence that go beyond the church walls. While a separatist and isolationist approach to Pentecostalism was once common, we have noted a decided shift toward social engagement throughout the churches included in our study.[10] Our last profile provides an illustration of a highly unusual "progressive" congregation, one that is truly a "church of" the poor and homeless rather than one that simply "ministers to" the needy.

Rescue Atlanta: Loving Like Jesus

In terms of our typology, Rescue Atlanta is clearly in the traditional quadrant, with high scores on Pentecostal identity (regarded by 37 percent of members as extremely important) and walking in the supernatural (regarded by 34 percent as extremely important). Beyond that, some of our typical descriptors begin to fade. Rescue Atlanta is located in one of Atlanta's most troubled inner-city neighborhoods. Many of its regular 400 congregants are picked up from public parks by one of the pastors or volunteers who drive the church buses each Sunday. Once they arrive at the church, these poor and often homeless members are greeted with a hot, nutritious breakfast and the opportunity to shower and wash their clothes. Seventy percent of the church family consists of homeless men and women, and another 25 percent are from troubled inner-city neighborhoods. The other 5 percent include the paid and volunteer staff members who serve in Rescue Atlanta's outreach.

Like many of our profiled churches, Rescue Atlanta has a complex history—with many twists and turns, full of supernatural interventions and sound strategy, and co-workers who share the vision of lead Pastor Mel Rolls and co-pastor Teresa Rolls—that cannot be captured adequately in a short sketch. As noted on the congregation's Website (www.rescueatlanta.com; accessed on March 11, 2009), whether in church or on the streets, "it is a common thing for the Holy Spirit to draw someone to us in need of salvation, healing and deliverance. These are powerful times of ministry!" Ministry is provided not only by the pastors and paid staff, but also by church adherents who are homeless. In 2005 Rescue Atlanta made national news as the "needy helped the destitute" with its ongoing work in New Orleans, which included homeless men and women from Atlanta coming to the flood-ravaged city to assist others who had just lost their homes.

The vision for Rescue Atlanta was born out of the youth work that Pastors Mel and Teresa did in Florida in 1982, a time during which "God began to give us a passion for evangelism . . . [and] began to speak to us about going to the inner city." During an interview, Pastor Mel shared the success he enjoyed in the position he relinquished in Florida: "I had hundreds of kids; I had more money than I ever needed; the church loved us; my family was well taken care of." But one day he had a strong sense it was time to leave: "I heard the Lord say, 'What I have called you to do here is over today.' I heard it so strong—I even stopped and said, 'What's over?'" With a sense of divine leading, they left that paid position in 1989 for another in Atlanta—but within six months Rolls was fired. "So I left; but to this day, I know it was God's way of getting me here [to minister to the homeless]—I know it was." Rolls's story continues with account after account of God's ongoing direction and miraculous provision as he began full-time ministry on the streets of Atlanta.

When Rolls first started the church, he had to do it without the Assemblies of God. He reported that when he first went to the leaders of the Georgia District, they said, "We don't have any churches like this. We're going to be your board, and we don't know how to advise you." So Rolls told them that he was starting the church and would send them all the required reports; then they could decide if they wanted to be his "covering and accountability." Only after the district leaders saw that the church was functioning without any help from them was Rescue Atlanta accepted into the denomination.

Evangelism remains the heart of Rescue Atlanta's mission. When Rolls first took to the inner-city streets and parks, it was to evangelize. He was troubled, however, when new converts would return, telling him how they were not welcome in most downtown churches. Rolls said that he then "cried out to God," only to hear God say, "You take care of them,"—and "taking care" seemed to mean more than getting a homeless man "saved." Rescue Atlanta's mission statement reads: "To inspire, motivate, and restore a passion for Christ in the hopeless"—a mission that embraces the goal "to love as Jesus loves."

Summary

Although the Assemblies of God is clearly a leading historic Pentecostal denomination, the profiles suggest that it includes different types of pentecostalisms and a wide diversity of congregations within its permeable boundaries. The profiles presented in this chapter clearly illustrate that there is no single type of AG church. Furthermore, given the relatively small number of congregations in the study, any generalizations about the entire denomination from the profiles should be made tentatively and with caution.

The four-fold typology was developed to illustrate not only the diversity within the denomination but also the ongoing dynamic processes of routinization and revitalization that continue to shape and reshape congregations. The profiles can be regarded as a backdrop against which the rest of the story of the AG plays out.

The survey research on pastors and congregations that serves as the focus of the remaining chapters is grounded in theories that guided the collection of data and the interpretation of the findings. We temporarily remove the spotlight from our empirical findings in the next chapter to present the major theories that shaped our research and provided insights for data interpretation.

2

Charisma and Structure in the Assemblies of God

Theoretical Overview

> America has changed dramatically since [the early twentieth century], and pentecostals have changed with it, but only superficially. At the end of the twentieth century the creative tension—or creative complementarity—between the primitive and the pragmatic persisted as productively as ever. . . . In the late 1990s millions—literally millions—reportedly flocked to the nonstop revival churning at the Brownsville Assembly of God Church in Pensacola, Florida. If one looked in the right places, miracles continued to dance before believers' eyes as frequently and as wondrously as ever. (Wacker 2001, 266–67)

Although most traditional Pentecostals have been wary of new revivals outside the denomination, the AG has been revitalized at least in some degree by them. Tension has always found a home within the AG; in fact, it can be argued that a degree of tension between what we have been calling the primal and the pragmatic—or, to use sociological concepts, between charisma and social structure—has been an important factor in the AG's vitality (Poloma 1989; Poloma and Pendleton 1989). Social scientists have long recognized that tension and conflict can have positive institutional consequences (see Coser 1956; 1967). Tension with an out-group (external conflict), for example, can serve to establish a strong group identity, and pentecostalism's status as a "third force" within Christianity may be indebted to the hostility Pentecostalism experienced as a newly emerging sect during the first half of the twentieth century. Tension within the group (internal conflict) can also have positive repercussions, especially for loose-knit structures such as the Assemblies of God. The potentially positive effects of conflict notwithstanding, however, maintaining a free flow of charisma requires skill not unlike that of a unicycle rider; despite great aptitude, there is always the risk of a fall.

As we have seen, this fear of falling into the abyss of "carnal," unregulated religious experience has commonly led traditional Pentecostalism to quench fresh revival fires in order to protect its emergent structure.[1] Charismatic outpourings seem to find more receptivity in the growing numbers of parachurch networks and independent churches rather than in Pentecostal denominations. These newly formed networks and emerging congregations appear to be more willing to risk embracing fresh experiences. Within the AG, as we saw in the congregational profiles, renewalist (charismatic) churches actively seeking revival are few in number and generally short-lived in that form, tending to shift into one of the other three congregational types we outlined within the AG, or into a revival network outside the denomination. Although renewalist congregations are difficult to maintain, charisma does continue to flow in traditional congregations, the vast majority of which (judging from our research) tend to be ethnic churches. As the congregational profiles illustrate, charismatic experiences are less desired and less frequently experienced in Euro-American congregations than in Hispanic and other non-Anglo churches.

This trend notwithstanding, a tolerance for a moderate amount of tension between charisma and institution is seemingly built into the DNA of pentecostalism, where religious distinctiveness centers on paranormal experiences believed to be generated by Spirit baptism. The inherent tension between what pentecostal historian Grant Wacker (2001) has called primitivism and pragmatism—the paranormal working of the Holy Spirit and the organizational matrix that promotes the Pentecostal mission—is rooted in its earliest history. Throughout this book, we use the tools of social science to explore the dynamics inherent in the dilemmas spawned by the tension between charisma (primitivism) and institution (pragmatism) as found within the AG.

Theoretical Concepts and the Presentation of Empirical Findings

Overview

Just as we have drawn upon a triangulation of data-collecting techniques (surveys, interviews, observation) and of respondents (pastors, congregants, exemplars of Godly Love), so too have we found it necessary to triangulate theoretical frameworks for presenting and interpreting these findings. The first is the Weberian approach to studying charisma and its routinization that was applied to pentecostalism in *Crossroads*. In this book we again employ

Max Weber's work on the routinization of charisma as further developed by sociologist Thomas O'Dea, this time to frame the pastoral data collected on the organizational work of the denomination. While O'Dea's thesis deals with routinization, we have modified it to contribute to our account of revitalization in the AG. We posit that what the brilliant but little-known sociologist Pitirim Sorokin has called "love energy" is driving the revitalization process in a theoretical model of Godly Love. Recognizing that emergent institutional forces tend to stifle charisma, this model suggests that charisma can be revitalized by perceived experiences of divine love, which in turn energize acts of human love. We also employ the work of philosopher Rolf Johnson on the "faces of love" to refine the concept of love and its relationship to the charismatic gifts and Spirit baptism (often called the "baptism of love") that are the hallmarks of pentecostalism. In sum, the theoretical model of Godly Love posits a *dynamic interaction between human responses to perceptions of divine love that affects personal lives, interrelationships with others, and social institutions* (Poloma and Hood 2008). In the case of pentecostalism, Spirit baptism and the charismata ("gifts of grace") are an integral part of the model. To further assess cultural facilitators and impediments to the flow of charisma, we draw on the recent posthumously published work of sociologist Philip Rieff that asserts that charisma has been "taken away" from modernity. Rieff's thesis on the role that interdicts (divinely sanctioned rules) and guilt have historically played in support of charisma is particularly relevant for exploring the relationship between charisma and love. O'Dea posits five institutional dilemmas as a base for assessing the routinization of charisma, while Sorokin, Johnson, and Rieff provide theoretical insights useful in testing the model of Godly Love and describing its potential as a revitalizing force within pentecostalism.

Charisma, Structure, and O'Dea's Dilemmas

Despite the evidence of ongoing religious experiences and intermittent revivals, few observers would question that the charismatic fervor of the early American Pentecostals has been domesticated over the decades. Although charisma is very much part of the Assemblies of God in theory as well as practice, a noteworthy shift has taken place from an emphasis on what might be called "magical charisma" supported by prophetic leaders to priestly or more routinized forms. While some leaders may tout the AG's nearly unchanged list of "16 Fundamental Truths," for example, many of the charismatic experiences associated with them (especially speaking in tongues) have become less common. The very success of the AG and the inevitable development of "routinized charisma" have contributed to the longstanding tension between the primitive and the pragmatic.

The AG has struggled against the same forces that have led other once-charismatic religious institutions down the path of over-institutionalization and over-regulation, forces that have been inimical to charisma. Birthed in the "charismatic moment" of the Azusa Street Revival and periodically tasting of revival, the AG has experienced, as have countless other religious groups throughout history, the sociological trek from prophetic to priestly leadership and from the free flow of charisma to its routinization. This process has been well defined by O'Dea (1963, 74):

> The most subtle of insights, the most unusual—most charismatic—of experiences, the most supraempirical aspects of human cognition and response and their implications for belief, attitude, and behavior cannot be given social regularity without becoming embodied in institutional structure. But, on the other hand, precisely because of the inherent antinomy which Durkheim showed to be involved between the sacred and the prosaic, such institutionalization raises the sharpest form of the possibility of emasculating the basic content of the religious experience or at least its serious curtailment and distortion.

O'Dea's theory of "institutional dilemmas" refined Weber's classic theory of charisma, particularly Weber's discussion of the transition from prophetic and playful action to a more routinized and institutionalized priestly form. The dilemmas can be regarded as barometers to assess the balance between the *primitive* (charisma) or intuitive dimension of pentecostalism and the *pragmatic* (institutional) or strategic dimension. We do not suggest that charisma can exist without a degree of routinization, but only that the genius of pentecostalism was that it purposively sought to retain the charisma found in its revival history even as it moved into the ranks of America's top ten denominations. The danger in routinization is not in the development of the pragmatic side of pentecostalism (thus facilitating its rapid growth and longevity) but in eclipsing the distinctive and extraordinary qualities that mark pentecostal charisma. O'Dea has provided us with an important theoretical tool with which to appraise the balance between charisma and institutionalization we found in the pastoral survey.

Building on Weber's discussion of charismatic routinization, O'Dea advances five specific paradoxes or dilemmas: mixed motivation, administrative order, power, delimitation, and symbolic. *Mixed motivation* arises as the single-mindedness of purpose characteristic of the earliest devotees is gradually replaced by more self-interested motivations. One of the "signs" of mixed motivation is that the religious body becomes marked by careerism, where the charismatic movement gives rise to a stable institutional matrix with attendant statuses and goals. The rise of a related dilemma, that of *administrative order*, can precipitate an over-elaborate structure that causes the religious organization to become an unwieldy machine. Not only can an organization grow to become unmanageable, but structures that were set in place at an earlier time may refuse to bend and change in response to charisma. A third dilemma—that of *power*—occurs as a religious movement matures and gradually becomes intertwined with the public, nonreligious culture (as happened when many in the AG aligned with the politically active "religious right"). O'Dea (O'Dea and Aviad 1983, 84) cautions about the "subtle temptation for religious leaders to avail themselves of close relation between religion and general cultural values in order to reinforce the position of religion itself." The fourth dilemma is identified as that of *delimitation*, or concrete definitions that substitute the letter of the law for spirit of the original message. O'Dea (1963, 83) observes that in the process of applying the religious ideal to "the prosaic and concrete, the content of the message may itself appear to take on a prosaic quality and lose those characteristic elements that originally moved men [*sic*]." There is a pit on either side of the narrow charismatic road: one dilutes the original message while the other has a rigid position that kills the spirit. The dilemma of delimitation is related to the fifth dilemma, whereby the symbol becomes a substitute for the sacred object. The *symbolic dilemma* involves the problem of trying to objectify the original charismatic moment in stable forms and procedures without creating routine rituals that "mold the personal dispositions of the worshippers after its own model" (O'Dea and Aviad 1983, 59). The routinized symbol loses its effectiveness to elicit and affect attitudes and emotions.

We employ O'Dea's thesis on charisma and the five institutional dilemmas as the theoretical framework for the presentation of pastoral data. For each of the dilemmas, we have identified a specific issue in Pentecostalism and used survey responses to explore its "core" and "peripheral" dimensions. A *core* value is a central component of the relationship between the individual and the structure, an attack upon which threatens the social group (Coser 1956). An attack on a core value threatens the organization with a single line of cleavage that may have seriously negative consequences. Peripheral conflict, on the other hand, often has positive functions as it serves as a medium for needed changes in the structure.

Loosely structured organizations like the AG thus may actually be strengthened by the tension that develops around multiple peripheral issues, conflict which tends to diffuse an attack on a core issue. Coser (1956; 1967) contends that when stress mounts within a group, making allowance for tension may become a positive force in "sewing" diverse factions together. Alliances made on different peripheral but potentially divisive issues can, paradoxically, further group integration. The problematic face of conflict arises when a single core issue is made focal and threatens to bifurcate the group.

Although O'Dea's five dilemmas were explored in *Crossroads,* the quantitative assessment in that work was done using congregational surveys that offered limited access to data beyond the local churches included in the study. Pastors, whom we regard as linchpins between their respective congregations and AG polity, play a key role in the AG. The nationwide pastoral survey thus provides data that extend beyond the twenty-one congregations in this study to complement the congregational surveys used later in our analysis. O'Dea's five institutional dilemmas point to the inherent tension found to some degree in all religious organizations. The ongoing tension between spontaneity and stability that permeates all five dilemmas can be described as "transforming the religious experience to render it continuously available to the mass of men [*sic*] and to provide for it a stable institutional context" (O'Dea 1961, 38). Once free-flowing, non-normative, and seemingly chaotic, charisma must (at least to some extent) be transformed into something that is stable, normal, and ordered. Although charisma has been an important catalyst in the development of all world religions, it is usually quenched in favor of the patterned and predictable institutional features of social life.

Pastors at the Crossroads

Pastors play a vital role in the balance of power between their local congregations and central administration. Pastors and other ministers find themselves bound by doctrine and required financial commitments to the larger bureaucracy, while simultaneously being accountable to their congregations. Our data suggest that the felt loyalties of most pastors rest first with their congregations, followed generally by an allegiance to their local district, and last to the judicatory organization. Pastors understand, perhaps far better than most congregants, the dilemmas posed by the intersection of charismatic vitality with institutional norms and practices. The pastoral data we present here can be succinctly summarized as follows: *The Assemblies of God has a solid core around which there are varying levels of ambiguity.* The ambiguity that exists on peripheral issues appears to function as a safety-valve mechanism feeding the ongoing dialectical interrelationship between charisma and institution building (Eisenstadt 1968). In sum, it appears that the AG continues successfully to balance charisma with institutionalization, as it has for much of its history. Institutionalization has not sounded the death knell for charisma, nor has revitalization of charisma brought about organizational anarchy.

Our empirical findings suggest a healthy tension between charisma and organization persists within the AG, and that this tension may be conceptualized as a kind of "emotional energy" for creativity and change. Although the reports of pastors provide an important link between congregational life and the judicatory, the charismatic process is played out not in AG board rooms but in the lived religion of its congregants. In raising serious question about the possibility of charisma in contemporary society, the late sociologist Philip Rieff has provided a sub-thesis for us to test as we explore the facilitators and inhibitors of the revitalization process in AG congregations.

Has Charisma Been Taken from Us?

In a posthumously published work, Rieff (2007), cultural critic and theorist, addresses the issue of charisma and traces how "the gift of grace" has become a casualty of modern/postmodern culture. At the heart of the dynamic charismatic process is a dialectical dance between faith and guilt once held fast by interdicts, divinely given cultural mores that impose limits on behavior and demand unqualified obedience. Rieff viewed charismatic grace as a function of interdicts. Although Rieff's (2007, 21) illustrations are derived largely from the creedal order of ancient Judaism, which "drew the Jews out of the welter of individual possibilities and established their corporate identity, their covenant," his descriptive theory would apply as well to the legalistic culture that developed in early Pentecostalism and characterized much of its history for the first half of the twentieth century (cf. Blumhofer 1993; Wacker 2001). This call to separatism—to being "a people set apart" and adhering to restrictive interdicts that resisted the larger culture—broke down during the latter half of the twentieth century under the weight of what Rieff calls the "therapeutic culture." For Rieff, the "therapeutic culture," the conceptual thesis for which he is best known, is synonymous with "unbelief." It is "a destroyer of genuine charisma because it undermines divine authority and substitutes a moral relativism that allows individuals to make virtually unlimited life choices guided only by what they believe will contribute to their 'self-actualization.' . . . Therapeutic culture is a 'releaser from interdicts'" (Rieff 2007, p. 4).

Is Rieff correct—has charisma been taken from us? More specifically, has charisma been taken from pentecostals? Based on the interviews that Lee and Poloma (2009a; 2009b) have conducted with pentecostal exemplars of Godly Love, Rieff's unqualified proclamation of the death of charisma and its interdicts seems unfounded. For pentecostals, the Bible remains a source of interdicts and named transgressions. Repentance (and accepting divine forgiveness), for example, is at the core of being "born again," but the narratives of the exemplars read more like transformations into love than adherence to set interdicts. Divine healing—both physical and emotional—arguably can be seen as an antidote for the guilt Rieff purports arises from human transgressions. Instead of accepting Rieff's thesis about the demise of interdicts and the corollary death of charisma, we raise it as an empirical hypothesis that we test using congregational data, especially in chapter 7. Reflected through the prism of the interviews conducted with exemplars of Godly Love, it appears that the paradoxical interdict that enhances pentecostal charisma may be the law to love—love even enemies and the seemingly unlovable—as empowered by what pentecostals call baptism in the Holy Spirit.

A Theoretical Context for Understanding Divine Love as Love Energy

Pitirim Sorokin's (1954/2002) concept of "love energy" provides a social-scientific theoretical base for studying love, specifically the construct we are calling Godly Love. According to Sorokin (1954/2002, 36), "love can be viewed as one of the highest energies known," and he contends that social scientists can study "the channeling, transmission, and distribution of this [non-physical] energy." Sorokin observes that love energy is continually being produced through human interaction and that it can be stored within cultures through religious and cultural norms, ideals, values, and rituals. Although his focus is on the love energy produced by human beings, Sorokin (p. 26) does acknowledge the "probable hypothesis" that "an inflow of love comes from an intangible, little-studied, possibly supra-empirical source called 'God,' 'the Godhead,' 'the Soul of the Universe,' 'the Heavenly Father,' 'Truth,' and so on." He also recognizes the existence of "inventors and engineers of love production"—that is, "exceptional individuals who themselves have been filled with love . . . and who deliberately endeavored to improve the production of love in groups and in humanity at large" (p. 38).

Although Sorokin's work on love has lain fallow in the discipline that he helped to establish in the United States more than seventy-five years ago, newer sociological theories have plowed ground into which Sorokin's seeds can be planted. One such theoretical development is Interaction Ritual (IR) theory, especially as explicated in the prominent work of sociologist Randall Collins (2004). In order to appreciate the importance of Collins's approach as a contemporary heuristic device for making sociological sense of Sorokin's concept of love energy, we must consider the possible explanations of behavior more generally. Human behavior can be explained in terms of static or dynamic forces. A partial list of such influences includes fixed biological predispositions, relatively stable personality traits, variable socialization experiences, dynamically changing situations, and the larger influence of enduring social institutions. In contrast with static theories of human behavior that account for differences among people based primarily on fixed traits (e.g., genes, income, age, race), Collins's IR is a dynamic theory that explores behavior by including lived situational co-presence, mutual focus of attention, and shared mood or affect as found within the dynamic human interactions of everyday situations.

This focus on dynamic situations is central to the study of Godly Love because it opens up the possibility that *anyone* has the potential to be affected by a perceived mystical experience of God. We found that experiencing the divine is not commonly limited by standard fixed demographic measures. Mystical experiences are dynamic situational interactions with often ambiguous meaning. Therefore, we cannot know in advance how any given individual will be affected by experiencing such an encounter. This also suggests that we cannot simply study the personality traits of saints to understand why they have loved with such generosity. It is important to pay special attention to the situations in which divine love energy may be transmitted and amplified not only in the lives of canonized saints but in the lives of believers found in congregational pews. After all, the Christian tradition is replete with stories of ordinary people becoming extraordinary leaders as a result of a compelling interaction with the divine. Pentecostals believe that epiphany experiences (especially conversion and Spirit baptism) empower adherents to live out stories in the modern world similar to those recounted by saints of old (the classic case being St. Paul's life-changing vision of Jesus on the road to Damascus, which was pivotal in the rise of Christianity).

Unfortunately, Collins and other social scientists working in the IR tradition have failed to take seriously the impact of commonly reported perceived interactions with the supernatural, as they have also ignored Sorokin's important thesis on love energy. Using our congregational data on spiritual experiences in the AG, we seek to move beyond the methodological atheism that has plagued social science by bringing God into the perspective that Collins has developed on the energy-producing and -sustaining features of ritual interactions. By drawing on Sorokin's concept of love energy, we also hope to reintroduce social scientists to his important theologically sensitive work. By taking this step, we move past the stalemate that has hindered the development of an empirically grounded and theologically informed understanding of love energy. Although testing Collins's comprehensive general theory is not our intent, his work does provide important theoretical components that guide our analysis. Collins's framework of dynamic interaction rituals that are ongoing in everyday life offers a contemporary theoretical grid for re-presenting Sorokin's work on the "ways and power of love" to twenty-first-century social scientists. Taken together, these two sociologists divided by a half century provide us with a strong foundation for systematically exploring and testing the relationship between perceived experiences of the divine and benevolent action.

Collins's IR theory has its roots in the early work of social scientists on religious rituals, particularly in Émile Durkheim's *Elementary Forms of the Religious Life*. Of particular relevance for our discussion is Durkheim's concept of "effervescence" (a concept akin to Sorokin's "love energy") that arises in religious rituals. This effervescence motivates and sustains behavior by investing those who participate in a ritual with emotional energy. Collins couples this Durkheimian insight on ritual with the theoretical works of the sociologist Erving Goffman (cf. 1961; 1963; 1971; 1974), who enlarged the concept of ritual beyond religion to include all human behavior, with an emphasis on the importance of the situation (context) in which the ritual is enacted. For Goffman, behavioral outcomes were largely a product of dynamic features of situations, not the static traits of individual personality or biology, or the top-down influence of unalterable, monolithic institutions. In other words, who we are and how we behave is a function of the situations in which we find ourselves, not fixed properties of individual or social structures. This is an optimistic perspective when applied to love energy because it can be experienced regardless of individual predispositions or social constraints, as the story of St. Paul demonstrates.

Although Durkheim's concept of "effervescence" is often cited in scholarly discussion, it has not been subject to systematic study within the IR framework. Even Collins has failed to explore its relevance for contemporary religious rituals. Moreover, social scientists from Durkheim to Collins have failed to take seriously the claims of theologians that interactions occur not just among people, but also between people and a perceived divine presence (see Collins 2004, 33). To date, social scientists have failed adequately to conceptualize and measure the effervescence that is generated in the perceived interaction between an individual and the divine, as in solitary prayer or mystical experience. Instead, scholarship has limited itself largely to group interaction rituals (e.g., speaking in tongues at a church service, preaching styles of ministers, the use of music in worship). Durkheim, for example, focused his analytical lens on the effervescence that was generated by group rituals rather than interaction between humans and perceptions of the divine.

We regard "effervescence," "emotion energy," and "love energy" as members of the same conceptual family, while Sorokin's discussion of "love energy" provides a more specific theory that is a good fit with Collins's more general IR theory. A complete understanding of love energy, to the extent that this is humanly possible, requires an empirical exploration of perceived interactions with God and with other individuals. Perceived vertical interaction with the divine and horizontal interaction with other people are both integral components of the Godly Love model.

Pentecostal Gifts of the Spirit

Sorokin's concept of love energy provides a sociological window to explore a theological question, namely, how "a connection between Spirit baptism and an expansive array of spiritual gifts helps us focus on the relatively neglected vocational dimension of Christian life" (Macchia 2006a, 32). In his *Baptized in the Spirit: A Global Pentecostal Theology,* AG theologian Frank Macchia has provided social science with a significant pentecostal theological insight that connects empowering experiences of God with a sense of call and mission. Macchia (p. 14) asserts that "God intoxication," described in the Christian Testament books of Acts and Ephesians, is a description of self-transcendence involving "a consciousness wholly taken up with God so that one feels especially inspired to give of oneself to others in whatever gifting God has created within." We use Macchia's theological reflections as a basis for the social-scientific model of Godly Love to present and interpret the findings from the AG congregational survey. Our analysis of the congregational data is grounded in empirical accounts of pentecostal spiritual transformation with a focus on Spirit baptism and glossolalia or speaking/

praying in tongues. In the Assemblies of God, Spirit baptism *with the initial physical evidence of speaking in tongues* is regarded as the key transformative experience. Using the lens provided by Godly Love, we empirically explore the interrelationship between vertical God–human interaction (Spirit baptism, glossolalia, healing, and prophecy) and horizontal forms of benevolence, including those centered in personal care-love, organized religion, and social welfare.

Faces of Love

In studying the relationship between human and divine love and its potential effects on interpersonal relations, we deliberately seek to sidestep the significant but sticky philosophical and theological questions raised over the centuries about the nature of love. Following philosopher Rolf Johnson (2001, 23), our focus is on relationships "between a subject and an object that inclines the lover toward the object." We use Johnson's typology of the "three faces of love" to explore the meanings and objectives of love relationships included in our definition of Godly Love. Following Johnson, we recognize that there are different distinguishable phenomena that bear the label "love," with the three primary kinds of "love relationships" being "union-love," "care-love," and "appreciation-love." *Union-love* has as its objective the union of the lover and the beloved. Although romantic love may be the first example of union love that comes to mind, as Johnson (2001, 25) has noted, "romantic love and mystical love are both examples of this form of love."

Testimonies of religious experiences that accompany pentecostal meetings and rituals are ripe with examples of "union-love" or mystical relationships with God—perceived experiences that we have effectively measured in scales created out of the responses to the congregational survey. *Care-love*, according to Johnson (2001, 24), "embraces all forms of concern for the well-being of the loved. Its objective is simply the good of the love object." Examples of this love relationship with others include feelings (e.g., compassion), cognitive concern (e.g., about another person's wellbeing), and behavior (e.g., benevolent acts). The third face of love, *appreciation-love,* is less active and more abstract. Included in this love relationship is the reverence, cherishing, and appreciation of "ideals, principles, or abstract qualities" (Johnson 2001, 25). For example, it is possible to be in "love" with cultural Pentecostalism—often seen in the pride over the denomination felt by family members who trace their roots back to Azusa Street—without any signs of mystical experience and little evidence of exemplary compassion. Traditional values, doctrine, pentecostal culture, or institutional well-being can all serve as objects of an abstract appreciation-love, which may or may not be related to union-love or care-love.

Ideally, as we will see, all three faces work together for strong Pentecostal identity, experience, and practice. Union-, appreciation-, and care-loves can be regarded, to use an overworked analogy, as three legs supporting a stool. When all three legs are present and balanced, charisma continues to flow within pentecostal organization; when out of balance, charisma falters. Johnson's "faces" of love relationships help us to explore how pentecostalism has been subject not only to institutional "routinization" but also to an ongoing process of "revitalization." The potential of revitalization is present to the extent that union-love— particularly the belief in and experience of Spirit baptism—has remained an explicit value and lived experience. In sum, union or mystical love is a source of "love energy" with the potential to enliven normative forms of benevolence (such as those characterized by organized denominational programs and policies) as well as relational congregational forms (where care-love is a dominant love relationship).

Godly Love as Theory and Praxis

The prime catalyst in our model of Godly Love is personally knowing the love of God and experiencing its energizing power. We found that perceived mystical experiences of the divine, although not the only factor, play different but significant roles in benevolent service. Humanly perceived encounters with the Holy Spirit may thus energize the charismata. Spirit baptism and attendant paranormal gifts of glossolalia, prophecy, healing, and other "signs and wonders" are empowering (i.e., producing "love energy") and reflect union-love with God. Such empowerment may also be positively related to empirically measurable acts of benevolence found in social structures ("appreciation-love") and social relationships ("care-love").

We use Sorokin's theory of love, juxtaposed with Collins's theory of interaction ritual chains and Johnson's thesis on the three faces of love, to assess the two primary axes of Godly Love—a vertical (union-love) relationship with God and horizontal (care-love) relationships with others. Although exploring relationships between and among people is basic social science, introducing the possibility that God can be conceptualized as an actor in human lives is somewhat controversial. The conceptualization and measuring of Godly Love require a methodological stance that shifts away from the assumptions of "methodological atheism," which have rarely been questioned in the social science of religion, toward what has been called "methodological agnosticism." Despite the normative stance of methodological atheism in social science, we contend that methodological agnosticism is more appropriate—even essential—for an understanding of pentecostalism as a lived religion.[2] Methodological agnosticism neither denies nor brackets reports of the supernatural, nor does it ignore or categorically dismiss the possibility of perceptions of divine grace having an impact on human action. Instead, it treats the topic of Godly Love as a challenge for empirical investigation that can further social-scientific knowledge about human behavior.

Divine Love and Human Love in Interaction: Preliminary Evidence

A plausible empirical relationship between the charismata (paranormal "gifts of the Holy Spirit") and human benevolent action can be found in the survey data reported in *Crossroads*. Experiences of glossolalia, healing, prophecy, miracles, and other "gifts of the Holy Spirit," discussed by St. Paul in 1 Corinthians 12–14, were positively related in statistical analyses to evangelistic outreach (Poloma 1989; Poloma and Pendleton 1989). Those who scored higher on the charismata scale were significantly more likely to invite new members and to support existing ones. These believers did more than pass out tracts on street corners. They went out of their way to share their faith in meaningful ways, making it possible and comfortable for friends and acquaintances to become more involved in the congregation. Such caring evangelistic activities, empowered by the experience of the charismata, were identified as an important factor in AG congregational growth.

This very preliminary and tentative finding informed later studies on prayer that explored the effects of other religious experiences. Experiences of God during personal prayer were found to have positive effects on personal well-being measures in two random samples, one of a local community and another a national survey (see Poloma and Pendleton 1991a; Poloma and Pendleton 1991b; Poloma and Gallup 1991). In these studies of prayer, God could be conceptualized as what Marvin Pollner (1989) called a "significant other" in the lives of many who pray. The perception of a personal and interactive relationship with God was a decided factor in accounting for higher levels of existential well-being and personal satisfaction.

A non-random survey conducted during the revivals of the 1990s (Poloma 1998a; 2003) provides yet another opportunity to explore the perceived divine–human relations that are the cornerstone for the theoretical construct of Godly Love. A 1995 survey collected data on religious experience from nearly one thousand pilgrims from around the world who visited the Toronto Blessing pentecostal revival site; a 1997 follow-up of these respondents included measures of acts of benevolence, or "care-love." Experiencing God's love in fresh and new ways during this neo-pentecostal revival proved to be a significant factor in reported acts of outreach and kindness to family, friends, co-workers, and strangers (Poloma 1998a). It was this link between religious experience and altruism that provided the foundations for the development of the theory of Godly Love.

Using the preliminary empirical findings just noted together with Sorokin's sociological theory of love, Poloma and Hood (2008) prepared a research proposal specifically directed toward the study of the relationship between the pentecostal charismata and empowerment for benevolence.[3] It was through the use of grounded theory in guiding the data collection and subsequent analysis of the findings that the concept of Godly Love with its present definition emerged. Poloma and Hood developed a complex longitudinal research plan to empirically examine the relationship between the charismata and care-love in Blood and Fire, an Atlanta-based ministry to the homeless. Under the prophetic leadership and vision of the coming kingdom of God provided by the founder, a social context existed in which "walking in the supernatural" was normative. Volunteers in this urban ministry to the homeless and their beneficiaries alike claimed to experience God guiding, protecting, providing, and empowering them to bring down a bit of heaven to the parks and projects of downtown Atlanta. The researchers sought to contextualize and frame within this extensive social network and situated action the reportedly "supernatural" experiences claimed to be "natural" and normative within this ministry. Their observations—especially as found in the survey data from volunteers, addicts in the program, and the homeless—fit well with earlier empirical findings that suggested a link between religious experience and compassionate living. Those who scored higher in their experience of the gifts of the Spirit also scored higher in altruism (Poloma and Hood 2008). As reflected in the surveys, Godly Love clearly had potentially powerful effects on human interaction, but the outcome of the four-year ethnographic work also uncovered a dark side.[4] Poloma and Hood's work pointed to a viable new model for an ongoing exploration of a social science of love. Applying the concept and model of Godly Love to an analysis and interpretation of survey data from Assemblies of God congregants is but one of several projects involved in exploring the role that experiences of God play in accounting for benevolent action.[5]

Summary

This chapter has laid out the theories that have guided our research, our interpretation of the findings, and our presentation of the account of the Assemblies of God that follows. In the following pages, we will describe and assess the judicatory portrait of the AG using O'Dea's five institutional dilemmas. We will use the tension between charisma and organizational development to frame the pastoral survey findings that show the AG still to be at the crossroad between what Wacker has called the *primitive* and the *pragmatic*, though increasingly leaning toward the pragmatic. We then turn our attention toward the AG congregants as we look for signs of ongoing revitalization that may be at work to balance the routinization of charisma. The interdisciplinary theoretical model of Godly Love, influenced by Sorokin, Macchia, Johnson, and Rieff, guides this analysis and interpretation of the congregational data. Through the lenses of this dynamic model we are able to present the steps of a dialectical dance that is ongoing between routinization and revitalization in this Pentecostal denomination. Our social-scientific story speaks both caution and hope for the future of Pentecostalism in the United States.

3

Pentecostal Identity and the Charismata

Mixed Motivation and Religious Experience

> [Contemporary] Pentecostals should mine their past for a vision of their future. While rejecting discrimination based on class, race, or gender, Pentecostals should reinvigorate discussions of cardinal Pentecostal doctrine and biblical authority. . . . Likewise, contemporary American Pentecostals must reconnect with the vibrant experiential nature of their faith and recover the awe and expectancy of charismata in their individual and corporate spiritual experience. It is simply impossible to be Pentecostal without the charismata, and yet classical Pentecostal denominations seem to have handed off their gift to younger movements such at the Vineyard and non-denominational charismatic churches. (Patterson 2007, 206)

The concern expressed by Eric Patterson in the above epigraph, found in the conclusion of his and Edmund Rybarczyk's edited volume *The Future of Pentecostalism in the United States* (2007), serves as a fresh reminder that the AG remains at an intersection. In *Crossroads* Poloma (1989) used the sociological theory of Thomas O'Dea to explore in detail the dilemmas inherent within a denomination struggling against the routinization of charisma that some sociologists would say is inevitable in all religious groups. Would routinization and institutionalization lead to the demise of distinct Pentecostal experiences in modern Pentecostalism? Is it possible for charismata to continue to play a defining role in the future of the denomination? Or would the AG morph into modern, plain-vanilla evangelicalism that emphasized cognitive "knowing" over the affective experiences that characterized Pentecostal "knowing"? A fresh look at O'Dea's "institutional dilemmas" provides a framework for presenting and analyzing the data from the pastoral survey.

The Dilemma of Mixed Motivation: Assessing Identity

According to O'Dea's theory, the emergence of a stable structure in a religious community brings with it the capability of eliciting a wide range of individual motives. This transition typically marks the denouement of the charismatic leader's single-minded vision and the rise of mixed motivation (O'Dea and Aviad 1983). The pentecostal movement,[1] however, has never had a single charismatic leader such as Methodism's John Wesley, Quakerism's George Fox, Mormonism's Joseph Smith, or Christian Science's Mary Baker Eddy. Pentecostalism is a movement that has democratized charisma, so the relationship between a charismatic leader and his disciples described by O'Dea has not been the prime motivating factor. Rather, the "single-mindedness" of the movement has been energized by a common experience of the *baptism in the Spirit.*

Although the dilemma of mixed motivation can be illustrated through the rise of an ordained clergy and the correspondent development of leadership roles, it can also be assessed through a discussion of religious identity issues found in pentecostalism's distinctive worldview. A passage from Zechariah 4:6 that serves as a motto for the AG provides a succinct statement about Pentecostal identity: "'Not by might, nor by power, but by my Spirit,' says the Lord." This simple profession reflects what AG theologian Frank Macchia (1999, 16) describes as a "paradigm shift from an exclusive focus on holiness to an outward thrust that invoked a dynamic filling and an empowerment for global witness."

As routinization extracts its due, however, this emphasis on "dynamic filling" and "empowerment" increasingly has shifted from personal experience and testimony to the profession and expansion of doctrinal decrees and position papers. The testimonies of lived experience that empowered early believers have taken a back seat to a selective reconstruction of AG history and doctrine, which often fails to capture the diversity that found expression in the larger pentecostal movement. As Robeck (1999a; see also Hollenweger 1997) has effectively argued in his discussion of pentecostal identity, pentecostalism has demonstrated a host of "indigenous entries," including "Oneness Pentecostalism," "World Faith Pentecostalism," "Feminist Pentecostalism," and even "Gay Pentecostalism," all of which have been rejected by the Assemblies of God. The AG has increasingly defined itself primarily as "Evangelical Pentecostalism," or perhaps a better description, "Evangelicalism plus tongues." Robeck (1999a, 5) goes on to state:

> Pentecostals have historically disagreed with one another on what constitutes a real Pentecostal, and as a result, on what constitutes genuine Pentecostalism. The fact may not be easy for some Pentecostals to accept, but it is true nonetheless. Each group seems to want to identify its own specific character as providing the best, if not *the only legitimate identity* for all real Pentecostals. Insofar as their distinctives become all that define Pentecostalism, the real character, contribution, and impact of the whole Movement may be lost.

Such diffusion has led one Pentecostal scholar to assert that such change in identity has resulted in pentecostalism's becoming an "American Evangelical pot of goo" (Rybarczyk 2007, 7).[2]

What appears to happen, particularly in more established classical Pentecostal denominations such as the AG, is that the breadth and depth of pentecostalism is eclipsed as each segment identifies with a single appendage, much like the blind men in their respective attempts to describe the proverbial elephant. The essence of pentecostalism as a "new paradigm"—with the natural and supernatural engaged in a dialectical dance—is compromised by accommodative forces that threaten to dilute pentecostal identity. As evangelicals find a prominent place in the American religious pantheon, some would put aside the "new paradigm" to embrace a modernist religious identity that downplays the controversial issues that come with "dynamic filling" and "empowerment."

Spirit-filled Christianity, unlike Christian fundamentalism and evangelicalism, represents more than a cognitive or doctrinal reaction to modernity. It has proactively developed certain characteristics that taken together make its worldview distinct from other forms of Christianity, both liberal and conservative. The pentecostal worldview is experientially centered, with followers in a dynamic and personal relationship with a Deity who is both immanent and transcendent. According to Pentecostal scholar Jackie Johns (1999, 75), "The Spirit-filled believer has a predisposition to see a transcendent God at work in, with, through, above and beyond all events. Therefore, all space is sacred space and all time is sacred time." God is seen as active in all events past, present, and future, which work together in a kind of master plan. It is a worldview that tends to be "transrational," professing that knowledge is "not limited to realms of reason and sensory experience" (ibid.). Consistent with this transrational characteristic, Pentecostal Christians also tend to be suspicious of creeds, believing that "knowing" comes from a right relationship with God rather than through reason, or even through the five senses. Theirs is a God who can and often does defy the laws of nature with the miraculous and unexplainable. Without a doubt the Bible holds an important place in their worldview, but for many it is a kind of catalyst and litmus test for the authenticity of personal and corporate experience rather than a manual of rigid doctrine and practices. As Johns (1999, 79) succinctly states: "A Pentecostal paradigm for knowledge and truth springs from an experiential knowledge of God which alters the believer's approach to reading and interpreting reality."

This "paradigm for knowledge and truth" is shared by traditional Pentecostalism as well as by more recent and divergent pentecostal streams, in which followers reflect the early forefathers and foremothers in their reluctance to embrace particular religious labels. The newcomers, as well as some once-traditional Pentecostals, may self-identify as "charismatic," "Spirit-filled" Christians, or even simply as "in the river" (of ongoing revival experiences). As products of more recent renewals and revivals, they are often stronger in Wacker's (2001) *primitivism* (and sometimes, but not always, weaker on *pragmatism*).

The primary distinction we have observed between the Pentecostal and neo-pentecostal streams in North America is in different overt expressions of a common core pentecostal spirituality (Albrecht 1999). At the risk of oversimplification, those who self-identify as "charismatic" or "third wave" are more likely to accept a *range* of paranormal experiences (including prophecy, miracles, healing, and physical manifestations of an altered state of consciousness) as signs of Spirit baptism, while most Pentecostals, including the AG, tend to place a doctrinal emphasis specifically on the gift of tongues. Furthermore, established classical Pentecostal denominations tend to have well-developed bureaucratic structures, while thriving neo-pentecostal organizations tend to be non-denominational, with members focusing on relational ties expressed in loose-knit networks.[3]

What can be said about the larger pentecostal movement, regardless of the stream, is that it is more about a distinct spirituality than about religion (Albrecht 1999; Land 1993). Members share a common transcendent worldview rather than particular doctrines, defined ritual practices, or denominational involvement. This worldview is a curious blend of premodern miracles, modern technology, and postmodern mysticism in which the natural blends with the supernatural. Signs and wonders analogous to those described in premodern biblical accounts are expected as normal occurrences in the lives of believers (Poloma 2001); Johns (1999, 74–75) asserts that what underlies Pentecostal identity is a Pentecostal epistemology "congruous with the ancient Jewish approach to knowledge"—one that represents an alternative to modern ways of knowing:

> Pentecostals have an alternative epistemology because they have an alternative world-view. At the heart of the Pentecostal world-view is transforming experience with God. God is known through relational encounter which finds its penultimate expression in being filled with the Holy Spirit. This experience becomes the normative epistemological framework and thus shifts the structures by which the individual interprets the world.

Pentecostal identity is the core of our assessment of mixed motivation, an issue that impacts each of the other dilemmas.

The survey findings on the Pentecostal identity of AG pastors enhance this brief description of Pentecostal identity and the importance of its worldview in maintaining the dialectical tension between charisma and organization that has been at the heart of Pentecostalism's success. The survey responses allow us to explore identity issues empirically to reveal core tenets as well as attendant ambiguities. What does it mean to be Pentecostal (specifically AG) in the twenty-first century? Is there congruence between the reported identity self-perceptions of pastors and of the congregations they represent? Is there congruence between these perceptions of identity and the denominational work performed by national and regional administrative offices? We can use these and other related questions to tap the perceptions of core identity and the ambiguities that exist around it, including the importance of being a member of the AG and Pentecostal. We also explore the social distance between AG adherents and the larger pentecostal movement, non-pentecostal Christians, and non-Christians.

Pentecostal Core Identity

AG scholar Everett Wilson (1999) asked: "What makes a Pentecostal?" Difficulties of providing a simple description are deeply embedded in Pentecostal history. Wilson (1999, 88–89) concludes that the Pentecostal social identity is rooted in a worldview based on the "mystical, the 'supernatural' and the allegedly miraculous," which tended to stigmatize and marginalize early Pentecostals. For Wilson, being labeled a Pentecostal was the result of more than a confessional act—it signaled a worldview that separated these believers from other Christians. As Wilson (1999, 88–89) comments:

> Like the proverbial duck, if the person looked like one, walked like one and talked like one—especially if one were supportive of the beliefs and practices that Pentecostals advanced—friends and neighbours could assume that he or she in fact belonged. At least the often-sung refrain, "I'm so glad I can say I am one of them" apparently gained favour not just to establish identity or to convince believers that they were with the right crowd, but because adherents gave assent to the Pentecostal way of looking at reality, something about which they may have felt deeply even when their convictions were not overtly displayed.

Although professing to be a Pentecostal certainly does not tell the whole story of AG identity, it is a good place to begin a discussion of single-mindedness. Are pastors still singing "I am one of them" as the denomination has taken a more accepted place in the religious mosaic? For the vast majority of pastors, the answer appears to be "yes." Self-identity can be gleaned from a survey question that instructed respondents to "indicate how important it is to identify with each of these groups": Assemblies of God, Pentecostalism, Revival/Renewal, Charismatic Movement/Third Wave and Evangelicalism (see appendix A, table A.1).

As can be seen in table A.1, pastors were most likely to report their primary self-identity as being Pentecostal (55 percent claimed it was "extremely important," with another 33 percent saying it was "very important"). Nearly identical figures were reported for a personal identification with being a part of "Renewal/Revival," implying a conscious decision to support a revitalization of Pentecostal identity through fresh religious experiences. Figures for self-identification with the AG were only slightly lower than those for being Pentecostal and in Renewal/Revival. Forty-nine percent reported self-identification with the AG as "extremely important," and another 36 percent said it was "very important." The vast majority of the pastors thus reported having a religious identity that can be described as Pentecostal and being a member of the Assemblies of God. These same pastors also identified very strongly with the need to be involved in revival/renewal, suggesting that Pentecostalism is largely regarded as a dynamic process rather than a staid structure. These labels of self-identity, however, need to be further explored. Probing into the nature of Pentecostal identity reveals some of the ambiguities that beset the denomination.

Ambiguity around the Core Identity

Despite the pastors' strong approval of retaining and reviving Pentecostal identity, an old dilemma lurks beneath the "single-mindedness" reflected in their responses. The AG historically has found itself in the paradoxical position of promoting a distinct Pentecostal perspective while seeking a rapport with fundamentalism and later with a more moderate evangelicalism, sectors of which have been very critical of Pentecostalism (Menzies 2005). Within two years after its initial gathering in 1914, the AG's message and mission, as Edith Blumhofer (1993, 135) noted, "would be held within the boundaries drawn by traditional evangelical doctrines." Its attempt to become "fundamentalism with a difference" (fundamentalism plus Spirit baptism) was not always well received, and Pentecostals, including the AG, became the target of a resolution of the World's Christian Fundamentals Association in 1928 that went on record as "unreservedly opposed to Modern Pentecostalism." Not until the development of the more moderate National Association of Evangelicals (NAE) in the early 1940s did the AG find acceptance in this newly formed transdenominational conservative network. However support for the NAE by AG constituents was far from universal. Blumhofer (1993, 187) reports the critical response of one influential AG pastor to AG membership in the NAE:

> This association is not Pentecostal and many of their speakers who are listed for a convention . . . not only do not favor Pentecost, but speak against it. This [cooperating with the NAE] is what I call putting the grave clothes again on Lazarus, while the Scripture says: "Come out from among them, and be ye separate, saith the Lord, and touch not the unclean thing; and I will receive you and will be a Father unto you, and ye shall be my sons and daughters, saith the Lord Almighty."

The old controversy appears to be far from resolved, and it is here that ambiguity surfaces. Clergy remain divided about the threat that evangelicalism poses to the Pentecostal worldview that provides the AG with its distinct identity. A clear majority (60 percent) of pastors agreed or strongly agreed with the statement "Too many AG churches have stressed a general evangelical identity at the expense of their Pentecostal heritage." AG congregations that clearly downplay their ties to the denomination often select a name for their congregation that gives the impression of its being an independent evangelical church. Ritual in such congregations often follows an evangelical format in which Pentecostal practices are discouraged—or at least their public display is not encouraged.

However, as can be seen in table A.1, more than two-thirds of the pastors responding to the survey self-identified as being evangelical, a nomenclature that is somewhat less important for most respondents than Pentecostal, AG, and Revival/Renewal identities. The evangelical label is clearly more important, however, than is self-identity with cousins in the charismatic/third-wave (neo-pentecostal) sector of the larger pentecostal movement.[4] Despite the pentecostal worldview of charismatic/third-wave churches, only 28 percent of the pastors reported that self-identity with these newer streams of pentecostalism was "extremely important" or "very important."[5] While Pentecostal and evangelical are thus central to the self-identity of a clear majority of AG pastors, only a minority self-identify with newer streams pentecostalism where revitalization and renewal is accompanied by a range of "signs and wonders" that are strikingly similar to those reported in the history of traditional Pentecostalism (Wacker 2001).

Further ambiguity may be observed in the response to the question about belief in a dispensationalist interpretation of the scriptures—a fundamentalist "fundamental" of longstanding tension within the AG. What is known as *dispensationalism* has been used to disparage Pentecostalism as at best delusional and at worst heretical. As Blumhofer (1993, 107) has noted of dispensationalists:

> Dispensationalists generally held that miracles had ceased with the Apostles; Pentecostalism thus could not be authentic, for its premise that New Testament gifts would mark the end-times church was false. Rejecting the latter-rain views by which Pentecostals legitimated their place in church history, dispensationalists effectively eliminated the biblical basis for Pentecostal theology.

Despite the fact that dispensationalism has been used by fundamentalists and some evangelicals to condemn Pentecostalism, 58 percent of the pastors strongly agreed or agreed with the statement "I believe in a dispensationalist interpretation of Scripture" (see appendix A, table A.5).

Ideological ties with fundamentalism go back to the earliest days of the AG. As Blumhofer (1993, 159) has observed, "The causes espoused by fundamentalists seemed to coincide in meaningful ways with Assemblies of God denominational interests and to offer as well an opportunity for declaring Pentecostal sympathies with doctrinal 'fundamentals.' It was not long before 'right belief replaced right experience,' causing even further erosion of AG distinctiveness." The danger that fundamentalism (and its softer evangelical expressions) poses for Pentecostal identity has been noted by Cox (1995), Hollenweger (1997), and Spittler (1994), among other scholars. Although the AG can be placed securely within the walls of larger evangelicalism, there is evidence that such positioning threatens to fragment its identity and, as O'Dea's dilemma of mixed motivation suggests, leaves the denomination with dissonant agendas that may not be easy to resolve.

As reflected in table A.1, dissonance between what AG ministers say and what they do to live out the pentecostal paradigm can be seen in the groups with which they and their congregations are willing to cooperate in promoting issues of common concern. Although over a quarter of the ministers surveyed professed to want strong ties with the charismatic/third-wave movement in other sectors of Christianity, a decisive majority preferred to keep their ties limited to other Pentecostals and evangelicals. When pastors were asked to indicate the "extent you would like to see the AG cooperate with different religious groups," they were most likely (65 percent) to choose full cooperation with other Pentecostals.

Clearly, widespread support exists among AG pastors for an identity that is Pentecostal and evangelical—but not necessarily pentecostal, as most decline to embrace charismatics and newer revival streams of the larger movement. The marriage of Pentecostalism and evangelicalism has generated some ambiguity in identity, especially when considered in light of fundamentalist opposition and evangelical indifference to a distinctive supernatural worldview. Yet despite initial opposition, the partnership between these seemingly strange bedfellows appears to have survived concerns of a generation past. Part of the explanation for the success of blending a modernist evangelical with a pre-postmodern pentecostal worldview may come from an increasing acceptance of a modified version of pentecostalism by the larger Christian church. A popular dispensationalist teaching, sometimes called *cessationism*, which insists that the supernatural gifts were meant only to jumpstart early Christianity (and then ceased), seems to be losing ground in many evangelical circles. The evangelical perspective rooted in a modernist worldview seems to have been found wanting in a postmodern culture hungry for a vital spirituality to counter the inadequacies of materialism and rationalism. Some scholars have gone so far as to contend that much of the old argument about the availability of "signs and wonders" for contemporary Christianity appears to be about semantics and doctrinal statements rather than popular belief. As Jon Ruthven (1999, 156) noted in a review of Wayne Grudem's (1996) edited volume *Are Miraculous Gifts for Today?*:

> One is left with the feeling that the whole debate could be resolved by a simple change in labels (not "prophecy," or "a word of knowledge," but "leadings"; not "*gifts* of healing," but "healings"). Here the issue is not so much what God actually *does* today, so long as one avoids identifying these events as "miracles" accrediting new doctrine.

The acceptance of a modified pentecostal identity shared with evangelicals notwithstanding, the marriage of the two distinctive worldviews is at the expense of the distinct identity that has characterized pentecostalism. An important and relevant issue underlying the controversy that surfaces in Grudem's collection concerns *how frequently and how intensely* these events should be expected. It may be that a version of the early Pentecostal worldview is widely accepted by both Pentecostals and non-pentecostal Christians, but it is a domesticated version that has diluted the original paradigm. As we shall see shortly, the twin issues of frequency and intensity not only are relevant for dialogue between Pentecostals and non-Pentecostals but also point to an identity crisis within the AG.

An analysis of how a converging of seemingly distinctive identities translates into theology and religious cooperation reveals some AG fragmentation. Pentecostal support for fundamentalist theology and evangelical alliances (after the founding of the NAE in 1943) has sowed seeds of ambiguity that continue to this day, preventing established Pentecostal denominations like the AG from being on the cutting edge of the larger pentecostal movement that includes charismatics, independent neo-pentecostals, and contemporary revivalists.

The Symbolic Dilemma: Assessing the Prevalence of Pentecostal Experience

The worldview of the early Pentecostals not only accorded ideological legitimacy to the paranormal experiences reported in biblical times, it also restored them to a normative position in the twentieth-century Western world. Although glossolalia or speaking in tongues became the pivotal experiential doctrine in the AG, accounts of divine healing, prophetic words, miraculous myths, and demonic exorcisms were also part and parcel for the Pentecostal package. More controversial were the strange physical manifestations that generated the pejorative label "holy rollers" ascribed by outsiders to Pentecostal believers, who sometimes fell in a faint to the floor, jumped pews, violently jerked and shook, laughed, barked, or rolled in the aisles under the alleged influence of the Spirit. Although many contemporary Pentecostals deny their occurrence in early Pentecostalism, these same controversial manifestations erupted again during the New Order of the Latter Rain movement of the 1940s, developed to a degree in the "second wave" as Pentecost came to mainline denominations during the 1970s, and intensified during the contemporary "third-wave" revivals that continue as we write (cf. Wacker 2001; Taves 1999).

A dilemma facing Pentecostal believers from the earliest days of Azusa Street was how to allow the Spirit free movement while controlling excesses judged to be fanatic. This challenge was met by sorting out the more controversial physical responses (often difficult to justify from biblical texts) from the less controversial experiences (more readily defined as "biblical") that frequently have accompanied the perceived presence of the Holy Spirit. In the Assemblies of God doctrinal statements, glossolalia and healing became two of the sixteen "Fundamental Truths," while many other alleged expressions of the Spirit's presence were eventually labeled "fanaticism" and "heresy." Despite the solid ideological support for revival expressed in pastoral responses to the Pentecostal identity issues already discussed, much ambiguity continues around the embodiment of this ideology. What is perceived to be "fanatical" and "heretical" has fluctuated in AG history, thus contributing to a mixed message about the current streams of revival, including the Pensacola Outpouring of the 1990s and the Lakeland Outpouring in 2008. This ambivalence about once commonly experienced revival phenomena can be gleaned in reviewing the survey data through the lens of the symbolic dilemma.

At the heart of the symbolic dilemma is ritual—"the cultic re-presentation of the religious experience [that] is central to the life of the religious group" (O'Dea and Aviad 1983, 58). In Pentecostalism, however, the goal was never simply to remember the past but rather to provide a forum for ongoing religious experiences. The report card on this dilemma is mixed, as Poloma (1989, 206) has noted:

> The symbolic dilemma is deemed one of the most important in maintaining charisma, yet it is, paradoxically, perhaps the most difficult to keep alive. In an attempt to minimize the dangers of both disorder and inauthenticity, some pastors are placing less emphasis on experiences in their services. Opting for set programs, well-timed services, and a high level of professionalism, these pastors are often openly critical of "emotionalism" in services. The dilemma is further jeopardized by the fact that some very successful Assemblies of God congregations have exchanged charisma for institutional techniques to promote church growth.

Core Ritual Expressions within the AG

Debates within the Assemblies of God about choirs and choir robes, printed bulletins, and ritualized services have increasingly been resolved in favor of order and predictability. Pragmatic decisions to have multiple services, to make services more inviting for non-pentecostals, and to shorten services to accommodate time-conscious Americans have produced a ritual in many churches that is indistinguishable from non-pentecostal evangelical services. Mechanisms used to maintain order are the same ones that stifle the free flow of pentecostal experiences. Some recall with fondness and longing the distinctive early pentecostal ritual, when congregants commonly "tarried," waiting for the Holy Spirit to move in the gathering, sometimes with unpredictable results (see Wacker 2001); others are more cautious about the feared "fanaticism" and "wildfires" found in unregulated meetings. As a result, the pentecostal spirit is distributed unevenly, a pattern that can be discerned from statistics on the personal religious experiences of pastors as well as from pastoral reports about congregational services.

As can be seen in table A.2, the most frequently practiced Pentecostal expression reported by pastors is speaking in tongues. All AG ministers must sign a document annually when their credentials are renewed certifying to the fact that they accept the doctrine of tongues as the "initial physical evidence" of Spirit baptism. Although this doctrine has repeatedly been challenged by those outside the denomination as well as by some within, it appears to have strong support among pastors. Eighty-five percent of the pastors agreed with the statement "A person who has never spoken in tongues cannot claim to be Spirit baptized" (table A.5). However, the number of pastors who do not agree with the AG position on tongues as initial evidence of Spirit baptism appears to have increased significantly over the past two decades, from 2 percent (Poloma 1989) to 15 percent (table A.5). Although increasing numbers of AG congregants do not speak in tongues, and a significant percentage of pastors disagree with the doctrinal statement, the experience of glossolalia and professing the creed of "initial evidence" continues to be a prerequisite for receiving and retaining AG ordination papers.[6]

The overwhelming majority of pastors in this survey (82 percent) reported praying in tongues weekly or more, with no pastor reporting not having prayed in tongues this past year. Tongues (at least on occasion) is a nearly universal part of the prayer lives of AG pastors. Pastors are somewhat less likely, however, to use this gift in a church service. Eighteen percent reported that they never gave an utterance in tongues or an interpretation of a glossolalic word in a church service during the past year, with another 36 percent indicating that they did so only a few times. Forty-seven percent expressed glossolalia in a congregational setting more regularly, reportedly giving an "utterance" or an "interpretation" once a month or more. The fact that pastors *pray in tongues* in private ritual but are less likely to use the *gift of tongues* in a corporate setting suggests a dissonance in this expression of pentecostal identity. Despite a more vocal yet clear minority who expressed reservations about the *doctrine* of tongues, it appears that the *use* of glossolalia is nearly universal for pastors in private prayer. Less than half the pastors surveyed, however, regularly practice its corporate form of expression as "tongues and interpretations," in which one person speaks out in tongues and the congregation waits for a prophetic interpretation of the message to be given in the vernacular by one or two others.

Glossolalia, though central to AG doctrinal identity, is only one of many paranormal expressions found in early Pentecostalism and in contemporary neo-pentecostal revivals. Experiences of other gifts and manifestations common at Azusa Street during the early history of the AG, and during subsequent renewals, outpourings, and revivals, are now seemingly few and far between in the AG. This narrowing range of Pentecostal experiences held true for the pastors' accounts of their personal experiences (table A.2) as well as for their reports of corporate experiences within their congregational services (table A.3).

Only a minority of pastors regularly experienced prophecy, healing, deliverance, or other phenomena believed by many to be signs of the activity and presence of the Holy Spirit. For example, 34 percent claimed to have given a prophecy once a month or more. Forty-six percent reported being a prayer facilitator for a physical healing, and 41 percent for a mental and emotional healing. Only 13 percent, however, claimed regular involvement in deliverance from demonic oppression as a result of prayer. Put another way, 66 percent responded that they never or rarely gave a prophecy, 55 percent never or rarely witnessed a physical healing through their prayer, 60 percent were never or rarely a witness to emotional or mental healing, and 88 percent never witnessed deliverance from demons (see table A.2). Other physical manifestations common to contemporary revival meetings outside the AG were similarly less likely to be part of experiences reported by AG pastors: 94 percent were never or rarely slain in the spirit; 83 percent had never or rarely experienced holy laughter; and 76 percent had never or rarely experienced the bodily manifestation of shaking or jerking, all of which were commonly experienced during the recent revivals.

A similar pattern was found in pastoral reports of corporate ritual experiences among congregants (table A.3). Tongues and interpretation was reported as a regular experience for only 43 percent of the congregations. While only 2 percent of the pastors reported that tongues and interpretation (which are dictated by Pentecostal protocol) were never a part of their public ritual, for the remaining majority it was an infrequent occurrence. Only one-third of the respondents reported regular experiences of prophecy, a gift that serves a function similar to that of tongues and interpretations. Both are regarded as inspired words or messages from God delivered to the congregation, with prophecy being a simple message without the glossolalic prelude.

Although prayer for healing was a regular feature for 90 percent of congregational services, less than half of the congregations (41 percent) provided regular opportunity for sharing healing testimonies. It appears that healing prayer has become a nearly universal ritual in AG churches but that fewer churches include opportunities for testimonials commonly used to encourage and build faith for miraculous healing.[7] The fact that testimonies about healings received were far less likely to be reported than regular prayer for healing may point to underlying ambiguity about healing ritual as well as glossolalia. The differing frequencies of pastoral involvement in the expression of charisma during worship services and congregational use of gifts during worship (tables A.2, A.3) demonstrate the extent to which ongoing charismatic practices vary widely within the AG.

Ambiguity and the Ritual Dilemma

The history of the AG, as we have seen, is one of a revitalization movement that emphasizes an experiential baptism distinct from baptism with water. In the words of David du Plessis, an AG minister dubbed "Mr. Pentecost" by neo-pentecostals for his influence in the charismatic movement of the 1960s and 1970s, "God has no grandchildren." Because the identity of Pentecostals is rooted in paranormal religious experiences, their children cannot rely on their parents' experiences to claim Spirit baptism. Many adherents, however, appear to be lapsing into a cultural Pentecostalism that increasingly assumes an evangelical identity at the expense of pentecostal experience. This shift may be demonstrated by the changes in Pentecostal ritual over the decades, particularly the decrease in revival meetings where signs and wonders draw both the faithful and potential converts to be refreshed by pentecostal experiences.

In a recent discussion of the history of Pentecostalism, scholar Everett Wilson (1999, 92) emphasized the important role revival plays in the spread of this global movement:

> Whatever success the historian has in identifying the succession of Pentecostal outpourings in the early century, the issue is not 'who begat whom', but who or what brought to life and enthusiasm those many different specimens of Pentecostalism in diverse settings and sequences. A pedigree can show the relationship of each ascending generation to its predecessor, but each new generation still has to be born in reproductive passion. Revivals last not because the movement had an impressive beginning, but rather because periodic renewal keeps the enthusiasm vibrant despite energy-sapping generational, organizational and circumstantial changes.

Revivals, once common in the AG, have gradually taken a back seat to "seeker-sensitive" churches and well-promoted programs in many sectors of the denomination. They were first banished from Sunday morning time-slots and relegated to Sunday evening church gatherings and summer camps, and they increasingly have been replaced by other rituals in many AG churches, lingering only as rumors from a seemingly distant historical past as fewer pastors and their congregants experience the range of charisma found in early Pentecostalism. When new outpourings of charismata come along, the AG has been reluctant to recognize them as authentic moves of God.

Blumhofer's (1989, 57) observations about the similarities between early Pentecostalism and a revival from the 1940s called the New Order or the Latter Rain (which began in Saskatchewan and quickly filtered into mid-twentieth-century Pentecostalism) provide some insight for understanding the ambivalence of the AG toward fresh outpouring of charisma:

> Some first-generation Pentecostals had begun within a decade to bemoan their movement's waning power and had pointed to future, more copious showers of the latter rain. Consequently, there was even precedent for the eschatological innovation by the New Order [i.e., Latter Rain] advocates. Daniel Kerr, for example, noting a declining focus on healing as early as 1914, had heralded a coming dispensation in which healing would have the prominence accorded to tongues at the turn of the century. As Pentecostal groups had organized and charismatic fervor had waned in some places—or was largely confined to revival campaigns and campmeetings—voices had been raised asserting that the turn-of-the-century Apostolic Faith

Movement had seen only the beginning of a revival where more copious latter rains were yet to come.

While Blumhofer goes on to describe the AG rationale for rejecting the Latter Rain movement, particularly the movement's rejection of religious organizations and its indictment of old Pentecostal practices, the fact remains that the AG has been at times ambivalent or even hostile to pentecostal experiences that were introduced in other streams of the movement. The Latter Rain of the 1940s, a subsequent healing revival of the 1950s, and the charismatic movement of the 1960s and 1970s all, for the most part, occurred outside the Assemblies of God. They had a positive effect on AG growth during this period largely through pastors who risked the criticism of their peers and sometimes censure from leadership for their support of these newer movements

As can be seen in table A.4, most pastors do seem to be aware that the Pentecostal worldview is in continual need of revitalization. A vast majority (84 percent) agreed or strongly agreed with the statement "The AG must actively seek to revitalize its early Pentecostal roots." Very few (5 percent) agreed that in order to reach the unchurched "the AG must downplay the public use of the gifts of the Spirit" that are believed to accompany baptism with the Holy Spirit. The overwhelming majority of pastors verbally support AG identity as a Pentecostal denomination in which paranormal gifts are openly displayed, even if these manifestations might cause some discomfort for first-time visitors. Moreover, 85 percent of the respondents reported that their congregations are of "one mind" regarding "expressive worship practices," which have at times caused divisions and disagreements in the past.

Yet despite the verbal acquiescence, an unresolved paradox appears to exist between the widely acclaimed support for revival and openness to paranormal gifts, on the one hand, and the absence or near-absence of Pentecostal vitality in at least half of the AG churches, on the other. With the possible exception of tongues and interpretations (experienced regularly in 43 percent of the congregations included in this study), other gifts and manifestations commonly witnessed in large sectors of pentecostalism do not appear to be a regular part of AG ritual. The discrepancy between sentiments and behavior—between what people say and what they do—has long been observed by social scientists (cf. Deutscher, Pestello, and Pestello 1993; Deutscher 1973) and can be once again seen in the responses to questions about the Pensacola Outpouring and other renewal tributaries (see table A.4).

As we have seen, 86 percent of pastors identify with Pentecostal renewal/revival (R/R), reporting that being involved in R/R is extremely important or very important to them. Nearly all (98 percent) were aware of the R/R movement found at the Pensacola Outpouring and at other congregations in North America through reading articles in AG literature (100 percent) or in other Christian magazines (86 percent) and by talking with AG leaders/pastors (72 percent), with church members (70 percent), or with other persons who have visited popular R/R sites (86 percent). The overwhelming majority of the pastors appeared to be aware of contemporary revivals and seemed to have a single mind about the importance of reviving authentic Pentecostal spirituality. This does not necessarily mean, however, that AG pastors are of one mind about the Pensacola Outpouring and the other revivals of the 1990s. Pastors were evenly divided on the issue as to whether "America is in the midst of a revival similar to the one that gave birth to Pentecostalism." Despite the fact that the national leaders of the AG have given cautious approval and support to the revival at Brownsville Assembly of God (BAOG) in Pensacola, the average pastor appears to be reluctant to embrace it.[8]

While nearly all the pastors surveyed support revival in principle, and nearly all had heard about the Pensacola Outpouring and the larger revival movement, far fewer had experienced this latest outpouring of charisma for themselves. It is noteworthy that despite their verbal assent to the importance of revival, approximately two-thirds *have not* personally attended the nightly meetings at the BAOG in Pensacola or any of the other AG and non-AG renewal sites that dot the nation. The vast majority has not invited revival speakers to their churches (67 percent), nor have they attended an Awake America Crusade sponsored by BAOG in various U.S. cities (80 percent). Given this lack of first-hand contact, it is not surprising that only 30 percent of the pastors report their churches "to be actively engaged in the Renewal/Revival."

Summary

It is clear that most pastors perceive a decline in Pentecostal practices within the denomination: 70 percent either agree or strongly agree that "the gifts of the Holy Spirit are losing their prominence in AG churches as a whole." They report concern about the loss of pentecostal power, an embracing of a renewal/revival identity, and being informed about the various renewal sites, but surprisingly most have made little effort to investigate the rumors of revival for themselves.[9] Being of one mind around the core value of revival has apparently not translated into an acceptance of revival in contemporary dress. Present-day pastors, much like their predecessors, have been reluctant to accept charisma as it has taken flesh in periodic revivals of the latter half of the twentieth century and into the twenty-first. At least among some pastors, revitalization in traditional Pentecostalism is being relegated to doctrine rather than personal experience. Revivals are often acknowledged to be "messy," even by their supporters. It seems that established Pentecostal denominations like the AG may well prefer the safety of doctrine to the unpredictability of religious experience.

4

Structure and Charisma

Doctrine, Power, and Administration

> Most people lose or forget the subjectively religious experience, and redefine Religion as a set of habits, behaviors, dogmas, forms, which at the extreme become entirely legalistic and bureaucratic, conventional, empty, and in the truest meaning of the word, antireligious. The mystic experience, the illumination, the great awakening, along with the charismatic seer who started the whole thing, are forgotten, lost or transformed into their opposites. Organized Religion, the churches, finally may become the major enemy of the religious experience and the religious experiencer. (Maslow 1970, viii)

Although the humanist psychologist Abraham Maslow penned the above epigraph nearly sixty-five years after the Azusa Street Revival, the early Pentecostals would wholeheartedly have agreed with his thesis. Having experienced Pentecost like they believe the early Apostles did, they did not want to see it fall prey to "dead religion." Well into the 1980s, when Poloma was gathering data for *Crossroads*, many AG leaders were openly resisting becoming a "denomination," preferring to refer to their faith as a "movement" or a "fellowship."[1] There is less talk of the AG not being a denomination these days, but like pentecostals of all streams AG pastors eschew the "religion" label and prefer to describe their faith in more dynamic and relational terms. Despite this resistance to bureaucratization and institutionalization, however, we know of no serious move to dismantle the organizational structure. As we shall see, for the most part, pastors gave high marks to the denomination's performance of its administrative functions. Using O'Dea's concept of *dilemmas of delimitation, of power, and of administrative order*, we can take a closer look at the structural dilemmas faced by the AG as it tries to maintain an efficient organization and its distinct worldview.

The Dilemma of Delimitation: Doctrine and Pentecostal Experience

The dilemma of delimitation addresses the threat to charisma posed by the relativizing of the original religious message in relation to new conditions. One horn of the dilemma is the danger of watering down the message to fit the times, often rendering commonplace what was originally a call to the extraordinary. As we have seen, the AG runs a risk of grabbing onto this horn with its long history of courting non-charismatic evangelicals who are indifferent and often hostile to the distinct pentecostal worldview. Primitive charismatic tendencies are tamed as favor is bestowed on more pragmatic ritual and organizations. The other horn of the dilemma is the creation of rigid doctrines and religious legalisms established in an attempt to capture and reproduce the charisma of the original movement. As we have seen, the early founders of the AG initially were resistant to forming any kind of doctrinal statement, but they soon found it necessary to produce a statement of faith.

The AG Statement of Fundamental Truths is basically a fundamentalist-dispensationalist creedal statement, with "initial evidence" added to the other largely eschatological concerns. The adoption of this creed from fundamentalism precipitated the unfolding of the dilemma of delimitation; the stage was set for replacing right experience with right belief—a move that tends to water down the distinct Pentecostal worldview in which the Spirit of God moves freely, openly, and creatively in the lives of ordinary believers. O'Dea and Aviad (1983, 61) described the dangers of delimitation as follows:

> While the dangers of distortion of the faith require these definitions of dogma and morals, once established, the definitions themselves pose the possibility of another kind of distortion. They become a vast intellectual structure which serves not to guide the faith of untrained specialists but rather to burden it.

In theory, it is the task of the Holy Spirit to ensure that Pentecostalism neither sinks into the abyss of content-less mysticism nor becomes rigidly doctrinaire. Pentecostalism in its various faces has continuously needed to balance experience with biblical teachings, with adherents describing themselves as both people of the Spirit and people of the Word. At the heart of Pentecostalism is a conviction that the Bible is the inspired word of God. Pentecostals differ, however, in their hermeneutics, with scholarship tending toward an evangelical rational/propositional theology. They have, as Timothy Cagel (1993, 163) has noted, "aligned themselves with Evangelicals in their move toward adopting the methods of higher criticism," whereby the biblical text is reduced to the meaning intended by the author of the scripture without sufficient exploration of how it relates to the lived religion of the believer. Traditional Pentecostalism, despite its official fundamentalist creed, tended to place greater "emphases on the immediacy of the text and multiple dimensions of meaning" (ibid.) that made room for religious experience. Through its populist narrative theology it allowed for subjective experiences and interpretations to exist alongside the more objective critical-historical-literary methods. Even the doctrine of tongues as "initial evidence" emerged not from the pens of theologians versed in higher criticism but from the accounts told by those who experienced glossolalia and sought to align this experience with their reading of the Bible.

Today's official Pentecostalism is more likely to appear dressed in the rationalism of contemporary American society, devoid of the colorful and emotional accounts that found expression through the anointed preaching and testimonies of its earlier days. As we have seen, the seeds for this condition can be found in the early history of the AG, as its leaders sought to find acceptance and legitimation from the dispensationalist fundamentalists. Pentecostal scholar Gerald T. Sheppard (1984, 6) has commented on this "uneasy relationship between Pentecostalism and dispensationalism," observing how embracing evangelical views has "raised new problems for the identity of Pentecostals—hermeneutically, sociologically, and politically." Other scholars have also cautioned against the danger of an uncritical wedding of Pentecostalism with evangelical/fundamentalist theology. Harvey Cox (1995), for example, noted the paradoxical relationship between fundamentalist Christianity and modernity, cautioning that fundamentalism is but a crude form of nineteenth-century rationalism that is not compatible with a pentecostal worldview.

Evangelical rational thought, with its propositional truth, can undermine the importance of religious experiences, the stuff out of which pentecostalism is made and through which it maintains its vitality. At the same time, it has provided a useful form for professing the faith, one that has enjoyed common and uncritical acceptance by most AG pastors. This present study as well as an earlier one (Guth et al. 1997) suggest that AG pastors are of a near single-mind on most common theological issues. Of the eight Protestant denominations included in the study by James Guth and his colleagues, the AG is clearly the group in most accord on basic doctrine. This theological core and some attendant ambiguities provide the foundation for discussing the delimitation dilemma.

The Bible, Fundamentals, and Orthodoxy

On matters of biblical orthodoxy, AG pastors score higher than clergy in the Southern Baptist Convention, Evangelical Covenant Church, Christian Reformed Church, Reformed Church in America, United Methodist Church, Presbyterian Church in the USA, or Disciples of Christ (Guth et al. 1997). On basic biblical beliefs coupled with premillennial eschatology (the idea that Christ will return to earth *before* the prophesied worldwide tribulation to take his followers to heaven in what is known as the *rapture*), AG pastors responding to the survey demonstrated almost unanimous agreement (see appendix A, table A.5). One hundred percent agreed or strongly agreed that "there is no other way to salvation but through belief in Jesus Christ," 99 percent believe "the devil actually exists," and 98 percent agreed or strongly agreed that "Scriptures are the inerrant, literally accurate word of God not only in matters of faith, but in all matters." Ninety-four percent agreed or strongly agreed that the "Bible clearly teaches a 'premillennial' view of history and the future," and 98 percent reported believing in the immanent "rapture" of the church.

Widespread agreement on basic Christian tenets, which appears to be stronger in the AG than in other denominations, may be due in part to its tendency to downplay the refinement of doctrine. As AG historian William Menzies (1971, 376) observed nearly thirty years ago, the AG "has been surprisingly free of theological controversy, possibly owing to the relative unconcern of the fellowship with the niceties of doctrinal distinctions."[2] Menzies goes on to state: "The traditional emphasis has been experiential and practical, not ideological. Absolute trust in the Bible and general agreement on fundamentals of the faith have served to furnish a fairly tolerant basis of fellowship."

Once removed from theological orthodoxy, however, some ambiguities can be seen lurking beneath the surface of the seemingly placid doctrinal waters. As we saw earlier, the survey suggests an ambiguity about a dispensationalist hermeneutic that speaks of a major potential cleavage. While 58 percent reported accepting a dispensationalist interpretation of Scripture, 42 percent rejected this approach. The wedding of dispensationalism and Pentecostalism by a majority of pastors points to the downside of not wrestling with theological "niceties" within the denomination. A de facto theology has emerged, but one that fails to mirror the lived religious experiences inherent in the pentecostal worldview. Of particular concern in exploring the dilemma of delimitation is the degree to which the "definitions of dogma and morals" within the AG contribute to maintaining or quenching a distinct Pentecostal identity.

Ambiguity and Dissent on Select Doctrinal Issues

Traditional Pentecostalism has birthed a movement that it has been unable to monitor. The Spirit blows how and where it will, and much of the activity within the past fifty years has been outside of classical Pentecostalism, within the so-called Latter Rain, charismatic, and third-wave sectors of the Spirit movement. AG scholar Cecil M. Robeck (1999b, 8) describes the dilemma faced in the wake of an expanded pentecostal movement as follows:

> While it is indisputable that the needs of some people are being met in these newer congregations, sometimes the very categories with which they choose to identify suggests a new form of elitism. Older Pentecostals are now being portrayed as *passé*, while these groups promise that God is on the move in their midst. They are the latest "wave" of what God is doing. Older "waves" have been passed by. As members of the first "wave" of what God is said to be doing in the Church today, Pentecostals must now deal with the same feelings that members of the historic churches had when they were first faced with the claims that Pentecostals were proclaiming the "Full Gospel." For some older Pentecostal groups, this has introduced questions of self-doubt or very human desires to discredit the "new" as not sufficiently up to God's standards.

Of significance for this discussion is that many of these newer streams have tended to de-emphasize the importance of glossolalia for Spirit baptism, much to the chagrin of classical American Pentecostals.[3] This simultaneous downplaying of speaking/praying in tongues while emphasizing the presence and power of the Holy Spirit appeals to neo-pentecostals (although there is recent evidence that more leaders are taking note of the importance of glossolalia in maintaining a supernatural worldview). Popular American Baptist sociologist/theologian Tony Campolo raises the issue in *How to Be Pentecostal without Speaking in Tongues* (1994), a book written for a larger evangelical audience. Campolo joined others outside the Pentecostal camp in rediscovering the power of the Holy Spirit. They adopted and adapted the Pentecostal worldview of Spirit baptism, suggesting that there is more to being a Christian than believing the accepted doctrines and practicing the right rituals. Glossolalia, which for most Pentecostals became the symbol of distinct identity, is being eroded by the influence of the larger pentecostal movement, in which many refuse to accept the centrality of tongues as "initial evidence." This seems to be causing AG leaders to cling more strenuously to this one plank of doctrine that makes them different.

Christians are increasingly aware that the Pentecostal perspective is no longer marginalized but has gone mainstream. G. Menzies (1998, 175) commented that whereas most Christians once "regarded glossolalia in particular as a token of fanaticism and emotional excess," now,

> due to the eruption of the charismatic movement in the 1960s and its widespread success in popularizing this Pentecostal understanding of spiritual gifts outside Pentecostal circles, the notion that all of the gifts of the Spirit are available to the contemporary church no longer constitutes a "distinctive" of Pentecostalism. And while Pentecostals rejoice that in this regard the rest of the church has moved in their direction, this "success" has only intensified the need for Spirit baptism and evidential tongues to provide distinctive identity and internal cohesion to Pentecostalism.

The logic of the AG leaders, who until a recent turnover in top leadership had been trying to tighten up the doctrinal wording, thus minimizing the mental gymnastics that some pastors engage in annually to renew their ordination credentials, runs something like this: the key to Spirit baptism is tongues, the key to revival is Spirit baptism, the key to church growth is revival.[4] Without tongues there can be no Spirit baptism, no revival, no church growth. To back down on what is increasingly becoming a controversial doctrine in some sectors of the AG, according to this logic, would send the AG traveling down a slippery slope of losing its Pentecostal identity and jeopardize the institutional well-being of this thriving denomination. At the same time that this particular symbol is being sharpened, the actual use of glossolalia and other experiences that birthed Pentecostalism seems to be waning within the AG.

While for many AG leaders and pastors (at least in North America) glossolalia remains a litmus test for "true" Pentecostalism, it is a doctrine increasingly held up for scrutiny. Although the vast majority (85 percent) of pastors affirmed the doctrine in their survey responses, a significant minority (15 percent) expressed disagreement with it.[5] If glossolalia is in fact the "initial physical evidence" attesting to Spirit baptism, how is it that others are experiencing a range of pentecostal-like phenomena without emphasizing tongues? Some answered the question by saying that eventually the Spirit-baptized person will speak in tongues, leading to the insertion of the word "immediate" before "initial physical evidence" to tighten the doctrinal reins. Even more disconcerting to those who would make tongues a litmus test for Spirit baptism is the fact, as we have seen, that in many AG congregations the majority of adherents do not report speaking in tongues. The combination of such observations with an evangelical hermeneutic have caused a small but growing number of pastors to question the biblical base for the doctrine. Although a majority of pastors state their support for the official position—and we have no way of determining how many of these are engaged in their own mental revisions of this plank even as they acquiesce to it—a significant minority opposition movement exists in the AG. Those who tackle the issue, however, do so at the risk of their own status as ordained AG ministers.[6]

The doctrine surrounding glossolalia is one of two major issues that have generated controversy over the years. The other is divorce and remarriage among AG laity and especially among church pastors. In the congregational survey that provided data for *Crossroads*, approximately half of the adherents of AG churches reported beliefs that were not in compliance with the stance of the denomination on divorce. The 1973 "Statement on Divorce and Remarriage" clearly proscribed divorce, but left the question of remarriage for adherents to "be resolved by the believer as he walks in the light of God's Word" (Poloma 1989, 148–49). While adherents were given permission to discern the issue of divorce and remarriage for themselves, until very recently divorced ministers were granted no such freedom of conscience about remarriage after divorce. Even if the divorce and remarriage occurred prior to conversion, a divorced and remarried person could not be ordained. (Rumblings could be heard, however, about annulments being granted that have enabled some high-ranking ministers to avoid the censure of losing credentials after divorce and remarriage or after marrying a divorced person.) After defeating similar measures in 1991 and 1997, in August 2001, the AG General Council passed a resolution that allows divorcees to become pastors *as long as the divorce occurred before their conversion.*

This recent action of the AG General Council partially resolved the divorce-and-remarriage issue. Many pastors appear to be in favor of increased flexibility in dealing with divorce and remarriage in their own ranks, just as there has been for laity. Pastors responding to the survey reported considerably less support for the official AG position on ministers divorcing and remarrying than at the time of the first pastoral survey in 1985, when only 10 percent of pastors disagreed with AG policy of defrocking divorced and remarried pastors. The present survey found that 43 percent agreed or strongly agreed with the statement "Persons who have been divorced and remarried should be permitted to serve as AG pastors"; however, only 19 percent reported a *strong disagreement* with the statement that divorced and remarried pastors should be banned from the ministry, suggesting that most desire increased flexibility in dealing with this thorny issue. Further, only a minority of pastors (23 percent) would prohibit divorced and remarried persons from assuming leadership in local congregations—a position that further illustrates the denomination's inability to withstand accommodative forces stemming from a widespread acceptance of divorce and remarriage in the larger culture.

Another set of moral proscriptions remains as a vestige from the past, when all worldly amusements were shunned by Pentecostals, who set themselves apart from the larger world to live "holy" and "separate" lives. The survey asked about four practices that represent the last remains of a former extensive behavioral "holiness" standard: drinking alcohol, gambling, dancing, and attending movies. Attitudes toward such behavior remain fairly strong among pastors (although sermons are rarely preached on these issues in most urban AG churches). A clear majority disapproved of "gambling, including lotteries" (98 percent); even "the occasional use of alcoholic beverages" (82 percent); social dancing (80 percent); and Christians patronizing "movie theaters" (51 percent) (see appendix A, table A.5).

More strikingly than in other well-established Protestant denominations, a seamless robe surrounds Christian orthodoxy in the AG, extending even to its particular eschatology and most moral and behavioral taboos. The garment wrapping distinct Pentecostal theology, however, does show some signs of wear. Pastors seemingly are divided on some remnant moral issues that once seemed central to Pentecostal identity—behavior and practices that set Pentecostals aside as a "peculiar people." Attempts to select any doctrinal items, as the leadership has done with glossolalia and divorced ministers, to prevent further slide down the proverbial "slippery slope," appears more likely to cause division than to reinforce Pentecostal identity. What seems needed to deal with the slippery slope is not a tightening of doctrinal reins but rather continued flexibility that allows controversy around issues peripheral to the larger Pentecostal worldview. Perhaps the best way to deal with controversial issues is to frame them theologically within a new pentecostal paradigm—one that reflects an openness to personal experience and narrative that aligns with Pentecostal identity as a Spirit-led people (Ma 1999).

Spirit baptism remains a core feature of Pentecostal identity, but increasingly it is not equated with the first experience of glossolalia. Spirit baptism (or "infilling") is often treated as an ongoing process in which pentecostals of all streams experience the power of God not only for personal pleasure and edification but also for empowerment for service (Macchia 2006b). Power and empowerment cannot be legislated or mandated by doctrinal decrees or denominational edicts, but rather depend on hospitable terrain that allows the wind, rain, and fire of the Holy Spirit to fall as it will. A fertile environment can be created, but the desired work of the Spirit is in every sense *charisma* or gift—an observation that takes us to the dilemma of power. The accommodative forces at work in O'Dea's dilemma of power are important for understanding the interrelationship between attempts to enforce doctrinal decrees on pastors and the empowerment sought by early Pentecostals.

The Dilemma of Power: From Pilgrims to Citizens

The theme of accommodation to the larger culture is one that runs through all of the institutional dilemmas, but perhaps no dilemma focuses on a more important facet of accommodation than the dilemma of power. O'Dea and Aviad (1983, 63) succinctly describe the dilemma of power as follows:

> Religion cannot but relate itself to the other institutions of society and to the cultural values. Yet such accommodation tends toward a coalescing of religion and power. The alliance of religion and secular power creates a situation in which apparent religiosity often conceals a deeper cynicism and a growing unbelief.

Although the early Pentecostals were not trained in sociology, they seemed to have a natural instinct for the importance of separation from the larger world for retaining their distinct worldview. As Blumhofer (1993, 42) noted, "Early Assemblies of God members professed little interest in contemporary society; they had either not yet glimpsed a broader social world or had consciously turned from it." They began their sojourn as pilgrims, but slowly and steadily moved toward becoming citizens. Nowhere is this better illustrated than in the move from an apolitical stance with a strong sense of Spirit-led destiny to embracing the political agenda of fundamentalism/evangelicalism. A premillennial eschatology proclaiming the imminent end-times and rapture of the church, which once kept Pentecostals at bay from politics, now seems to undergird a staunchly conservative political agenda (Guth et al. 1997).

The Core and the Periphery: Consonance and Dissonance in Political Thought

As the Christian Right began to flex its political muscles during the 1980s and 1990s, the AG struggled with its role in the political scene. Few AG pastors plunged into partisan politics (although a significant majority of them are self-reported Republicans), but they did begin to speak out on select issues. Based on both congregational and pastoral data as well as other research on conservative religions and politics, Poloma (1989, 157) noted a distinction between private morality and public political issues that continues among AG pastors:

> Although the dividing lines are somewhat blurred, it appears that the Assemblies of God is quite concerned about private moral issues, such as divorce, pornography, drug and alcohol abuse, and abortion, that touch on "personal purity." Its leaders, however, are much more reluctant to step into the area of "public issues," including economic problems, social welfare legislation, and international affairs. Most appear not only to oppose political involvements that focus on the public sphere but also carefully to eschew partisan politics.

The increased visibility of and attention paid to the Christian Right has prompted many AG pastors to take a role alongside other evangelicals in politics as well as in theology, a stance that Blumhofer (1989) has linked with the AG's one-sided involvement with the National Association of Evangelicals. Not only are pastors now more likely to express concern over select political/moral issues, but many reportedly expect the judicatory to lead the way in conservative political action. For example, 86 percent of the pastors in the present survey indicated their belief that the National Office should "serve as a political voice to combat homosexuality and abortion," with another 3 percent relegating this task to the District Offices, and only 11 percent indicating that such activity should be performed by neither judicatory. Fewer pastors, although still a clear majority, support judicatory action to promote select political candidates; 59 percent assigned this task to the National Office and 8 percent to the District Offices, with 33 percent replying that such political activity is not appropriate for either denominational administrative office.

AG pastors increasingly are being drawn into an evangelical political agenda that fails to mirror an earlier Pentecostal understanding of power. As

AG members have subtly transitioned from being pilgrims to citizens (Blumhofer 1989), a corresponding shift in emphasis has occurred from reliance on pentecostal power to one on political power. The passage from Zechariah 4:6 quoted earlier still can be found on the front cover of each issue of *Today's Pentecostal Evangel*: "Not by might nor by power, but by my Spirit, says the Lord." The classic Pentecostal understanding of that passage and the issue of Pentecostal empowerment warrants closer inspection for unpacking the relevance of the dilemma of power for the AG.

Power, Politics, and Empowerment: A Minority Report

The AG serves as a good illustration of the strong connection between theological and political conservatisms in American politics. The history of Pentecostalism suggests, however, that this relationship is due more to doctrinal issues than to pentecostal spirituality. When pentecostalism is in its charismatic moment, political agendas seem to lose significance as actual behavior may become (at least for the moment) somewhat radical. In the words of a popular renewal song that became a theme of the so-called "Toronto Blessing," Spirit-filled people will "break dividing walls"—walls that can be found between men and women, blacks and whites, Pentecostals and non-Pentecostals, old and young, and so on.[7] According to some Pentecostal historians, dividing walls fell at the Azusa Street Revival that birthed Pentecostalism but were quickly reconstructed during the years that followed. Gender, social class, race, ethnicity, and denomination all become less relevant (at least temporarily) when the power of the Spirit is sweeping over a gathering of people, leaving ecstasy in its wake.[8]

Despite the apolitical stance of the early Pentecostals, many seemed to understand that the pentecostal experience was meant for service (cf. McGee 2005; Macchia 2006b). Speaking in tongues, for example, initially was conceived as an infused knowledge of a foreign language for missionary activity. Those who tried to exercise their new language in foreign countries were usually disappointed, but their disappointment did not cause them to abandon glossolalia. Tongues was reconceptualized as a door that opened for the believer a storehouse of spiritual power, with missionaries coming to expect Pentecostal signs and wonders to provide for their necessities and to bring others to the Christian faith. Reports by missionaries then—and now—affirm this link between Pentecostal power and service. As AG scholar and veteran missionary Douglas Petersen (1999, 4) describes the situation in a commentary on Macchia's (1999) excellent article calling for a paradigm shift in Pentecostal thinking:

> From its inception, emphasis upon supernatural empowerment for ministry, observes Macchia, rather than academic formation was the motivational force behind the ever-expanding pastoral and missionary activity of the movement. Characterized by the active participation of its members as "doers" of the word, assessment of Pentecostalism by themselves or others, according to Macchia, usually focused on their enthusiasm, emotional expressions, or exponential growth.

Macchia (and seemingly Petersen) would encourage a shift in emphasis to include the spiritual power underlying Pentecostal missionary activity, particularly the pentecostal experiences of Spirit baptism and divine healing.

> These spiritual encounter moments serve as a corrective antidote for these distinctive theological beliefs which are traditionally embodied within the uncritical constructs and limits of doctrinal guides. When supernatural experiences are integrally linked together with the person of Christ, Macchia argues, they offer potential for Pentecostals to move beyond a personal experience of self-gratification toward becoming part of a prophetic movement for both spiritual and social liberation (Petersen 1999, 4).

The AG's uncritical acceptance of a conservative political stance, at least in the United States, is not consistent with the nature of the potentially radical Pentecostal experience. The Azusa Street Revival, the event that catapulted the Pentecostal gospel, according to some historical accounts, empowered blacks and women long before the Civil Rights and Feminist movements of the 1960s. However, this breaking down of dividing walls was short-lived as organized Pentecostalism mirrored the same problems of racism and sexism found in the dominant culture.

Sexism, social-class inequities, racism, ecumenism, and other issues that captured the attention of liberal Protestantism more than a generation ago are slowly finding their way into AG awareness, causing more ambiguity around the core. Some have heard the challenge offered by scholars like Ronald Bueno (1999), a Salvadoran Pentecostal anthropologist, to begin "listening to the margins"—to reflect on Pentecostalism as it has been constructed by different ethnic groups (see also Daniels 1999). Others are calling for greater openness to women's issues within Pentecostalism, noting how Pentecostalism's success has limited opportunities for women (Blumhofer 1995; Benvenutti 1995; Gill 1995; Everts 1995; Everts 1999; Poloma 1995). Still others have begun working on the challenge of interfaith dialogue as pioneered by the late David du Plessis as he shared his Pentecostal belief and worldview with non-pentecostal Christians—a mission continued today by Cecil M. Robeck, an AG minister and professor at Fuller Theological Seminary, who continues to serve as a Pentecostal representative to international ecumenical gatherings.[9] The isolationist mentality that has made the AG so wary of "ecumenism" has inadvertently cut off the denomination not only from traditions that could provide much-needed insight for developing a truly pentecostal theology but also from fresh revival experiences. As we have seen, the AG has tended to distance itself from those who are most likely to share its worldview, namely those neo-pentecostals in mainstream Protestantism, Roman Catholicism, and the independent charismatic movement.

There is evidence that the work done by Pentecostal scholars is slowly filtering through some pastors and into the pews, increasing an awareness of the importance of tackling issues beyond the narrow focus of so-called family values. This awareness is not shared by all, thus creating some additional ambiguity around the core of near-universal positions. Seventy percent of the pastors in our survey, for example, agreed that "issues of social concern really get to the heart of the Gospel." After years of encouraging black Americans to join the largely black "sister" organization, the Church of God in Christ, 93 percent of the pastors agreed or strongly agreed that the "AG should actively work to attract persons of color." Women's issues appear to be more divisive. Although the AG has ordained women throughout its history, only 72 percent of pastors support women serving as senior pastors. A smaller number (57 percent) would support women in leadership positions within the National or District AG government or on local church boards (53 percent).

Although the Assemblies of God has done an admirable job of establishing a loose-knit, cooperative worldwide network that is sensitive to regional and cultural differences, until recently the American church has been relatively homogeneous. The sample of pastors responding to the survey reflects this old homogeneity that lingers in AG leadership: Only 5 percent of the respondents were female and 97 percent self-identified as "white"; one respondent was African American, two were Hispanic, two were Asian American, and two identified themselves as "other." The congregations pastored by these respondents, not surprisingly, tended to be Caucasian, native-born American. Significantly, 6 percent of the congregations were either mostly (3 percent) or entirely (3 percent) comprised of Hispanic Americans. Less than 1 percent were primarily African American congregations, and 1 percent were primarily Asian. The pastor survey thus fails to capture a change underway in the ethnic composition of the American AG, a heterogeneity that can be seen in the congregational sample.

Figures on ten-year church growth of the Assemblies of God reveal a slight decline in white AG churches from 1990 to 2000, alongside a noteworthy increase in the number of ethnic churches (which is responsible for the overall increase in the number of churches and adherents claimed by the AG for the past decade).[10] A document titled "The Church in Transition," put out by the Commission of Ethnic Relations in 2000, notes:

> Change doesn't happen overnight. It occurs in small stages. It is usually so subtle that it goes undetected until we are overwhelmed by it. Because of this we don't always understand the affect [*sic*] of change and we don't always know how to respond to change. We don't see it happening and when we look back we wonder how we could have missed it and what we should have done.
>
> I say this because I believe the Assemblies of God is now in the midst of what could be the most dramatic change since the founding of our Fellowship in 1914. I also believe we need to recognize and understand what this change means to us as a fellowship of Pentecostal believers. The change I speak of is not a doctrinal change and it is not a change that poses a threat, but rather an unparalleled opportunity. The change I speak of is a change in the composition of the church. *We are becoming more ethnic minority* [emphasis in original].

Social forces have compelled Pentecostals to accept the increasingly pluralistic nature of American culture, with the AG being a beneficiary of the new waves of immigration that promise to "change the composition of the church." To date, however, the African Americans, Hispanics, Asians, and "others" are not commonly found in the mainstream of the American AG polity but are often relegated to "special language districts."[11] The change in composition currently underway in the AG will undoubtedly have repercussions for the power dilemma we have considered, as well as for the issue of delimitation.

The Dilemma of Administrative Order: Elaboration and Alienation

The final dilemma we will discuss brings us back to the emergence of the Assemblies of God and its transition from a "cooperative fellowship" to a denomination with a complex bureaucratic structure.

Charisma does not exist in pure form; some degree of organization is necessary to promote and protect her spirit. Despite an earlier resistance to organization, the AG is now a well-structured bureaucracy. At the top of the flow chart is the General Council of the Assemblies of God, made up of clergy and representatives from all member congregations, which gathers every two years. The overall administration of the AG is under the direction of the Executive Presbytery, six elected officers (General Superintendent; Assistant General Superintendent; General Secretary; General Treasurer; Executive Director, US Missions; and Executive Director, World Missions) and eleven other non-resident executive presbyters. The Executive Presbytery, together with various boards, directors, counselors, and committees, governs and ministers to the needs of the denomination. Growth within the AG has led to a proliferation of programs to mobilize groups and resources, including those with an evangelistic emphasis, such as missions, a drug program, university campus outreach, and military and prison chaplaincies; those that focus on education, including a division of Christian education, bible and liberal arts colleges, and a publishing house; and service programs adopted by most congregations to provide opportunities for fellowship and learning from cradle to grave (Blumhofer 1989). Buffered between the National Office and the local congregations are the District Offices, each with its own bureaus, most of them based on geography but others based on ethnicity or special need (e.g., churches of the deaf). This is the complex organization that attempts to maintain the vision and carry out the mission of the Assemblies of God—an organization that appears to have the respect and support of a vast majority of AG pastors.

Coherence around the Administrative Core

Our pastoral survey, as well as an ancillary survey of 250 leaders of regional judicatories conducted during the Organizing Religious Work (ORW) project, revealed solid support among AG leaders for the work being carried out by the national and regional governing structures. Those in the ancillary study tended to give high marks to the way the church has met ministry objectives, with only a small minority indicating that denominational effectiveness has decreased over the past five years. These objectives (and the percentage of respondents indicating approval) included providing resources for spiritual revitalization (98 percent); expanding overseas mission efforts and ministries (99 percent); attracting and keeping members in the denomination (86 percent); attracting ethnic minority members in particular (94 percent); maintaining high-quality clergy in local churches (93 percent); keeping unity of purpose within the denomination (90 percent); creating a financially stable national church (100 percent); developing an identity as a global church presence (98 percent); attracting ethnic minority clergy (92 percent); strengthening the health of local churches (91 percent); getting judicatories to share resources with one another (93 percent); and maintaining a denominational identity in local churches (80 percent). Whether reviewing this report card internally or comparing it to those of other groups included in the ORW study, the AG administration appears to pass with high marks.

Similar expectations for and satisfaction with the governance of the denomination can be found in the pastors survey. A majority of pastors indicated that the following tasks should be primarily the responsibility of the National Office:[12] marshal available resources for world evangelism (91 percent); provide press information on AG for the secular world (89 percent); serve as a political voice to combat homosexuality and abortion (86 percent); support seminary and bible colleges (80 percent); safeguard doctrinal conformity (78 percent); support denominational liberal arts colleges (72 percent); develop congregational programs such as Royal Rangers and Missionnettes (71 percent); coordinate missionary activities (66 percent); promote renewal/revival (60 percent); serve as a political voice to elect God-fearing candidates to public office (59 percent); and develop suitable educational resources for local congregations (58 percent).

The vast majority of the respondents were knowledgeable about and expressed strong approval of the denominational work being done in the realm of missions and evangelism.[13] Pastor awarded ratings of "good" to "excellent" to the Division of Foreign Missions, Teen Challenge (drug and alcohol rehabilitation), Speed the Light (ministries for young people), and Light for the Lost (a more general evangelical support program). A vast majority of the pastors also reported being knowledgeable about and gave positive ratings to publications and Christian education programs developed by the National Office. The weekly magazine *Today's Pentecostal Evangel* and the work of Gospel Publishing House both rated "good" evaluations, with the Division of Christian Education receiving a slightly lower approval rating, mid-way between "fair" and "good."

Two years after his election to the top church post in 1995, then general superintendent Thomas E. Trask noted that he wanted the denominational bureaucracy to serve churches rather than the other way around. Trask told *Charisma* magazine, the major publication for the pentecostal movement,

"We want to address the needs of the local church and the pastor. We want to be known as servants of the local church" (Ford 1995, 62). For the most part, it appears that pastors and leaders give high marks for such efforts. At the same time, as with each of the dilemmas, there are areas of ambiguity and potential alienation that merit some note.

Administrative Ambiguity and Potential Alienation

Given the history of the AG and its resolve not to become a denomination, perhaps it is not surprising that the report card provided by the pastoral survey on the administrative dilemma includes a few lower grades. There is a seeming and possibly increasing alienation among pastors from the National Office, particularly if alienation is measured by decreased attendance at the biannual General Council meetings. Only 40 percent strongly agreed (4 percent) or agreed (36 percent) with the statement "I always do whatever I possibly can do to attend General Council meetings." The key for understanding this seeming apathy toward once-important gathering may be found in the pastors' response to another statement: 46 percent either agreed (10 percent) or strongly agreed (36 percent) that the General Council "does not provide an adequate forum for discussing differing opinions on key issues." In informal discussions, some AG pastors are quick to raise the Pensacola Revival and "initial evidence" as examples of failures to hear differing opinions on these currently hot topics. These pastors have also commented that they prefer to use their time and money going to conferences (very often outside the denomination) that are more relevant to their ministries than those of the AG.

Pastors also indicated concern about the AG becoming a denomination in a post-denominational society. More than half (54 percent) agreed or strongly agreed with the statement that the AG needs to "focus more on being a religious network and less on being a denomination." Our informal discussions with pastors suggest that many would like the denomination to do more to provide opportunities for fellowship and spiritual growth.

The AG has historically been ambivalent about higher education, and the survey responses may reflect current ambivalence—or possibly indifference—to the sponsorship of higher education by the denomination. Although a majority of pastors agreed that it was the responsibility of the National Office to provide support for its colleges and seminary, more than 40 percent of the respondents did not feel they knew enough about the denomination's colleges in Springfield, Missouri (where the AG national headquarters is located), to provide a rating, and 38 percent were unable to rate the seminary. The mean ratings for Evangel University, Central Bible College, and the Assemblies of God Theological Seminary were "fair." Pastors were most familiar with Berean University, the correspondence course designed to train AG ministers, which they rated as "good," the highest rating given for AG work in the educational realm.

Silence, as suggested above in the discussion of AG institutions of higher education, may actually provide a porthole for discerning dissatisfaction. While fewer than 5 percent of respondents failed to provide a score card for ministries such as Gospel Publishing House, the Division of Foreign Missions, and *Today's Pentecostal Evangel*, this form of "no response" was fairly high for the Executive and General Presbyteries. Twenty-two percent of the pastors were reluctant (reportedly because of a lack of knowledge) to rate the job being done by the Executive Presbytery and the General Presbytery. Among those who did rate them, the mean scores for the Executive Presbytery and the General Presbytery were somewhere between "good" and "fair."

Despite some negative comments we have heard over the years about the increased centralization of the AG, such hearsay appears to be a minority report (31 percent). Most pastors strongly disagreed (8 percent) or disagreed (61 percent) with the statement that "too much power is being centralized in the National Office." Respondents were nearly divided in whether they used the services provided by the National Office, with (56 percent) either agreeing (51 percent) or strongly agreeing (5 percent) that their churches made "extensive use of the services provided by the National Office."

Pastors seem to be somewhat more supportive of their respective district offices than they are of the National Office. Given their dependence on and expectations of the district to provide networking opportunities (including nominations for church positions), they appear more likely to attend their district council meetings than the national General Assembly. Seventy-one percent strongly agreed or agreed that District Councils "are a good investment of my time." Use of District Office services appears to be strong, with 84 percent of the ministers strongly disagreeing (26 percent) or disagreeing (58 percent) with the statement "I cannot find any service provided by the District Office that is of particular use to my congregation."

The list of services that the majority of pastors expect from their district offices include the following: provide opportunities for pastoral fellowship (88 percent), provide workshops for ongoing pastoral training (73 percent), establish appropriate networks for pastors (70 percent), provide resources for smaller churches (68 percent), provide pastoral/congregational "covering" (64 percent), develop programs to encourage pastoral spiritual growth (52 percent), and provide credentials for ministers (51 percent). The last item is of special interest given that the National Office provides the credentials, having taken over even more authority after a disagreement between the Louisiana District and the National Headquarters over censuring AG televangelist Jimmy Swaggart in the 1980s after his penchant for pornography and prostitution was made public. Only 48 percent of the pastors indicated support for the national credentialing of ministers.

Charisma and Administration

From the AG's inception as a formal organization in 1914, its adherents have had a love-hate relationship with institutionalization. Although the leaders of this new religious movement recognized the need for organizing to carry on its mission, they also recognized the perils that structure would pose to their fragile, newfound gift of charisma. The healthy tension between charisma and organization that could be observed over the years in the AG continues today. Many are wary of the threat that administrative offices pose to charisma, but many also trust the Holy Spirit to lead both congregations and denominational administrative offices.

When pastors were asked, "To what extent does the manifest presence (e.g., prophetic leadings, tongues and interpretations, etc.) of the Spirit affect the decision making process of your local congregation?" only 19 percent reported "greatly," with another 54 percent replying "somewhat." Twenty-seven percent (a significant minority for a denomination whose identity is rooted in a worldview that has historically recognized the power of the Holy Spirit) responded "not at all." A clear majority of pastors report that the Holy Spirit guides the leaders and workers in various bureaus, agreeing (58 percent) or strongly agreeing (11 percent) that the "Holy Spirit directly affects the decision making process in most AG administrative agencies." Once again, however, a significant minority (31 percent) appears to regard the day-to-day operations of the denomination much like they might regard the workings of any secular modern organization.

Godly Love and the Crossroads

The Assemblies of God contains a solid core of beliefs and practices, with a healthy level of tension around peripheral issues. Its growing ethnic diversity positions it for an even more visible place in the American religious mosaic of the twenty-first century. The report cards provided by both the pastoral and judicatory surveys demonstrate a solid core of pastoral support for the administrative functioning of the denomination. Charisma and institutionalization, at least in the minds of a majority of pastors, are still interwoven nearly one hundred years after the AG's founding.

The ambiguity around the central core of each of O'Dea's five institutional dilemmas, however, provides some guidelines for charting the future. Perhaps the greatest challenge faced by the AG is what might be termed its "identity crisis." If the AG is going to be a major player in the American religious mosaic in the twenty-first century, it requires a paradigm that can reflect its unique qualities—qualities that better fit a postmodern culture than a modern one. Among other things, Pentecostalism has made the common experience of the divine available to a spiritually starved materialistic culture, taught the meaning of paradox to a Western world steeped in propositional logic, revived a sense of miracle and mystery among people trapped in the cage of rationality, and provided opportunities for catharsis in a civilization fearful of emotion. AG identity, however, is increasingly expressed in terms of rational doctrine that masques the playful creative Spirit that pentecostal believers have encountered throughout the last century. Pentecostalism is more than "evangelicalism plus tongues," and to limit its identity in this way robs the AG of its rich heritage.

The failure to develop a consistent Pentecostal theology within an appropriate paradigm has made it difficult to affirm revivals within AG churches and renewal movements outside its boundaries. As we have seen, while some congregations have embraced fresh wind and fire, the response of pastors and denominational leaders toward the new waves of charisma has mostly been to critique and to tighten control rather than to test the experiences by riding the waves. The tendency to quench charisma can most clearly be seen in our discussion of the dilemma of delimitation. On one horn of the dilemma we find the watering down of Pentecostal identity due to inevitable accommodative forces; on the other, attempts to control ministers through dogmatic edicts in hopes of making them more "Pentecostal."

Also to be gleaned from assessing charismatic routinization through the lenses of O'Dea's dilemmas is how accommodative forces have eroded a distinct prophetic voice that could have developed from a well-articulated Pentecostal theology and sense of Pentecostal history. The experiences of the Pentecostals who challenged the sexist and racist cultural norms of early-twentieth-century America could have paved the way for later disciples to make significant contributions to feminism and civil rights. Its early pacifist stance could have provided a plank for the peace movement. Its suspicion of rigid denominationalism in the face of a democratized baptism of the Spirit could have provided a platform for ecumenical activities. None of this happened, in part due to the isolation of Pentecostals during the first half of the twentieth century. As Pentecostals moved across the tracks to a more comfortable lifestyle, followers tended to lose sight of their movement's unique identity. Increasingly, they were no longer the marginalized people upon whom the Spirit released His power and presence in the earliest years of the twentieth century. As they made the journey from pilgrims to citizens, AG pastors seemed to take on the political voice of the fundamentalist-evangelical church as expressed through the Republican Party.

On the whole, however, the findings that indicate the AG to still be at the crossroads (a quarter century after Poloma collected the original data) are reason for guarded optimism. Within our assessment of O'Dea's institutional dilemmas and the routinization of charisma, we can see not only routinization but also revitalization. This process appears to be what we are calling Godly Love at work, with reports of divine–human interaction that are linked to benevolent outcomes. During the earliest years of Pentecostalism, when the revival fires burned brightly on Azusa Street and the movement was in its "charismatic moment," cultural norms that kept the races divided and women without a public voice were challenged not by edicts but by action believed to be divinely inspired. God, as promised through the biblical prophet Joel (2:28–20), appeared to be pouring out his Spirit "on all people," causing some believers to defy segregation norms, to make room for women leaders, and to refuse to serve in the military during World War I. Early Pentecostals regarded the baptism of the Holy Spirit as empowerment for ministry, particularly during what most believed to be the "last days" of the world as they knew it. This was no time for racial divides, denominational bickering, or limiting the work of women. It was important for all to labor together to spread the Christian faith, empowered by such spiritual gifts as tongues, prophecy, and healing. Early Pentecostal eschatology assumed that Jesus was returning to earth soon to usher in a new millennium of God's kingdom. Despite their countercultural stances on war, race, and gender, however, Pentecostals were not actively involved in condemning World War I, in questioning the racism of the time, or in promoting the feminist movement that granted women the right to vote. While some Americans were working to further equality and justice in American society, this was not the Pentecostal way. Theirs was a spiritual path believed to pave the way for a heavenly order on a new earth.

When talking about divinely empowered benevolence, as conceptualized in the theory of Godly Love, it is important to remember that benevolence often lies in the eyes of the beholder. Those who bring gifts are not always regarded as philanthropists, and today's heroes may become tomorrow's villains. Pentecostals had a gift to bring, and that gift was their understanding of Christianity, which included a belief in and experiences of the supernatural. Despite their affirmation of women, interracial gatherings, and pacifist stance, they would not have promoted changing the world either through peaceful legislation or through war. Benevolence for them was focused on the use of the spiritual gifts, including glossolalia, prophecy, and healing, which transcended time and space in empowering them to usher in the kingdom of God.

Summary

Throughout our discussion of Godly Love within Pentecostalism, we have seen that benevolence generally consists of a blend of Rolf Johnson's "care-love," or compassion, and "appreciation-love," or vision. The vision for Pentecostals has always been rooted in their understanding of and love for the Bible, but this understanding has been altered over time. One hundred years after the Azusa Street Revival, Pentecostal believers still profess the second coming of Jesus with the reign of Christ to follow, but for most it is no longer the guiding vision. The focus of appreciation-love continues to be on the Bible, but *on the Bible as understood by groups of believers* acculturated into twenty-first century America, where pragmatic action commonly trumps more primitive beliefs. For example, pacifism as understood by many Pentecostals during the First World War was shaped not only by the biblical passages related to war and peace, but also by expectations about the second coming of Jesus. As eschatological expectations shifted away from Jesus's imminent return, a pragmatic support of preemptive military action would eclipse pentecostal pacifism (Alexander 2007). Serving in the military to protect America would take precedence over a biblical call to "love your enemies." A related and more recent shift in appreciation-love and its accompanying vision can be seen in the drift of the denomination toward the "religious right" or conservative (commonly Republican) politics and the decline in the number of AG women ministers despite the AG's long history of ordaining women. The judicatory and pastoral leadership of the AG has continued the move away from an emphasis on spiritual forces that were once believed to have the power to bring in the new millennium toward supporting the concrete political agenda of contemporary evangelicalism and of the religious right. This stance includes actively challenging the teaching of evolution, support for preemptive military action, condemning homosexuality, and constraining the roles played by women as congregational pastors and in the judicatory.

A biblically-based vision, at the foundation of Pentecostal appreciation-love, is thus an indicator of Pentecostal benevolent action. As we will see in the congregational data, however, AG adherents have been shifting away from the negative "thou shalt nots" toward an emphasis on serving both physical and spiritual needs. This command to love as empowered through the work of the Holy Spirit reflects an AG where experience of the mystical is ongoing, and where the pragmatic and the supernatural can dance together in a worldview that transcends the premodern/postmodern dichotomy. Our assessment of the judicatory suggests that AG structure and polity is permeable enough to provide a medium for the charismatic play of the Spirit within the congregational life of the church.

We will begin our exploration of pentecostal paranormal phenomena and their relationship to living out the gospel of love—namely, the Great Commandment to love God and love one's neighbors—with a discussion of Spirit baptism. Using the survey voice of the congregants, we will see that the theoretical construct of Godly Love empirically demonstrates the significance of pentecostal experiences (especially glossolalia, healing, and prophecy) for benevolent action. Of particular interest are the effects that Spirit-filled experiences have on attitudes and behaviors that serve not only to reflect but to revitalize Pentecostal identity.

5

Spirit Baptism and Spiritual Transformation

An Exercise in Socio-Theology

> Many Pentecostals, especially in the United States, consider speaking in tongues as evidence of the experience [of Spirit baptism]. Not all Pentecostals globally hold to the doctrine of speaking in tongues as the initial evidence of Spirit baptism, however, the *experience* of glossolalia is arguably still fairly widespread in the movement. . . . [William J.] Seymour regarded tongues as a sign of the empowerment of the church to reach out to all nations, implying a boundary-crossing experience that produces a diverse church. He noted, "God makes no difference in nationality, Ethiopians, Chinese, Indians, Mexicans, and other nationalities worship together." He later regarded love as the primary sign of Spirit baptism. (Macchia 2006a, 35)

Baptism in the Spirit, identified as the "crown jewel" of pentecostal theology by AG theologian Frank Macchia (2006c), is at the heart of pentecostal spiritual transformation. An experience subsequent to Christian conversion or being "born again," it opens believers' eyes to a dimension of reality that is a-rational and supra-empirical. Spirit baptism marks the beginning of a journey of empowered spirituality for service that is at the core of Godly Love, with "signs and wonders" that reflect a "supernatural" dimension of daily life. Its main functions have been described in a position paper by the General Council of the Assemblies of God (2000, 2) as follows:

> The baptism in the Spirit is not an end in itself, but a means to an end. The scriptural ideal for the believer is to be continually filled with the Spirit (Ephesians 5:18). Baptism in the Holy Spirit is the specific event that introduces the believer to the ongoing process of living a Spirit-empowered life.

> Although speaking in tongues is the outward sign of Spirit baptism, it is designed by God to be much more than evidence. Subsequent speaking in tongues brings enrichment to the individual believer when employed in private prayer (1 Corinthians 14:4) and to the congregation when accompanied by the interpretation. (1 Corinthians 14:6-25)

The concept of Spirit baptism, like other theological tenets found in the AG Statement of Fundamental Truths, is grounded in the Christian scriptures (McGee 2008; Macchia 2006a). Its early modern roots can be traced to John Wesley's quest for "perfection" (unwavering loyalty of the will to the love of Christ)—a crisis experience also reflected in nineteenth-century American revivalism and called "the baptism in the Holy Spirit" (Macchia 2006b). Pentecostalism arose in part in response to the Wesleyan Holiness movement and its emphasis on "sanctification" with an alternate interpretation of Spirit baptism. As Macchia (2006b, 109) notes, "Pentecostals came to view Spirit baptism as an empowerment for witness as evidenced by heightened participation in extraordinary gifts of the Spirit, especially speaking in tongues."

Despite the recognition that Spirit baptism is more than tongues, the primary focus has often rested on "the initial physical evidence" rather than on "empowerment for witness." This position has periodically met with controversy in the denomination. As early as 1918 one of the best-known leaders in the AG, Fred Francis Bosworth, submitted his resignation from the newly formed sect as he became convinced that "*any* of the gifts of the Spirit would suffice as evidence of Spirit baptism" (Menzies 2005, 116). As a result of Bosworth's questioning of the doctrine of tongues as the "initial evidence" of Spirit baptism, "a resolution adopted at the 1918 General Council made the teaching of anything contrary to the initial physical evidence doctrine a matter of 'serious disagreement'" (Menzies 2005, 116).

We focus here on the complex relationships among Spirit baptism, glossolalia, ritual embodiment, love, and empowerment as tested through the lens of the theoretical construct we are calling "Godly Love." Again, *Godly Love is the dynamic interaction between divine and human love that enlivens and expands benevolence.* With Godly Love as the theoretical frame, the congregational surveys provide the content as we statistically test the empirical relationship between the profession of Spirit baptism, the practice of glossolalia, the experiences of other revival manifestations, and evangelism, the primary measure of benevolence used in this chapter. Complementing the quantitative survey data are qualitative reports from interviews conducted with AG adherents from a related study of Godly Love that add "thick description" to the survey findings.[1]

Glossolalia and Spirit Baptism in Context

In exploring the earliest pentecostal descriptions of Spirit baptism and how speaking in tongues was regarded as a source of spiritual empowerment, AG church historian Gary McGee (2008, 128) offers this succinct and insightful summary: "Pentecostals consciously strove to model the spirituality of first-century Christians and conform their own experiences to scriptural norms. Yet, the spiritual and missiological unity they enjoyed did not prevent the surfacing of different perspectives on the linguistic nature of tongues, prayer in the Spirit, and the gift of interpretation. The populist bent of the movement encouraged participants to tease out the details for themselves." Although the AG soon developed a clearly defined position on the topic of Spirit baptism and its relationship to glossolalia, pastors and congregants continue today, as did their ancestors, to "tease out the details for themselves."

As we have seen, AG pastors are required to profess the experience of baptism in the Spirit with the accompanying evidence of speaking in tongues before ordination and to annually sign a statement to reaffirm this belief. Yet a significant minority of pastors who responded to our survey (16 percent) either strongly disagreed or disagreed with the official denominational position (see appendix A, table A.5). Moreover, even if they are in accord with the doctrinal statement on tongues as the "initial evidence" of Spirit baptism, many pastors fail to foster this belief and practice within their congregations. For example, less than half of the pastors (47 percent) said that they regularly offered congregational prayer for Spirit baptism (see table A.3). Despite the official theology on Spirit baptism, some pastors are admittedly fearful of offending newcomers with traditional Pentecostal rituals and practices, including speaking in tongues. Our congregational survey data show that AG adherents are even less likely than their pastors to agree with the official position of the AG that tongues is the "initial physical evidence" of Spirit baptism—84 percent of the pastors as compared with 62 percent of the congregants. Quite possibly some pastors who personally accept the AG position on tongues and Spirit baptism are concerned about offending not only visitors but also a significant number of their existing members.

Despite the noteworthy departure from traditional belief and practice, the glass can still be described as approximately two-thirds full. The clear majority seems to accept, both cognitively and experientially, the AG position on tongues and Spirit baptism. Seventy-seven percent of our congregational respondents claimed to be baptized in the Spirit, with another 8 percent indicating they were uncertain (15 percent said they were not Spirit baptized).[2] It is significant that *69 percent of the respondents claimed that they spoke in tongues* (with another 5 percent saying they once did but no longer do so). For the most part, it appears that those who report being certain of their Spirit baptism also speak in tongues.[3]

Given the doctrinal emphasis on speaking in tongues, however, it is reasonable to point out that while the glass may be two-thirds full, it is still at least one-third empty. Less than half (49 percent) of the congregants regularly pray in tongues, suggesting that for many it is not a particularly meaningful practice or experience. Thirty-one percent of the sample reported that they never pray in tongues, and another 20 percent indicated that they do so "once in a while," with the remainder praying in tongues on a fairly regular basis. This finding stands in contrast with the survey of pastors, of whom 88 percent reported that they prayed in tongues at least weekly (see appendix A, table A.2). Clearly pastors are more glossolalic than AG adherents.

Although glossolalia is most frequently used as a personal form of prayer, the community plays an important role in fostering, modeling, and defining its use (Baker 1995). The interplay between the church community and the personal use of tongues is reflected in our finding that the frequency of glossolalia is clearly related to the type of congregation in which the respondent worships. Congregants in *traditional* and *renewalist* congregations, whose members are in greater agreement that it is important for them to "walk in the supernatural," are more likely to report frequently praying in tongues. Eighty-nine percent of those in either traditional or renewalist congregations have (at least at some time) prayed in tongues. This figure drops to 71 percent for alternative congregations and 74 percent for evangelical pentecostal ones, where congregants appear to be more wary of "supernatural" experiences.

A similar pattern is found when we look at those who pray in tongues "many times a day": 28 percent of the *renewalist* adherents and 21 percent of the *traditional* church adherents (but only 12 percent of the *alternative* and 15 percent of the *evangelical pentecostal* congregations) have made prayer in tongues an integral part of their daily lives. Of the demographic measures used in our analysis—age, gender, race, education, income, and whether or not the respondent was raised in a pentecostal church—only age was statistically significant. Older adherents are more likely than younger ones to speak in tongues and to be regular users of this gift of the Holy Spirit (see appendix C, table C.1).

These preliminary statistics suggest that those who fear that the AG may be losing its "crown jewel" of Spirit baptism may have good reason for their concern if the litmus test is glossolalia.[4] The shift of many AG churches from traditional to evangelical congregations in our four-fold typology suggests that there are fewer AG congregations in which glossolalia is modeled than there were a generation ago. Moreover, younger adherents in all types of congregations are less likely than older members to support the official doctrine or to experience glossolalia. The shift in the congregational typology and the fact that younger adherents are less likely to integrate glossolalia into their spiritual lives do not bode well for the future of the doctrine of glossolalia as the "initial evidence" of Spirit baptism.

Although our survey data does not include former AG adherents, in our research on exemplars of Godly Love (Lee and Poloma 2009a) we have encountered several respondents between the ages of twenty and thirty whose spiritual narratives shed additional light on what may be happening to glossolalia in the AG. We use an account provided by April (not her real name), a twenty-six-year-old elementary school teacher, who in the course of her interview spoke of intense experiences of the Holy Spirit as she walks in "power and love" in a neo-pentecostal network. Although we make no claim that April represents all young people who may have left the AG, her story reflects other similar accounts that we have heard both in that study and in interviews conducted with young neo-pentecostal volunteers in an inner-city urban ministry (Poloma and Hood 2008). These young people may have experienced Spirit baptism with tongues in the AG and may continue to be highly glossolalic, but they are dissatisfied with the AG emphasis on tongues as "initial evidence."

These respondents would concur with Heidi Baker (1995)—a popular neo-pentecostal evangelist and missionary to Mozambique who holds baccalaureate and master's degrees from an AG university and is herself highly glossolalic—when she unreservedly states in her Ph.D. dissertation: "The Pentecostal insistence of tongues as evidence of Spirit baptism must be rejected" (p. 73). While noting that Pentecostalism "is much more than a tongues movement," Baker insists that glossolalic prayer is a "unique element of Pentecostal spirituality" with greater significance for Christianity at large than was previously recognized. She adds, "It may be considered as a valid, nonrational, private and personal form of prayer which edifies the believer and is available to all Christians" (Baker 1995, 149). April's story provides an example of a young person raised in the AG who, like Baker, has rejected official AG theology on tongues being the "initial evidence" of Spirit baptism, but who paradoxically embraces and values the practice of praying in tongues.

April's Narrative

April enthusiastically shared her memory of how excited she was when her parents began attending an AG church when she was nine years old. She told of how she was "baptized at eleven at my own request," adding that she "had come to know the Lord and to know his voice at a young age." She continued talking about her early journey by describing the importance of Sunday school and her "most wonderful Sunday school teacher who taught us about forgiveness and the great love of God—that touched my heart pretty radically." She laughingly added, "After I was baptized, I immediately started evangelizing my friends. Although I told them all about hell, I never got anyone saved." The story of her pre-adolescent experiences and enthusiasm reflected an intimacy with God and a desire to please God by serving others. It was a time of ongoing "conversations and dialogue" in which she learned to discern the voice of God, including a vision and a call to ministry. Noting the importance of the AG in her early spiritual formation, the interviewer interjected, "So you heard the Gospel and learned about the power of the Spirit in your church." April corrected the statement with a prompt and decisive response:

> I learned a lot about praying in tongues! To be honest, I didn't learn much about the power of the Spirit. I did have a baptism-in-the-Spirit moment, but the only thing that people could talk about was my praying in tongues. It was so much more than that, but I didn't have words to express what had happened. When I was twelve or thirteen [at youth camp] I experienced a baptism in the Spirit. I felt the presence of God come on me so strong that I knew something had happened inside me. But I didn't have a language for it, and the only thing that was cultivated by people in my church was speaking in tongues. I didn't know how to explain what was going on in my body (physical manifestations) or what I was feeling emotionally, and nobody was talking about it. They were just talking about tongues and explaining the baptism in terms of tongues. So I set the experience aside, not really certain what to make of it. It was so much more than tongues. It wasn't until I had the experience again in a different setting that I knew that I had an experience of Spirit baptism or infilling, and this experience was so much more than the gift of tongues.

The interviewer then asked, "Am I hearing you correctly? What you are calling 'baptism in the Spirit' is an ongoing process. It can be experienced again and again, taking you deeper and deeper with different experiences. Does that make sense in terms of your understanding?"

> Yup. It does. I think that is the Greek meaning. I think when we did a word study in class, baptism in the Spirit means being consistently and continually filled. I have had and continue to have these experiences that have taken me deeper and deeper into the love and the power of the Spirit.

In the interview April shared how after abandoning the use of glossolalia as an adolescent, she later experienced a "resurrection of tongues" and was able to find a satisfactory meaning for the experience. She now prays in tongues daily and "feels called" to spend an hour a day worshiping God and building up her own spirit as she speaks in this "heavenly language." But before she came to appreciate the gift of tongues, she quit using it completely during her mid-teens, only to have it return after she began attending a Vineyard church, a third-wave denomination that is often accused of being "soft" on tongues.

> Because all I knew from the AG church was speaking in tongues, I started to resent it and started to be afraid of it. So I actually quit speaking in tongues. I would have dreams and hear myself speaking in tongues and I would be in worship service at the Vineyard church and feel my tongue start going, and I would bite my tongue—literally. So I silenced my tongue, but I would still hear it in my head but it wouldn't come out.

Tongues would eventually be "resurrected" for April during a deliverance service she experienced in the Vineyard church. April described the effects of the restoration of tongues as follows:

> So I got my gift of tongues back, which really revved up my spirit. I now use tongues every day—in fact I have a conviction that I should pray in tongues for at least an hour a day. Every time I feel physically sick, I pray in tongues. Anytime I feel depressed or spiritually attacked, I pray in tongues. It is my first line of defense because it edifies me—it builds me up. (Interviewer: And that was an understanding of tongues that you got in the Vineyard?) Yes, it was. The Assemblies never really taught me what to do with tongues. Once it was explained to me that tongues was a gift given to me to edify myself, I got that little tool that helped me to understand. Then

> I learned that was what I should be doing as I worshiped every morning. It wasn't something just to show off at church.
>
> That was the culture I grew up with in the Assemblies—who could pray in tongues the loudest was the game that was played. That's just how it was in my little church, to be honest. And it was the same obnoxious woman who was terribly mean who prayed in tongues the loudest. And I thought, "Wow, that's no fun" (laugh). So the transition happened in the Vineyard. And I think there was confusion [in the AG] between the "gift of tongues" and "speaking in tongues." The Assemblies teaches a lot about giving tongues from the platform so that someone can interpret the message. But I didn't hear about how tongues could edify myself and strengthen me. So I really thought you just did it in church.

Based on our interviews with April and others, it would appear that although most neo-pentecostal networks do not emphasize tongues apart from the other charismata, glossolalia may actually have more immediate spiritual relevance in some neo-pentecostal churches than in the AG. We have noted that many involved with neo-pentecostal networks may be "walking in the supernatural" in ways that reflect early Pentecostalism but without the doctrine of "initial evidence." Our statistical findings suggest that for many the AG doctrine may have actually stymied the use of tongues and the wider range of the charismata.

A Doctrinal Dilemma

Although the doctrine of "initial evidence" is still intact, it is increasingly questioned, especially by young adherents. The decreased significance and use of tongues among AG adherents is further reflected in a decline of traditional Pentecostal services that commonly promoted the experience of Spirit baptism. Sunday morning services are now more likely to take on the form of plain-vanilla evangelicalism rather than wild-fire pentecostalism; many Sunday evening revival services have long been canceled as commuter congregations replace local ones; summer camp meetings that once inaugurated youth into pentecostal experiences have given way to more programmed events; and revivals that periodically erupt in unlikely places are regarded with suspicion. As illustrated by the case of April, there are decidedly fewer opportunities in most congregations for those seeking the baptism of the Spirit to find a meaningful experience of it or a grid in which the experience can satisfactorily be placed.

The dilemma that even life-long AG congregants may encounter between their personal experience and the AG doctrine on Spirit baptism is illustrated by Ted's narrative. Ted, an elderly ordained AG minister, began his interview for the Flame Project saying that he didn't know if he had "any episodes that tower over others" in his spiritual experiences. When encouraged to share incidents from his spiritual journey as they came to mind, he began with his adolescence, in which he experienced the discomfort of not having spoken in tongues:

> It was something of a crisis—not having received the baptism in the Spirit. The most sensitive years were the high school years. There were people who were telling me they were praying for me—which they would do literally at the altar if I would let them. Some would say that I was "away from the Lord," which I did not think so (but at the time I guess I took their word for it). I even ran away at one time. Friends interpreted it as my running away from the Lord but I would interpret that it was running *to* the Lord and not *away* from him. Eventually I did receive the Spirit baptism at the age of fifteen, and that brought social relief from being hounded.

The interviewee then asked, "What was the experience of Spirit baptism for you?" Ted responded:

> Disappointing (pause). Disappointing in this way. When I began speaking in tongues my feet were firmly on the floor. In other words, I wasn't on a cloud somewhere. When you heard the testimonies, that is what the experiences sounded like. When I first started speaking in tongues (at the altar in church) an elder dragged me over to another boy saying, "You pray for him; you have just received the baptism." I had no interest in praying for him, and I slowly backed away. It was not what I expected by any means. It was not the peak experience of my life. I will affirm to this day that I did not gain any advertised values of the baptism of the Spirit—empowerment for service. I don't think that my service was any different than it was before. I don't.

As with many (if not most) of our Flame respondents, Ted did not regard Spirit baptism as one of the epiphanies of his spiritual life. Instead, his reported spiritual journey was much like most others in that study, in which respondents were more likely to single out their initial conversion and their call to service than the first time they spoke in tongues (if they spoke in tongues at all). It was generally only with further probing by the interviewers that tongues would be discussed.

Despite the attrition in the use of glossolalia, a clear majority in our survey of congregants does profess to be in agreement with the doctrine, to be Spirit baptized, and to speak in tongues at least on occasion. In order to explore the significance of tongues, its relationship to Spirit baptism, and the relationship between glossolalia and Godly Love, we compared responses from regular glossolalics and non-practicing glossolalics (those who never speak in tongues and those who rarely do). Does being highly glossolalic have an effect on Godly Love?

Pentecostal Glossolalia in Perspective

Glossolalia has been called a "universal religious phenomenon" that has taken a variety of forms (May 1956). Non-Christian varieties include *dramatic* glossolalia (occurring in "television situation comedies when actors spontaneously initiate a language then put the punch line into the vernacular"); *spiritualist* glossolalia among spiritual mediums; *pathological* glossolalia as found in schizophrenic disorders; and *pagan* glossolalia, both ancient and modern (Spittler 2002). In Christianity "sporadic accounts of glossolalia could be found among the [early Church] Fathers, the Catholic Saints, the Radical Reformers (Enthusiasts, Anabaptists and other groups), the Quakers (1624–1690), the Camisards (1685–1705), the Jansenists (17th–18th centuries), the Moravians (1722), the early Methodists (1730), the Shakers (1747), the Irvingites (1830), and the Holiness and Evangelical Movements (nineteenth century)" (Baker 1995, 170). Of particular relevance for us is Christian glossolalia as practiced by pentecostals and neo-pentecostals, a form that has experienced a global resurgence with the advent and spread of Spirit-filled movements since the beginning of the twentieth century.

Researchers have approached Christian glossolalia from differing perspectives and assumptions in their attempts to answer questions about its essence, functioning, and legitimacy. When the experience of glossolalia leapt across the tracks from the early classical Pentecostals like the AG (in the first half of the twentieth century) into mainline Protestant and Catholic churches in the 1960s and 1970s with the charismatic movement, the small body of literature on the topic (based mostly on spiritualist mediums) was expanded to reflect a growing interest in the phenomenon. Rather than reinforcing assumptions that glossolalia was a symptom of pathology, speaking in tongues was found to have possible positive psychological effects.[5] More recently, in part due to the decline of the charismatic movement in mainline churches and the decreasing emphasis on tongues in pentecostal and neo-pentecostal churches, social-scientific interest in glossolalia appears to have diminished.

In light of existing evidence, it would appear likely that the ability to speak in tongues is an innate one, generally requiring a voluntary yielding to the tongues experience and a decisive resolve for its regular use. Yet the motivation, form, and meaning clearly differ significantly across time, cultures, and subgroups due to learned behavior (Samarin 1969). What we do not know from social science—and can never prove through scientific lenses—is whether a transcendent God is actually pouring out divinity in Spirit baptism and the practice of glossolalia. We concur with Miller and Yamamori (2007, 158–59), who astutely draw the following conclusion after discussing their observations on pentecostal worship and prayer:

> While some Pentecostal experiences lend themselves quite nicely to functional explanations, it often seems like one is running up against a wall in trying to understand people's deeper motivations by simply appealing to rational choice models, deprivation theories, and the like. Perhaps some of the time, and for some people, there is "something more" at play in their experience. If one were to accept this hypothesis, it certainly would not mean that one is ruling out all the variables that social scientists enjoy manipulating, such as social class, geography, race and ethnicity, and so on. Obviously these variables provide the context within which religious pursuit occurs. Rather, one is simply adding a variable, the realm of the Spirit, to one's theoretical tool kit.

Clearly social science has been negligent in its disregard for potential spiritual factors and its tendency to reduce spirituality to material factors.

Glossolalia: Meaning and Practice

As early Pentecostals dealt with the controversies over linking glossolalia doctrinally to Spirit baptism as its attendant "evidence," they were seemingly seeking to "make sense" out of an anomalous experience. Some were quick to regard glossolalia as a known language that would equip believers "in these last days" to spread the gospel in foreign lands without the long arduous process of study and training in foreign languages. AG historian Gary McGee (2005, 38–39) notes that as early as 1906 some began to have reservations about this function of tongues for missions, and he notes an early shift toward defining glossolalia as primarily a prayer language:

> Most came to recognize that speaking in tongues, though still considered recognizable languages and intrinsic to Spirit baptism, represented worship and prayerful intercession in the Spirit. For the most part they seemed to accept the transition in the meaning of tongues from preaching to prayer since on either reading—glossolalia for functioning effectively in a foreign language, or for spiritual worship—the notion of receiving languages denoted zeal and empowerment for evangelism.

As we view glossolalia through the lenses of the survey data we see an ongoing shift in restricting the understanding of glossolalia to an unknown prayer language.

Even with this shift in meaning, however, praying in tongues still retained a social dimension in most AG churches. As we saw in the case of April (when she made a distinction between the "gift of tongues" and "speaking in tongues") AG churches have traditionally emphasized the use of glossolalia use in corporate worship in two ways: as communal prayer and as a form of prophecy.

Communal prayer was once widely practiced before the church service or during a time of congregational exuberance. It entailed praying together aloud (and loudly, often with sobs and wailing, kneeling with face buried in the pew) in intercession to God. Some prayed in tongues and some in the vernacular, with most alternating between the two, as the congregation interceded together for personal and corporate needs. Our site visits to churches over the years suggest that communal use of tongues, once a model of the practice for non-glossolalics, seems to be dying out in most larger, urbanized, Euro-American AG congregations where there is less room for pentecostal exuberance and spontaneity in worship gatherings.

A second corporate use of tongues (more often stressed than communal glossolalic prayer) can be found in the practice of "tongues and interpretation." The Holy Spirit is believed to empower the utterance in tongues and to inspire the interpretation by providing, not a translation, but a sense of a prophetic word for the congregation. God is thus believed to be speaking directly and prophetically to His people through human instruments. Forty-three percent of the pastors reported that this practice occurred regularly in their congregations. The congregational survey data suggests, however, that the practice may not be as frequent as reported by the pastors—or if it is, the same small group of people is usually involved. Only 7 percent of the congregants indicate that they regularly give a message in tongues at a worship service, while 71 percent report that they have never done so.[6]

In a survey conducted two decades ago a battery of items previously used in a local survey on prayer and prayer experiences (Poloma and Pendleton 1991a; 1991b) was included in a national Gallup poll (Poloma and Gallup 1991) to obtain information about experiences of God during prayer. Not surprisingly, pentecostals were more likely to score higher on prayer experiences than the average American. In *Crossroads* similar prayer experience items were found to be correlated with the reported use of glossolalia among AG congregants. Without exception, frequent glossolalics scored higher on each of the other commonly used prayer experience measures designed to tap perceived interaction with God.[7]

Glossolalics in our survey (as in the earlier *Crossroads* survey) continue to be more likely than those who do not speak in tongues (or who do so infrequently) to report experiences of the unmistakable presence of God, obtaining deeper insights into spiritual truths, receiving revelations directly from God, receiving answers to specific prayer requests, and hearing divine calls to perform specific actions.[8] They were also more likely to experience a more universal mysticism in which they felt everything disappear but consciousness of God, to have experiences of God that words could not express, to feel their selves merging with God, and to have experienced God and lost awareness of time.[9] Perhaps most important for understanding the relationship between glossolalia and the vertical (divine–human) dimension of Godly Love, glossolalics were more likely than non-glossolalics to report feeling God's love as the greatest power in the universe. Seventy-five percent of those who prayed in tongues "daily or more" also reported experiencing the power of God's love daily, while only 15 percent of those who *never* prayed in tongues reported similarly frequent experiences of God's love. In other words, those who prayed in tongues more frequently were more likely to be Christian mystics (Campolo and Darling 2007).

A Cautionary Caveat

When assessed in light of commonly reported prayer experiences, we found that those who seldom or never practice glossolalia may not enjoy the same depth of religious experiences as those who are regular glossolalics. This finding is significant for understanding the role the gift of tongues plays in the spiritual lives of pentecostals. It appears to be a physical sign of the non-material, deep and frequent mystical experiences enjoyed by believers, holding a key to the divine–human interactions that are hypothesized to be an energizing source of Pitirim Sorokin's 1954/2002) "love energy." Given that only about half of AG congregants regularly use glossolalia as a prayer language, a dilemma faces the denomination as it seeks to emphasize the doctrine of tongues. If it fails to provide opportunities for modeling tongues through its use in church rituals, through testimonials of frequent glossolalics, and in teachings that resonate with actual experiences, glossolalia may continue to slide into irrelevance with the increasing evangelicalization of AG congregations. On the other hand, if leaders and pastors seek to restore praying/speaking in tongues to the position it once held in denominational rituals and personal experiences, it will risk frustrating and alienating those who fail to have meaningful glossolalic experiences. As it is now, speaking in tongues is in danger of becoming "some kind of badge that we pull out once in a while as proof that we have been baptized in the Spirit" (Chavda 2003, 21) It appears that some pastors and many congregants—as we saw in April's story—may not be interested in a doctrine that is more of a "badge of proof" than a dynamic ongoing experience.

Glossolalia and Embodied Worship

While glossolalia is regarded by most AG clergy and congregants alike as the "initial physical evidence" of the unseen grace of Spirit baptism, other sacramental signs (alluded to by April in her account) have accompanied pre-pentecostal American revivals and are rekindled periodically during contemporary revival experiences. Such physical signs include jerking, shaking, resting in the spirit (or "going down under the power"), uncontrolled laughter and/or weeping, and even rolling on the ground. Glossolalia can thus be regarded as but one of several physical manifestations of Spirit activity experienced by pentecostals. What religious historian Ann Taves (1999) calls "fits, trances, and visions" have commonly been part of the American revival scene, bringing with them controversy, criticism, and critique.

The debates between religious "enthusiasts" and "intellectualists" have a long history in America, going back to the transatlantic awakening of the 1730s and 1740s, during which people experienced bodily agitations not unlike those that would later be seen in pentecostal revivals around the globe. The early debate brought criticism from various sectors, including from the Congregationalist minister Charles Chauncy, who was concerned with social order and commitment to an established church. Moderate defense of the bodily agitations, trances, and visions came largely from revivalists, including the cautious Jonathan Edwards and the more accepting John Wesley. The "enthusiasts" (from the Greek, literally "filled with God") believed that God could be encountered with one's whole being, while the "intellectualists" were convinced that any encounter with God was one of the mind. Meanwhile, the defenders differed among themselves in their judgments of the authenticity of various bodily demonstrations (Taves 1999).

A similar scenario played out during the early years of Pentecostalism, in which some sought to distinguish "true" from "false" revivals. The Chauncy-like position was taken by the Holiness and Reformed churches, from which many early Pentecostals were forced to leave once they experienced glossolalia. Another split later occurred between two of the most significant players in the outbreak of Pentecostalism in the early twentieth century. Charles Parham is often credited with conceptualizing the doctrine of tongues as the "physical evidence" of Spirit baptism after one of his bible school students in Topeka, Kansas, spoke in tongues. William Seymour, who studied briefly under Parham, is best remembered for his pivotal role in the Azusa Street Revival that launched Pentecostalism into global orbit. As Taves (1999, 328) notes: "If Charles Parham, preoccupied with counterfeits, was (loosely speaking) the Jonathan Edwards of Pentecostalism, then William J. Seymour was Pentecostalism's John Wesley." While Edwards and Parham both accepted limited somatic expressions as authentic work of the Spirit, Wesley and then Seymour were far more willing to let the weeds grow along with the wheat than to quench what they believed to be the activity of the Holy Spirit.[10]

Embodied Experience and Pentecostal Ritual

As sociologist Meredith B. McGuire (2008, 98) has astutely noted: "All religions engage the individual through concrete practices that involved bodies as well as minds and spirits." The embodied ritual practices, however, are more apparent in some religions than others, as in premodern religious practices of "drumming, dancing, vision quests, sweating and chanting." The worldview of pentecostalism, as we argued earlier and as demonstrated though the embodied practice of glossolalia, is holistic in its integration of body and spirit (cf. Hollenweger 1997; Land 1993). During times of revival, embodied experiences are more intense and varied, often becoming the center of controversy as in the revivals of old.

In order to explore the effect of revival influences on congregational members, we asked about four embodied religious manifestations that were commonly found in the revivals of the 1990s and that are still experienced periodically in AG church services. These bodily manifestations have been points of contention for many AG leaders, who are often closer to Edwards than Wesley in their wariness of the physical manifestations like falling down under the power of the Spirit, shaking, jerking, loud weeping, laughing, and occasionally rolling on the floor (as did early Pentecostals, a practice that led to the pejorative label "holy rollers"). A majority of the AG congregants (55 percent) had never experienced the physical manifestations of uncontrollable shaking or jerking that are common in many revivals (although 8 percent claimed to have them "regularly" and another 19 percent "sometimes"). A similar distribution of responses was found for "being slain," "falling under the power," or "resting in the spirit," with 52 percent saying they never had these experiences, while 9 percent claimed to have them regularly. Respondents were least likely to experience "dancing in the spirit," with 58 percent saying they "never had the experience" while 9 percent had it "regularly." "Singing in the spirit," commonly seen as corporate singing in glossolalia, is the practice most likely to be reported, with only 39 percent saying they had *never* experienced it and 19 percent responding "regularly."

Despite the reluctance of many AG leaders to support these embodied rituals as being authentic biblical experiences, evidence in this study and earlier work on revivals (Poloma 1998a and b; 2003) suggests that these somatic manifestations may be regarded as sacramental "outward signs" of an inner grace.[11] Glossolalia itself, as we have already noted, can be conceptualized as "sacramental," or as an embodied sign of the inner grace known as Spirit baptism. It is thus not surprising to find that regular glossolalics are much more likely than infrequent or non-glossolalics to report other somatic experiences during worship or prayer.[12] It would seem safe to say that glossolalia is not alone as a "sign" or "evidence" of the spiritual transformation that pentecostals call baptism in the Holy Spirit. However, glossolalia remains the most commonly reported embodied experience for AG adherents, and the only embodied experience accepted as "physical evidence" of Spirit baptism.

Experiences of the Divine, Evangelism, and Church Growth

Earlier analyses (Poloma 1989; Poloma and Pendleton 1989) noted the relationship between "evangelism" and experiences of the charismata or gifts of the Holy Spirit. Congregants who had more frequent and varied experiences of these gifts were more likely to score higher on the evangelism scale. Poloma and Pendleton (1989) argued that those who had more intense and varied experiences of the divine were more likely to have a story to tell about their personal relationship with God that is alluring and inviting to prospective members. Through accounts of divine encounters they are more likely to engage in behavior that leads to congregational growth.

This finding, reported in *Crossroads,* was replicated in this study. Among the congregants in our sample, 27 percent were likely to have talked with friends and neighbors about their church five or more times within the past six months, and only 13 percent reported never having done so. Seventy-five percent had invited at least one non-member to church, 70 percent helped someone get acquainted with their church, 66 percent offered church services to someone in need, 52 percent offered to transport someone to church services, and 51 percent invited an inactive member to return to the congregation. The majority was less actively involved in recruiting children of non-members; only 43 percent had ever invited a non-member's child to church. We combined the above items to construct an evangelism scale, which represents benevolent action taken to bring new believers into the church family and to retain them once they are there (see appendix B).

As proposed in the thesis of Godly Love, glossolalia and other embodied manifestations were found not only to have a strong relationship with reporting of frequent experiences of the presence of God (the vertical divine-human link) but also to be statistically related to evangelistic outreach (the horizontal or interpersonal link).[13] Those who talked with friends and neighbors about their church, invited non-members to church, helped them get acquainted with the church, offered transportation to church, and encouraged inactive church members to become more involved were more likely to pray in tongues regularly and to experience other somatic manifestations than were those not actively involved in promoting their congregation.

In sum, our statistical findings confirm that Spirit baptism (especially when measured by the use of glossolalia and other embodied revival experiences, rather than by a response to a question about being baptized in the Spirit) does account for differences in reports of both experiencing the presence of God and engaging in evangelistic outreach. Persons most likely to be evangelistic are those who are highly glossolalic and who have had other somatic experiences often linked with revivals.[14]

Glossolalia and Godly Love: A Tentative Assessment

Baptism in the Spirit as reported in narratives has often been limited to a "high-voltage experience with God, especially as evidenced by speaking in tongues" (Macchia 2006b, 112)—and undoubtedly many pentecostals' personal narratives fit this description. It would appear, however, that if Spirit baptism is evaluated in terms of "empowerment for service," it requires ongoing embodied experiences that empower the believer, rather than a one-time experience of glossolalia. In this our analysis would support April's contention that she has experienced "Spirit baptisms" that are ongoing and empowering for ministry.

Surveys such as ours can only dimly mirror the diversity and flow of embodied rituals, which are better captured through participant observation and interviews. However, this survey clearly demonstrates that praying in tongues is a meaningful experience for many pentecostals that is accompanied with a sense of the divine presence that may foster benevolence. Whatever else it is, glossolalia is a form of prayer. What is less clear from our survey is whether praying in tongues (1) originates in a one-way human cry to God rooted in feelings of fear, sorrow, or anguish; (2) flows from the pray-er's response to the sense of an overwhelming presence of God; or (3) represents an ongoing dynamic process of God's touching the pray-er and the pray-er's glossolalic response, which intensifies the sense of God's presence. The dynamics of glossolalic prayer raise questions that linger as we continue to explore the relationship that other religious experiences may play in accounting for benevolence.

Pentecostal missionary and revivalist Heidi Baker (1995, 56) has provided a theological description of glossolalia in which she defines prayer "as human communication and divine self-disclosure," which she distinguishes from "the more common method of regarding glossolalic prayer from the vantage point of human experience alone." As a theologian (not bound by the canons of social science) Baker draws on her own experience and understanding of glossolalia to say:

> The primary purpose of prayer in tongues is to serve as extraordinary communication with God and from God to humanity. This must mean that Pentecostal glossolalic prayer, theologically understood, may not be viewed as human capability utilized at will to achieve some religious end. Like all true encounters with God, it takes place primarily as the consequence of the divine resolution to act. The closer one draws to the divine mystery, the more pressing it becomes to express oneself, and simultaneously the less capable one is to achieve sufficient expression. This is the climax in which glossolalic prayer breaks forth (p. 56).

While it goes beyond our data and the capabilities of empirical social science to support or refute Baker's theological formulation, particularly in the implied ordering and causal sequence in the glossolalic process, our data provide some guarded support for her thesis. *In accord with the model of Godly Love that guides our statistical analysis, congregants who perceive a deeper relationship with God were found to be more glossolalic, with both a sense of divine presence and glossolalia being related to interpersonal acts of benevolence.* Throughout our analyses of congregational responses, we continue to use "outcome measures" that serve as proxies for human love, particularly what Rolf Johnson (2001, 30) has called *care-love*—which, put simply, is "a concern for the good or the welfare of someone or something."

Summary

Equating the metaphors of "baptism(s) in the Spirit" with "baptism of love" and relating Spirit baptism to glossolalia and other embodied manifestations are important for understanding Godly Love in the pentecostal tradition. Entering into the love of God through pentecostally normative spiritual experiences is, we suggest, a source of what Pitirim Sorokin (1954/2002) called "love energy," which empowers a person to live a life of love and service. The relationships between experiencing God, empowerment, and willingness to serve others have been demonstrated through our empirical findings. They suggest that Spirit baptism is more than simply a one-time experience of speaking in tongues. Rather it is an ongoing process of spiritual transformation intertwined with other charismata. Macchia (2006b, 117) describes this process as follows: "Pentecostals regard the baptism in the Holy Spirit as an experience of empowerment for witness. The experience is in my view akin to a 'prophetic call,' which allows believers to participate in various gifts connected with prophetic discernment, such as visions, dreams and various 'word gifts,' and other gifts of the Spirit highlighted in the New Testament."

In this sense, our exploration of glossolalia as an empirical marker of Spirit baptism serves as a foundation to introduce an important theological and experiential concept of AG theology. This "crown jewel" of pentecostalism, when understood as Macchia has described, provides a concrete illustration of Godly Love—that is, the "dynamic interaction between divine and human love that enlivens and expands benevolence." The following chapter builds on this foundation, as we expand our analysis to discuss the gift of divine healing, its relationship to prayer experiences (including glossolalia), the "word gifts," and empowerment for witness and service.

6

Spiritual Empowerment

Pray-ers, Prophets, and Healers in the Pews

> Christianity is not the only religion in the world concerned with healing and its connotations. . . . But even in the context of long-standing, worldwide demands for religious healing, Christians have distinguished themselves. Often borrowing techniques and ideas from other religions and from numerous forms of medicine, Christians have time and again disseminated their religion as a means to healing and eternal good health. Christianity's success as a world religion has much to do with its attractiveness in this regard and with its effectiveness in promoting a whole range of salutary benefits and behaviors. (Porterfield 2005, 8)

Early Pentecostals, including the Assemblies of God, intentionally ignored many of the theological distinctions that have marked various flavors of American Protestantism, but they soon found themselves embroiled in doctrinal squabbles of their own making. As AG historian Edith Blumhofer (1993, 4) astutely described the paradox, Pentecostals "are not doctrinally unconcerned, but they are suspicious of theological finesse." Instead of well-developed systematic theologies, they have opted for biblical terminology and their understanding of biblical precedent. Not always aware of the social scientific theories of the construction of human reality—including the social construction of religious reality that brought Pentecostalism into being and continually modifies its understanding of biblical texts—Pentecostal pioneers simply took select biblical texts and used them as significant markers for their beliefs and practices.[1] In addition to the core importance placed on speaking in tongues in its self-understanding of what made its gospel distinct from fundamentalism was the insistence that physical healing was "in the atonement" for all believers.

Pentecostals in the movement's first decades regarded themselves as spiritual kin to early-twentieth-century Christian fundamentalists, but theirs was a "full gospel" that added speaking in tongues and divine healing to the fundamentals of faith. Pentecostalism was described as "fundamentalism with a difference," as Blumhofer (1993, 5) explains: "They added to the standard fundamentalist profession of faith (which most basically included the verbal inspiration of scripture, the virgin birth, the substitutionary atonement, and the physical resurrection) two components that made their gospel 'full'—the insistence that physical healing was 'in the atonement' for all believers and the expectation that tongues speech and other spiritual gifts listed in 1 Cor. 12, 14 should be manifested in the contemporary church."

Pentecostalism's admiration for fundamentalism was hardly reciprocated; however, as fundamentalism morphed into a more moderate form of evangelicalism in the mid-twentieth century, the AG found a degree of acceptance. With the establishment of the National Association of Evangelicals (NAE) in 1943 the AG continued its struggle to retain a distinct identity with a slight modification: "fundamentalism with a difference" became "evangelicalism with a difference."

Divine Healing in Social Context

Early Pentecostals insisted that divine healing is firmly rooted in the Bible. This long-standing Pentecostal belief in divine healing has increasingly gained acceptance, especially among evangelical Christians. More recently, representatives of both religious sectors have come to use the newly emergent body of academic literature on the relationship between religious faith and healing to garner support for their belief that prayer is a powerful agent of healing. Although the contemporary practice of divine healing has roots in the nineteenth-century Holiness denominations, some Holiness leaders began to downplay the practice at the turn of the twentieth century—a time when newly emergent Pentecostalism made this practice one of its main statements of faith (Curtis 2007). Pentecostalism's medical mores have changed—no longer are doctors held in suspicion, nor is medical insurance taboo—but the practice of divine healing remains a strong differential feature.

Pentecostal healing beliefs and practices have many similarities with the alternative healing groups studied by sociologist Meredith McGuire (1988) in her research on healing practices in suburban America. McGuire noted how, for most healing practitioners, including Catholic neo-pentecostals, "the moral concerns pertaining to salvation are expressed in the idiom of health and illness" (p. 247). These concerns include the mental, emotional, physical, and even financial, the latter being best demonstrated in popular pentecostal prosperity teachings. Whereas the cultural trend has been to medicalize many human problems, the groups involved in alternative healing practices, including Pentecostals and their neo-pentecostal cousins, tend to spiritualize them. McGuire observed that most of the healing groups she studied "were vehement that the key issues underlying illness were not in the province of medical knowledge and treatment" (ibid.). According to McGuire, and in accord with many Pentecostal believers, "Most of the Christian healing groups studied considered personal sin a major source of illness, although they differed widely as to how much emphasis they placed upon individual responsibility, as opposed to general sin or diabolical influences" (ibid.).

McGuire and other ethnographers (see Koss-Chioino and Hefner 2006) have provided insightful "thick descriptions" of healing and healing practices that indicate a holistic perspective in which healing is much more than simply a mechanistic "curing" of illness. Prayer for health and healing is embedded in a holistic view of life that remains vibrant within Pentecostalism's spiritual perspective of possibilities—even when the medical prognosis and the dice of theoretical probability point to physical death.

Underlying Pentecostal healing beliefs and practices is a holistic worldview that allows for both the physical and the transcendent—what philosopher Philip Hefner (2006) calls the "double entendre." This double entendre is reflected in Poloma and Hoelter's (1998) analysis of a revival within neo-pentecostalism, through which they developed the implicit model found in McGuire's (1988; 1993) work. The double entendre places "spiritual healing"—experiences that can be conceptualized as (in McGuire's term) building a "right relationship with God"—in the center of a complex model that includes religious experiences and different forms of healing. Other forms of healing—physical, mental, emotional, and even financial—can be mediated through "spiritual healing," which is basic to an intimate personal relationship with God. Experiencing the presence and power of God is thus at the heart of divine healing in the pentecostal tradition.

Consistent with most other contemporary spiritual healing practices, healing for pentecostal Christians involves more than curing physical ailments. With an intricate interweaving of mind, body, and spirit, this perspective places a "right relationship with God" at the nucleus of well-being for pentecostal believers. *Healing*, as understood by pentecostals, thus differs from the common usage of the term (as equated with "curing" medical maladies) in at least two important ways: (1) in its understanding of "healing" as a juxtaposition of the ordinary and the sacred; and (2) in its holistic approach to healing, which encompasses soul, spirit, mind, and body. All forms of healing are energized through corporate and personal prayer.

For pentecostals and their evangelical cousins, the beginning of this restorative and healing relationship with the divine can be traced to "salvation" or the experience of being "born again." Ninety-five percent of our respondents said they were certain they were "born again." The clear majority of the respondents, as we saw earlier, also claimed to experience a second blessing of Spirit baptism with the "physical evidence" of speaking in tongues as an instrument of empowerment. As significant as Spirit baptism may be doctrinally for the AG, it is claimed by only three-fourths of the respondents—slightly less if one insists on glossolalia as the "initial physical evidence" of Spirit baptism. Divine healing, on the other hand, is increasingly being recognized by scholars as a significant pentecostal marker. It is nearly universally reported as a pentecostal prayer practice and an experience by survey respondents. Before exploring further the holistic nature of healing for pentecostal believers, it is useful to place this important belief and practice into historical context.

An Abridged History of Christian Healing

"Holiness" and "health" have the same etymological root, which reflects the ancient conviction that well-being and a right relationship with the deity go hand in hand. The separation of holiness from health among medical practitioners, however, has a long history, as indicated by Plato's concern: "This is the great error of our day in the treatment of the human body that physicians separate the soul from the body." The "great error" of Plato's day seemingly triumphed as the ills of mind, body, and soul were allocated to different specialists (Lee 1976, 23).

While Christian theologies that developed over the centuries stressed the separation of the body and soul, thus marginalizing belief in miraculous healings, the practice continued in folk religion. It found an outlet in Roman Catholicism through the use of relics and shrines, which provided a medium through which cures and tales of cures could be perpetuated. While such practices were tolerated and regulated, if not encouraged, in Catholicism, a less mystical and more rational post-Reformation Protestantism largely prohibited vehicles for spreading such "superstition." In the words of Francis MacNutt (2005), a former Catholic priest and theologian who has become a scholar of the contemporary healing movement, the demise of healing in Christianity was "the nearly perfect crime."

Rumors of divine healing, however, could be heard from time to time in new religious groups that encouraged its belief and practice. One of the earliest American-grown religions to advocate divine healing was the Society of Friends (Quakers), whose founder, George Fox, had a significant healing ministry. It was not unusual for American religious movements birthed in the fervor of revivalism (including the Quakers, Shakers, Mormons, Noyesites, and Adventists) to encourage the practice of healing prayer (Chappell 1988). It was from the revivals the late-nineteenth-century Holiness movement, however, that healers emerged who proclaimed divine healing and health rather than the virtue of illness and suffering (Curtis 2007), going as far as to make it a basic tenet of the Christian faith.

The Wesleyan revivals of the late nineteenth century added a theological rationale to the experiential base that served to restore divine healing as a normative Christian belief and practice. Leaders in the Wesleyan Holiness movement, a direct antecedent to the Pentecostal revivals of the twentieth century, began to link a doctrine of Christian perfectionism with divine healing, teaching that "Christ's atonement provided not only for justification but also for the purification of the human nature from sin." According to some perfectionist theology, this purification would "eliminate illness" (Chappell 1988, 357).

It is important to note that traditional Christians proclaiming divine healing were not alone. The same time and culture that gave rise to divine healing in the Holiness movement also birthed the metaphysical New Religious Thought movement, as Mary Baker Eddy (Christian Science), Charles and Myrtle Fillmore (Unity School of Christianity), Ernest Holmes (The Church of Religious Science), and others were promoting Christian healing as viewed through the lenses of metaphysical "new thought" (Darling 1992; Meyer 1988). At the same time, the disciples of a more orthodox Holiness movement began reporting miraculous healings occurring regularly during religious revivals that dotted the land. Nineteenth-century healing revivals led by Maria Woodworth-Etter, John Alexander Dowie, and lesser-known figures set the stage for Pentecostal healing ministries that would grow in popularity throughout the twentieth century.

Although healing had been and remains a central belief and practice for pentecostal believers throughout the twentieth and into the twenty-first century, the revitalization of dynamic healing practices has often been associated with famous healing evangelists—well-known "anointed" men and women like William Branham (1909–1965), Kathryn Kuhlman (1907–1976), Oral Roberts

(1918–2009), and Benny Hinn (born 1952). Alongside these healing stars were always common men and women, often inspired and motivated by the healing evangelists, who functioned as everyday media through whom the graces of divine healing flowed. Perhaps no single person did more to emphasize a populist theology of divine healing in the last quarter of the twentieth century than John Wimber, founder of the neo-pentecostal Vineyard Christian Fellowships (Wagner 2002). With its widespread appeal in the United States and abroad, Wimber-like teachings not only flowed into evangelical fellowships that were at best ambivalent to the practice of glossolalia but also served to revitalize healing in some Pentecostal churches as well. Divine healing was no longer limited to the realm of faith healers or even church pastors and deacons. Prayer for healing was the right and responsibility of all Christians.

Divine healing, notes pentecostal scholar Allan Anderson (2004, 30), "is perhaps the most universal characteristic of the many varieties of pentecostalism and perhaps the main reason for its growth in the developing world." But pentecostalism's belief in and practice of healing prayer has been an especially good fit for a contemporary American culture that has become increasingly wary of the adequacy of mechanized medicine. Although doctrinally speaking some Pentecostals have made glossolalia their main distinctive, healing has come to center stage in the lived religion of many pentecostals (as well as many evangelicals who find ways to be pentecostal without speaking in tongues).

Overview of Statistics on Healing

The National Center for Complementary and Alternative Medicine (CAM) reported that the use of prayer is one of the leading complementary health remedies. A survey of more than 31,000 adults on complementary and alternative healing practices found that 45 percent had used prayer for health reasons; 43 percent had prayed for their own health; almost 25 percent had had others pray for them; and almost 10 percent had participated in a prayer group for their health (Barnes and Sered 2005). Belief in healing prayer appears to be even more extensive than personal experiences and practice. A *Newsweek* poll found that 72 percent of Americans believed that "praying to God can cure someone—even if science says the person doesn't stand a chance" (Kalb 2003). This finding reflected an earlier Gallup poll showing 82 percent believing "in the healing power of personal prayer" and 77 percent agreeing that "God sometimes intervenes to cure people who have a serious illness" (Cole 1996). While belief in and prayer for healing is undoubtedly a *common practice* reflecting reported normative belief in contemporary American society, it is a near *universal norm* for Pentecostal believers, and they are undoubtedly one of the groups that help to account for the national findings in the CAM report on prayer as a health remedy.

Among the 1,817 congregants in our sample, all of the following activities were nearly universally acknowledged: "praying for the healing of family and friends" (99 percent); "praying with others for healing" (96 percent); "being prayed with for healing" (92 percent); and reporting that they have "heard accounts" of what they regard as "miraculous healings" (94 percent). Furthermore, 93 percent claimed to have personally experienced "an inner or emotional healing" at least once in a while; 70 percent reported a divine healing from a physical illness; 75 percent reported personally experiencing a (unspecified) "miraculous healing" touching their lives; and 85 percent said they had "witnessed a miraculous healing in the lives of family members and/or friends."

These personal beliefs and experiences do not exist in a vacuum; they are firmly rooted in the lived religion of most AG congregations and are supported by healing rituals that are more likely to be regularly practiced in congregations than are prayers for Spirit baptism. Eighty-five percent of the respondents reported that they were at least occasionally involved in prayer for healing in their church, with 28 percent reporting regular participation in this congregational ritual. Also reflecting the practice of praying with one another for healing is the finding that 67 percent of the respondents have sometimes been instruments of divine healing.

Older respondents (who are more likely to experience physical ailments) are more likely than younger ones to report having experienced healing from a physical illness, received prayer for healing, prayed for the healing of family and friends, prayed with others for healing, heard accounts about miraculous healings, and personally witnessed a miraculous healing.[2] Age is not related, however, to two other important variables, namely, having experienced an inner or emotional healing or in being used as an instrument of divine healing.

On Methodology

Healing Measures

We selected four survey items to further explore divine healing in the AG. Two are measures of personal healing experiences: reported frequency of healing from a physical illness, and the frequency of experiencing inner or emotional healing. The other two healing items are proxies for benevolent action: praying with others for healing, and the frequency of being used as an agent of divine healing for another person. All are single items included in a battery of questions with six response choices, ranging from "never" to "many times a day." Only 30 percent of the AG respondents had *never* personally experienced a divine healing from a physical illness, while 12 percent claimed physical healing to be a regular occurrence (most days or more often). Inner or emotional healing is a near-universal experience, with 94 percent of the respondents indicating they had experienced it at least on occasion; 22 percent reported that they experience inner healing at least daily.

Ninety-six percent of the AG respondents reported "praying with others for healing" at least on occasion. (This figure was second only to the 99 percent of respondents who said they "prayed for" the healing of others.) With regard to proxies for benevolence and healing "prayer with others," and to being used as an "instrument of healing" for others, the respondents who serve in the healing ministry are not driven by some unseen force, as this question might suggest, but rather are responding to what they believe to be a divine invitation to serve others. (They would not be comfortable with a question inquiring if *they* had healed another person; God is always regarded as the healer.) A clear majority of AG congregants reported that they had been instruments of divine healing at least on occasion (only 33 percent reported that they had never experienced this). Nearly one-half (49 percent) were intermittent healers, responding that they had the experience "once in a while" or "on some days," while 18 percent believed they were being regularly used by God as agents of divine healing.

A Statistical Note

While the narratives respondents provided are thought-provoking, and the basic survey results we have employed support lessons derived from these personal accounts, a systematic analysis is necessary to determine both the validity and strength of these relationships found in responses to our survey questions. For example, we can see from table C.1 in appendix C that those who frequently experience physical healing tend to be highly glossolalic, are more likely to experience a frequent sense of divine presence, and are more likely to be highly prophetic.[3] All three variables demonstrate statistically significant and positive relationships with answers to our question on experiences of divine physical healing. As we continue to review table C.1, we see that several of the demographic variables show statistically significant positive relationships with physical healing: those who are older and non-white and those with less education and income are more likely to report being physically healed through prayer than are their counterparts. This simple analysis provides a valid and systematic description of the relationship of the spiritual measures and healing for our survey of AG congregants.

While this descriptive information is well worth knowing, it raises an important question: which of these measures of spirituality has the strongest relationship with the experience of healing once the effects of the other factors are taken into account? Could the valid and positive relationships between the measures of spirituality and healing just be a reflection of the demographic factors, rather than the reported spiritual experiences? For example, poorer people are likely to have fewer resources to see a doctor than richer people. Thus, it is possible that income is the real reason for reports of divine healing among the poor, because poorer respondents have turned to religious services rather than physicians for help with illnesses. It is possible that the spirituality measures have no relationship with reports of divine healing, but rather that the "real" causes are less education and less income.

These questions can be addressed by means of *multiple regression analysis*, a statistical analysis that assesses the impact of numerous variables simultaneously (see the "Physical Healing" column of table C.2). Once the effects of other factors have been taken into account, the impact of spiritual measures on healing is clearly not just a reflection of the respondents' age, education, or income. The strongest statistically significant relationship is found between prophecy and healing (with a partial correlation or "beta" of .51), as compared to income (beta = –.07). These findings suggest that spirituality, especially prophecy, is more than just a description of those who experience physical healing; it is likely to be a cause of such as experiences as well.

In the rest of this chapter we will use the results of this statistical technique (in notes and tables) to assess the validity and strength of the various measures of spirituality on healing, as well as the independent strength of these measures taking into account the impact of other factors. The goals of this assessment are to better understand the nature of the healing practices in the AG and then to assess the role healing may play in revitalizing the AG through the experience of Godly Love. For ease of presentation, we will offer the results of this analysis without the special language of statistics; readers who are well-versed in these statistical methods may consult the notes and the appendices for this information. We will use this approach in the chapters that follow as well.

With this preliminary statistical information in place, we return to our narrative about April, the twenty-six-year-old woman we met in the previous chapter, who was raised in the AG and is now part of a neo-pentecostal ministry. Pentecostals are people of narrative, and reliance on numbers can too easily take us away from the Spirit that animates the lives of believers. Although April no longer is a member of the AG, her Pentecostal upbringing provided a solid foundation for her move to the neo-pentecostal revival community in which she is a leader. Her story can help us to establish another link between the divine–human relationship and human acts of benevolence. April's narrative thus sets the stage for further statistical analysis of the congregational survey data—specifically, of measures of spirituality that are said to empower the believer, and of being used as an instrument of healing.

April's Narrative: From Inner Healing to Healer

April's "spiritual healing" could be said to have begun, as we saw earlier, with her conversion ("accepting Jesus into her heart") at nine years of age and her Spirit baptism (when she first spoke in tongues) at age thirteen. Although her spiritual journey, as she recalls it, may have begun with these two events, her family life was shattered shortly after she had her initial intense experience of the Holy Spirit. Her mother discovered that her husband had been having an affair, and the family was forced into bankruptcy after the divorce. April, her mother, and her younger brother had to leave their much-loved home for a nearby town where "everyone knew about the affair and our bankruptcy." April said she felt acute pain during that time of turmoil, but her experiences of God and her AG church family kept the pain from overwhelming her. Although she was quick to praise her mother—"she is the person who has most shaped who I am today"—April was understandably estranged from her father (despite her mother's efforts to keep her connected with him).

April shared with the interviewer how nature and grace worked together to bring about an inner healing that transformed her young life. She recounted how her mother had sent her to professional counselors to help her adjust after the divorce: "I went to a Christian counselor and then to a secular counselor; they were not any different. In fact I liked the secular counselor better because I could be real with her. They both helped me to be aware of the problem and my pain, but that didn't help me with not being able to forgive my dad for what he had done to us." She emphasized, however, that "nothing really changed" through the counseling, but the secular counselor "did buy me another year until I started attending a Vineyard church," where April said she had "a real heart restoration." April shared the details of this spiritual transformation as follows:

I would like to tell you about a day when I had a most profound experience in the healing process. I started to go to the Vineyard when I was eighteen, in the middle of my senior year. Two years later, when I was a sophomore in college and living three hours away, I would still return to the Vineyard as often as I could because I had such growth and healing there. We were having one of Randy Clark's [a revival leader] associates teaching on deliverance. It was one of those occasions when the power of God was much greater than we were used to experiencing. It was the first time I saw people falling in the presence of the Lord!

So this day there was a small group of us who met with the associate. He laid hands on us and prayed for us. I don't remember what he prayed—it doesn't matter. But it was the first time I felt the power of God so strong that I fell down. I just lay there on the floor and someone knelt down—I don't know if it was an angel or a person, but someone knelt down and whispered in my ear: "You have not forgiven your father; it is time to forgive him."

I opened my eyes and saw this woman leaving. I don't know who she was and don't remember ever seeing her before. Whether she was an angel or not—it really doesn't matter—she helped to change my life. As she left, I just felt this really deep cry come up and out from within me. I just wailed and wailed. I don't know how long I was down there—an hour? A half hour? I don't know. But that was the day I forgave my dad. I had gone through the words and been prayed for hundreds of times. I desperately wanted to forgive him, but I couldn't stand to be around my dad. I could not be in his presence and be at peace. That day the Holy Spirit came on me in such a deep way that there was a deep release in my spirit and I didn't feel the burden any more.

I had wanted to have a bad relationship with my father so that he could feel the pain I felt. There was such a release that I arranged to see my father, and for the first time in eight years I volunteered to stay in his house overnight. So the next week I spent the whole weekend with my dad and stepmom. He saw the difference in me—and I knew the difference. It is the first time I enjoyed being around him. And ever since then I have been able to have a relationship with him. And let me tell you—he hasn't changed; he hasn't changed at all (hearty laugh). In some ways he has gotten worse! But I enjoy him now.

April emphasized to the interviewer that although the counselors, her mother, and caring members of her church family played important roles in the growth she was experiencing during these early college years, she would not have been able to forgive her father without this dramatic encounter with God. It changed her life, restored the vision of her childhood, and gave her a new sense of purpose and identity. Ultimately it released a gift of healing that enables her to effectively pray for the healing of others. April continued:

> I knew everything about forgiveness, but it took that experience to get me to forgive and set me free. It took two years of worship times [at the Vineyard church] when I was just in the presence of God and His Spirit was able to soften my heart, and finally I was really willing to let the Holy Spirit take the burden from me. You could say "I gave it up," but it was a spirit exchange; it was not an intellectual exchange. And there was fruit in my life from that time forward that made it very noticeable.
>
> That was a very big turning point in my life. I started to grow in security in my own skin and became more self-confident. A whole series of things began happening after that in terms of my call and my destiny and what I wanted to do. I began to sense God pursuing me; He was so faithful to me. He brought me back to a dream He put within me when I was young about being a world-changer. When I was in high school I would often go forward to rededicate my life to the Lord, and there were times I would see myself preaching to the nations. I would see the pain and the suffering and just find myself weeping. I would hear the stories of the martyrs and think "That could be me." So mixed in with the pain of the divorce were these experiences with the Lord. One was never too far away, and that was because of the Assemblies church.
>
> So when I was twenty and went through that deep forgiveness it was like a rocket booster. Everything that was stored up in me—all of the dreams and visions from the Lord—just began to explode. That day—when I fell in the Spirit for the first time and was able to forgive my dad—something had changed in my heart that I had worked on for six years and could not change. And then came a resurrection of the gift of tongues in a deliverance session. I felt a spirit leave that had been attacking me, began speaking in tongues, and never had night terrors after that. That all happened within a month or so after the initial forgiveness experience.
>
> So it was just like the Lord opened a box and took out treasures one by one. Another very powerful experience was the time there was this associate at our [Vineyard] church, and there was this time of ministry at the end, and he was praying for the impartation for the gift of healing. And I was standing in this church, and he looks at me and calls me out—"You

> in the turquoise sweater"—and I feel this hand behind me pushing me forward. I thought it was my pastor, but when I talked to him afterward, he said, "Nobody touched you"—it had to be an angel. You see, when he called me out, I thought, "Me, not me, it can't be me," but I did go forward. He prayed for me, I went down, and I felt fire on my face! I was just trembling. He started prophesying over me about being called to preach and to be in the ministry full-time. So he just prophesied this call on my life that totally registers with me. He then says, "Stand up and pray for people." It's bizarre—I am crying but my face is dry; I am shaking and trembling; I am feeling fire; I can hardly stand. And he is saying, "Get up and pray for people." And he takes my hand, and I would lay hands on people and they would fall. It was like popcorn! He was full of wisdom. In that moment I realized that everything I had thought about my call was real.
>
> This all took place within a half hour or an hour. I would pray for people and they would get healed. All I could do was pray in tongues. He would say, "Prophesy over them." But all I could do was pray in tongues! But people were reporting getting healed. There was so much power! It shocked me! I could not even keep my eyes open; I was so lost in the Lord. I actually had a picture of myself while all this was happening. It was being a Raggedy Ann doll draped over the arm of Jesus. Jesus was doing it. I said to the Lord, "I will go anywhere, just as long as you take me!"

April believed that this was the day she was commissioned for ministry. Dramatic spiritual things would happen every month or two at her church during her last two years of college. She also visited another nearby Vineyard that was "in revival" at the time. April noted, "I just kept praying for people and they were getting healed." She told of revival leaders who would continue to call her out to proclaim the anointing that was on her life. She insisted that this prophetic and healing anointing was not just about her: "I don't think it is just about me; I think when they say they are talking anointing and impartation, they are talking about a company of people who are being raised to proclaim the things of the kingdom." She felt strongly that she is but one person in a "company of people," a belief that led her to join Global Awakening (where she met and married her husband), a ministry founded by Randy Clark, the former Vineyard pastor who launched the Toronto Blessing (Poloma 2003).

April's narrative provides examples of both the "first blessing" conversion and subsequent blessings of Spirit baptism (or "Spirit baptisms," as April calls them), including what we are calling "inner healing." April's story reflects well the model of holistic healing presented by Poloma and Hoelter (1998) based on revival data in which "spiritual healing" and an ever-deepening mystical relationship with God are at its core. Spiritual healing serves as a kind of divine energy through which forgiveness is extended, changes occur in self-image, relationships are "healed," and visions of personal destiny are birthed. Life-changing spiritual experiences occur in perceived experiences of God, which often came through a process old Pentecostals called "tarrying" and neo-pentecostals refer to as "soaking" in the divine presence (Wilkinson and Althouse 2010). It was in pentecostal worship rituals, April reported, that her "heart was softened" and she was able to receive the gift of being able to forgive her father. Since receiving that inner or emotional healing, April has frequently been used as an "instrument of healing" in the United States and in mission trips abroad. April's story not only fits well with the Poloma and Hoelter's model of holistic healing but it allows this model to be incorporated into the dynamic framework of what we are calling Godly Love. The emotion energy generated by perceived encounters with God, its impact on self (sense of destiny and general well-being), and its empowerment to serve as an "agent of healing" who reaches out to others can be used to cast interpretive light on our AG healing data. The statistical findings can be likened to a skeleton, with its bones being arranged with the help of theological reflection and social-scientific paradigms. Thick descriptions found in stories like April's help in interpreting the findings and can add flesh to the dry statistical bones.

Holistic Healing and Godly Love

In our discussion of spiritual transformation we have already used Spirit baptism and embodied manifestations (with a focus on glossolalia) as empirical indicators of the vertical relationship claimed by pentecostals to exist between humans and the divine. Glossolalic and other embodied religious manifestations serve as proxies for the empowering experience of divine love, while we conceptualized the evangelism scale as a measure of human benevolence or "care-love." We hypothesize that interactions in the divine–human (vertical) relationship provided "love energy" that empowered benevolent action in human–human (horizontal) relationships. Using the lens of a holistic model of healing, we now explore additional variables from the survey that tap into the vertical relationship with God and its potential effects on human benevolence. They include often interrelated elements that are reflected in April's narrative—the giving and receiving of prophecy, and experiences of divine presence and of emotional and physical healing. Our proxies for benevolence in this analysis reflect service in the healing ministry, including "praying with others for healing" and "being used as an instrument of healing."

Prophecy and the Prophetic

According to the pentecostal worldview, the gift of prophecy is not reserved for the spiritually elite; it is available to men and women, young and old, rich and poor. As pentecostal scholar Gerald T. Sheppard (2002) correctly notes, a wide range of activities can be referred to as "prophetic" by Pentecostals. Prophecy may "take the form of 'interpretation' by one person in a familiar language immediately following incomprehensible tongues (or glossolalia) delivered usually by another person." It can also include other variations, such an "anointed preaching," when the preacher feels like a channel of the Holy Spirit and words seem to flow in an effortless manner"; the words of a "'healing evangelist' [who] might sense special prophetic insights accompanying healing manifestations of the Spirit"; or a "'word of knowledge' most pertinent to a single individual, delivered by one person to another." Although prophecy is commonly understood as a prediction of future events, Sheppard insists that "prophecy does not typically predict the future, but gives assurance, confirmation, warning, or spiritual encouragement" (p. 64).

Prophecy is also more than simply a personal mystical experience through which God speaks to humans; it is also one in which humans interact with God, often in a collaborative way. It reflects a corporate dimension, having meaning only as its content is shared with another person or a larger community, and as it is confirmed by the community. We created a *prophecy scale* comprised of five individual survey items that we have used in this analysis.[4] The items (with the percentage of the AG respondents who have experienced them within the last six months in parentheses) are as follows: gave a prophetic word to another person (46 percent), received a personal prophecy from another person (71 percent), received a revelation directly from God (81 percent), had an experience of God accompanied by a lost awareness of time and surroundings (73 percent), and heard a divine call to perform a specific act (73 percent).[5] It is worthy of note in April's story how prophecies (personal revelations and corporate messages) were experienced in the process of "inner healing" as well as in the "impartation" of the gift of healing others. April's account also points to the role that experiencing the divine presence plays in creating the milieu for prophecy and impartation for healing.

Divine Presence

April credited her years of worship at a Vineyard church with "softening" her heart to receive the gift of forgiveness at a powerful revival service in which the divine presence was palpably felt. Divine presence, however, can be experienced in different intensities, in countless forms, and in ordinary or extraordinary places. Four items make up the *divine presence* scale used in our statistical assessment. These items and the percent of the AG respondents who have experienced them at least on "some days" are as follows: felt God's love as the greatest power in the universe (87 percent); felt the unmistakable presence of God during prayer (85 percent); had everything disappear except consciousness of God (57 percent); and obtained deeper insight into a spiritual truth during prayer (72 percent).[6] Unlike prophecy, which involves a perceived collaborative work directed by a divine call requiring a human response and may involve other collaborative human actors, sensing a divine presence measures a one-way action in which God is perceived to make the divine presence a felt one. Reporting such feelings says nothing about the response of the person to this mystical encounter.

Divine Healing in the Assemblies of God

Physical Healing

While AG adherents nearly universally claim to pray for the healing of others and report personal experiences of inner healing, fewer have ever experienced a divine healing from physical illness for themselves. Twenty four percent reported fairly regular experiences of physical healing, with 8 percent claiming such healings daily or more often. Thirty percent reported that they had never had such an experience, with another 46 percent saying it happened "once in a while." While we have no survey data on what kinds of physical problems were believed to be divinely healed, we do know that some pentecostals use prayer as a first line of defense whenever dis-comfort or dis-ease is perceived. If one cannot successfully receive healing for a headache or a stubbed toe, how can one accept it for something more serious? This, at least, is the argument for ongoing healing prayer. Those who claim to receive a physical healing every day (or multiple times per day) most probably use this "first-line-of-defense" reasoning and believe that God is always about the work of "healing" them and others around them.

Multivariate analysis enabled us to determine the role that demographic measures and spiritual factors play in reported experiences of physical healing.[7] Our findings reflect an observation that can be gleaned from April's story, which includes accounts of prophecy: a strong relationship seems to exist between a collaborative relationship with God—found in hearing a prophetic word and giving prophecy—and a strong sense of God's presence. Although spirituality factors were the most significant descriptors of those who reported physical healing, demographic information also played a modest role. *In sum, those who reported more frequent experiences of physical healing were likely to be older and to have less education and income, but they were more likely (regardless of these demographic factors) to have a strong sense of a divine presence and (most significantly) to be highly prophetic.*

Inner Healing and Mental Health: Fred's Narrative

Fred is a pentecostal and a psychiatrist who, like April, was interviewed as an exemplar of Godly Love. In private practice as a mental health provider, Fred is also a gifted healer. When asked about Spirit baptism, he replied, "I got into all this backwards. In traditional Pentecostal thought, the first gift is praying in the spirit. I got it all backwards—first I was healed and then I was being used to heal others. Eventually I received all the gifts, but they came out of order." The healing Fred shared with us was being completely healed of clinical depression, an affliction he had suffered all of his adult life.

The healing came through a pentecostal inner-healing conference in the mid-1990s. A good friend and pentecostal believer challenged Fred by asking him why he was satisfied with taking medication to keep his depression in check. He then invited Fred to a Theophostic conference led by the movement's founder, Ed Smith. Theophostic is one of the newer forms of inner-healing prayer that were commonly practiced in the pentecostal revival world of the 1990s. Like other inner-healing techniques, it centers on prayer rather than on providing counsel. Smith teaches the practitioner to use Theophostic (literally "light of God") principles that instruct the client to "invite Jesus" into past painful memories. It is Jesus who reveals the "lies" inherent in the memories and provides the healing (Garzon and Poloma 2005). The Theophostic experience proved to be both powerful and healing for Fred:

> No one asked me if I wanted to be filled with the Holy Spirit when I received my healing—and I was not—but I no longer require medication. I started doing inner healing with others, and every time I did, Jesus showed up in the room—the Holy Spirit showed up. He started working through

> me, healing through me as spirits were being delivered out of people. So I got into it backwards. I didn't go through the official Pentecostal way (laughs).
>
> For those who are willing to do it—not just pharmacology management, not just medication, not just traditional therapy, and not just traditional Christian counseling—healing happens. I have come to conclude over the years that most Christian counseling is nothing more than secular counseling with the Bible tacked on. I have to be careful and try to be sensitive; I don't mean to put down Christian counseling. It is not a bad thing; it can be a first step in coming to healing. But I want to say there is a more excellent way—there is more.
>
> Now when I do healing—and my wife sees the difference in me; I used to come home drained—I come home and say, "Jesus showed up. This person got healed and this happened to that person." Now I come home more energized than when I started the day.

Fred expressed excitement that some other psychiatrists, including recognized names in the field of religion and psychiatry, have consulted with him. He has shared his experiences with them, together with accounts of clients healed of depression, bipolarity, and post-traumatic stress disorder. He spoke of how he is now energized rather than drained by his work. "So we got to share a lot of good stories. I like getting the message out that healing is available—it's more than getting someone into maintenance mode. We don't have to say, 'You are going to have to be depressed the rest of your life, but we can take the edge off of it.' I have a different message—a full restoration message—a message of healing." Fred's account provides an illustration of the interrelationship between mental health, mental health therapies, and inner or emotional healing. Whether through Christian counseling therapy or prayer, pentecostals believe that God is about a healing work. As demonstrated in April's and Fred's narratives, they prefer inner healing that is driven by prayer in a collaborative act between the pray-er and God.

Inner Healing and AG Congregants

The frequency of reported inner healings—for many daily or more—suggests that much inner or emotional healing may occur through self-administered prayer in which a perceived interaction occurs (without other human mediation) between the person needing healing and God. Inner healing may also be carried out in rituals—in a therapist's office (as illustrated by Fred) or in a congregational service (as illustrated by April)—where other pray-ers play a role in the process.

Only 7 percent of the respondents said they had never experienced inner or emotional healing, while 36 percent said they experienced it "most days," "every day," or "many times a day." Inner or emotional healing undoubtedly encompasses a wide range of human experiences that our survey data do not permit us to unpack satisfactorily. As we saw from April's story, it can include deliverance from the hold of an evil spirit, being empowered to forgive (and released from the bondage of unforgiveness), and an increased self-acceptance and sense of destiny. Inner healing is also commonly used to refer to "healing of memories," that is, a release from painful memories that have negative effects on the human psyche. It may include forms of Christian counseling (the efficacy of which was questioned by both April and Fred), or it may take place suddenly and memorably at a revival service (as it did for April) or through a particular technique (as in Fred's case, with Theophostic). Numerous models of inner-healing prayer have developed over the years, particularly in the neo-pentecostal communities that have filtered into pentecostal churches. They all stress how inner healing is a process with the goal of holistic restoration. Jesus, through the power of the Holy Spirit, is regarded as the ultimate healer and deliverer, regardless of the technique or the human agent who may be used in the process (see Poloma 2003, esp. chap. 4).

To determine which variables might best account for differences in reports of inner healing, we again turned to multivariate analysis.[8]

What we found was that those who reported more frequent experiences of inner healing were also more likely to have an abiding sense of the divine presence and to be prophetic—with no differences found for age, gender, race, education, or income. Praying in tongues unexpectedly showed a significant but *negative* relationship with inner healing, indicating that those who prayed in tongues most frequently *without deep experiences of an abiding divine presence and with few experiences of prophecy* were *less likely* to report experiences of inner healing. As we interpret this finding, when the volitional act of praying in tongues is frequent, *but the pray-er experiences neither the immanence of God nor the prophetic, inner healing is actually less likely to occur.*

Congregants Ministering Healing to Others

Praying with others for a divine healing is a basic component of the healing ritual process. Only 4 percent of the AG congregational respondents reported that they *never* prayed with others for healing; 39 percent said they did so "very often"; 29 percent "fairly often"; and the remaining 28 percent "once in a while." Although praying with others for healing is nearly universally practiced, a profile does emerge in an analysis of those who are most likely to be frequent pray-ers.[9] The best single descriptor of someone who prays frequently with others for healing is someone who has an abiding sense of the presence of God and is highly prophetic. Our findings can be conceptualized in terms of the model of Godly Love in which benevolence or care-love is expressed in terms of interceding for the healing of others *and* where glossolalia, prophecy, and experiencing the divine presence "empower" the pray-er to pray selflessly for others.

The Godly Love model provides a heuristic device for interpreting a related analysis found in table C.2, in which "being used as an instrument of divine healing" is employed as one measure of benevolence. Although the demographic measures of race (non-white) and education (less education) are modest descriptors of someone who reports being frequently used as an instrument of divine healing, prophecy is by far the best descriptor. Those who are highly prophetic are far more likely than those who are not to say they have been used to heal others.

The findings reported for "praying with others" and "being used as an instrument of healing" reflect different ways in which prayer can be experienced by pentecostals, namely, as one-way talk or two-way interaction. When conceptualized as a vertical relationship with the divine, prayer can originate with the pray-er talking to God or it can begin with divine empowerment (i.e., God seemingly acting upon the individual). It would appear that much prayer, including praying in tongues, begins with the person crying out to God, during which God may or may not be perceived by the pray-er. As we have noted in discussing glossolalia, it is common for prayer—even prayer in tongues—to be entirely voluntary. Glossolalic pentecostals generally can choose to pray in tongues or in the vernacular. But sometimes the sense of God's presence can be so overwhelming that the line between voluntary and involuntary becomes blurred. Revival leader and theologian Heidi Baker (1995, 56) has described this seemingly involuntary process as follows: "The closer one draws to the divine mystery, the more pressing it becomes to express oneself, and simultaneously the less capable one is to achieve sufficient expression. This is the climax in which glossolalic prayer breaks forth." For many pray-ers, however, prayer exists primarily as a one-way voluntary action, with the pray-er speaking to God (and not expecting an answer). Pentecostals are taught that prayer is a two-way conversation and are instructed to wait expectantly for God to speak. This "hearing from God" and the human response to a divine call are what we measure in the prophecy scale.

Simply "praying with others" can be a totally voluntary act and an example of a one-way communication with the divine. Those who describe being used as an instrument of healing suggest that something more may be going on—namely, a two-way interaction that includes divine empowerment as mirrored in the prophecy scale. Our statistical analysis suggests that commonly experiencing prophecy is by far the leading descriptor of a person who acknowledges being an instrument of divine healing. In short—and relevant to our thesis on Godly love—our findings imply that spiritual experiences involving divine-human interaction may be facilitators of benevolence, including effective prayer for the healing of others (see Poloma 2006c). In short, *divine collaborators who hear the voice of God and respond to it are also the most likely to perceive themselves as functioning as God's instruments of healing in the church.*

A careful reading of April's narrative can illustrate the potential relationship between prophecy and being used to heal others. It was a prophetic word from the minister at a church revival meeting—calling out the woman "in the turquoise sweater"—that brought April forward to be prayed with and filled with a sense of divine power. As she lay trembling on the floor, he started prophesying a word calling her to ministry and preaching that she had heard in personal revelation as a child and young adolescent. It resonated with her. He stood her up and instructed her to prophesy (which she reportedly could not do), but she experienced people falling down as she prayed. She began to pray for others (in tongues), and she later reported that people were being healed. April's experience was more than a one-way divine action of experiencing God; it marked the beginning of a collaborative work. Empowered by interactive prophetic words confirmed by corporate or public prophecy, April was slowly able to launch into a ministry where she frequently finds herself being used as an instrument of divine healing.

Divine Healing and Godly Love: A Tentative Assessment

The pentecostal worldview—a worldview that runs counter to the hegemony of rationalism and modernism in the wider society—provides a context in which to explore the human experiences of divine love at the heart of the concept of Godly Love (Macchia 2006a). Benevolent action (at least for pentecostals) is frequently accompanied by experiences of the divine that appear to empower the believer, as suggested in Sorokin's (1954/2002) concept of "love energy." This pattern is evident in our exploration of the healing rituals and experiences reported in this chapter. Through multiple regression analysis, we have described demographic traits and aspects of spiritual experiences as they relate to healing, specifically to benevolent acts of healing prayer. Our findings clearly point to the special role that prophecy—hearing the voice of God and responding to it—plays in the healing process.

In the previous chapter we established that glossolalia was a contributing factor to increased benevolence as measured by evangelistic practices. Glossolalia or speaking in tongues, however, is also related to the other spiritual experiences included in our survey. The spiritual experience measures (as seen in appendix C, table C.1) are also related to the questions about healing that are the focus of this chapter. When we explore these preliminary statistics further through the use of multivariate analysis (appendix C, table C.2), the relationship between glossolalia and the healing measures are nonsignificant for experiences of physical healing or for being used as an instrument of healing. What can this mean? We suggest that speaking in tongues is important for those who experience divine healing or who are agents of healing, but that it functions in an indirect way. That glossolalia appears to be a silent partner to the experiences of prophecy can be summarized as follows: *those who prophesy usually pray in tongues, but glossolalia without experiences of the prophetic is not significantly implicated in healing experiences.* In biblical terms, this finding reflects the Apostle Paul's admonition: "Follow the way of love and eagerly desire spiritual gifts, especially the gift of prophecy" (1 Corinthians 14:1). While tongues is for "self-edification," Paul continues, prophecy is meant "for the church." *In terms of our analysis, the prophetic is not limited to human interaction with the divine; it also serves as a catalyst for "divinely inspired" interpersonal interaction* (i.e., benevolence). Two-way interaction with God—*hypothesized to be the source of Godly Love*—is in turn a factor in benevolent interaction with others. The interaction of the human and the divine expressed through prophecy and its effects on healing can be expressed in social-scientific terms as Godly Love or in theological terms in doctrines of Spirit baptism as *"empowerment for mission or service."*

Summary

What has emerged consistently in our statistical analyses thus far is the important role that an intimate relationship with God—whom the believer senses as a real presence and as a divine collaborator—plays in benevolent action. Survey research can be lifeless when compared with the vibrantly rich, thick descriptions found in pentecostal narratives, but it does something that narratives cannot do, namely, going beyond anecdotal evidence to establish findings that can be generalized beyond interesting observations. *The statistical evidence on healing rituals and practices points to the importance of Godly Love as a revitalizing force within Pentecostalism.* With a worldview that has traditionally emphasized religious experience over religious institutions and formal doctrine, Pentecostalism has created space in modern society in which the sacred is encountered. Judging from our survey data, most AG adherents, albeit with differing frequency and intensity, experience the charismata of tongues, healing, and prophecy—charismata that directly or indirectly appear to affect benevolence. The statistical findings reported in this chapter reflect the normative expectations of pentecostals that God is intimately and powerfully present in their lives—and that encounters of the divine make a difference in their lives and in the lives of others.

7

Law of Love and Love of Law

Beliefs, Mores, and Faces of Love

> Charisma opposes the lifestyle of transgressiveness, not in the infinite, but in the finite. It is for this reason that the true charismatic is always an interdictory figure, closing down the openness of possibility, narrowing the human passion for the infinite into a particular culture or way of life. (Rieff 2007, 228)

In a posthumously published work that is painstakingly difficult to read, sociologist Philip Rieff (2007) critiques aspects of the Weberian theory of charisma as he writes a treatise on "the gift of grace, and how it has been taken away from us." At times reading like the work of a scholar with a mind far beyond most mortals, while in other sections sounding like the ranting of a curmudgeon about the loss of a world that never was, Rieff's (2007) *Charisma* can be mined for golden nuggets to enrich sociological comprehension of a poorly understood and often misused concept. Of particular relevance for our understanding of the relationship between charisma and benevolence is Rieff's discussion of interdicts—that is, divinely given cultural mores. We use some of Rieff's insights to explore the relationship between Jesus's Great Commandment—an interdict that can be referred to as the "law of love"—and the "love of law," interdicts that contextualize the norms and practices of Godly Love. Paradoxically, loving the law and its interdicts can both enliven and distort the law of love.

There is no question that Rieff believed that charisma has been taken away from us. What he calls the hegemonic "therapeutic culture"—for him, "synonymous with unbelief"—is a destroyer of genuine charisma.[1] To mix Rieff's descriptors, what passes for charisma today is merely "'sprayed-on'/'publicity,'" devoid of both faith and guilt. Some of the examples Rieff posits of the therapeutic culture's role in the destruction of charisma would apply to sectors and practices of the pentecostal movement; but were he alive to respond to us, he probably would take us to task for marrying his insights with our theoretical discussion and empirical observations of Godly Love. We believe, however, that our use of charisma in relation to Godly Love aligns with this Jewish scholar's observations—or, at the least, through them Rieff has provided a heuristic tool complementing concepts already used to assess the dynamic nature of charisma in the AG.

For Rieff (2007, 4) "there is no charisma without creed." "Fresh interdicts" break through the existing order to proclaim "something to be true and important," providing prescriptions and prohibitions to guard faith. In Pentecostalism (with no single charismatic leader but rather a charismatic message and experience that immediately drew disciples) the charismata brought to life the creed of the Holy Spirit found in all orthodox Christian proclamations. The Bible is the source of Pentecostalism's interdicts and named transgressions, and repentance (and accepting divine forgiveness) is at the core of being "born again." Furthermore, although charisma is not uniformly distributed among believers, it is not regarded as the property of a single leader or leaders in the movement. As we have seen, however, according to Pentecostal tenets charisma requires a second experience of grace (available to all believers) known as the baptism of the Spirit to open the channels through which the charismatic gifts of the Spirit are released.

Although Pentecostals would be slow to admit any debt to Catholicism, similarities can be found between pre–Vatican II Catholicism and the charisma of Pentecostalism.[2] Rieff (2007, 193) acknowledges that although charisma in Catholicism has been *structured*, its sophisticated structure allows for charisma to emerge in *nonstructural* form. What he says about Catholicism could just as easily be used to describe early Pentecostalism, as well as the movement's contemporary struggles to be "sophisticated enough to allow the interdicts to freshly communicate themselves," essentially making a way for "nonstructural forms" to emerge within denominational practices:

> Non-structural charisma is a term which describes the activity of the free and autonomous Spirit operating through other than structured channels. In every age, the Spirit raises up saints, founders of orders or movement, members of both hierarchy and laity who speak to their age by virtue of a divine mandate personally received through revelations or vision and effectively legitimized through miracles and works of wonder. For Catholics still aware of the richness of their tradition in this matter, the results of non-structured charisms may be seen in the martyrdom of Christians, in personal dedication to the service of the church, in the missionizing activity of its members, and in its social reform movement.

At the outset of the twentieth century, the Spirit seemed to have risen up to unleash the paranormal charismata commonly believed to have ceased with the rise of Constantine and the politicization of Christianity in the Western world. Glossolalia, prophecy, healing, miracles of faith, and other paranormal experiences were declared normal for believing Pentecostals—gifts of the Spirit to enhance mission and ministry. We have already explored the role charismatic experiences play in the lives of many AG congregants and how they affect benevolence. In this chapter we explore whether interdicts—rules that enhance guilt to find resolution in faith—are in fact essential for charisma. Rieff's thesis provides a frame for looking back on the Pentecostal interdicts of old in light of the vestiges found in our congregational survey, and for determining whether these interdicts are part of the dynamic process we have been calling Godly Love.

"Almost Pentecostal": An Empirical Assessment

In her article "The 'Almost Pentecostal,'" theologian Kimberly Alexander (2007) plays on John Wesley's distinction between being an "almost Christian" and an "altogether Christian" as she explores the future of Pentecostal identity in the United States. Is Pentecostalism in danger of becoming primarily a religion set in its institutional norms and doctrinal statements—or has it been able to retain its spiritual fluidity as a form of Christianity rooted in the experiential love of God and neighbor? She questions whether increasing license has been given "to see few absolutes" in matters of practical living except for "issues such as the sanctity of life and marriage" (i.e., anti-abortion and anti–gay marriage). Issues such as "modesty and simplicity" and problems like "materialism and consumption" are rarely addressed (Alexander 2007, 141). Alexander effectively argues that "It is not enough to profess to be a Pentecostal. One must *be* a Pentecostal" (p. 152).

Modernism has always posed a dilemma for those seeking to be "altogether Pentecostal" in a culture where dynamic experiences of the Holy Spirit have the tendency to morph into particularistic religious doctrine. With a worldview that has more in common with ancient Israel and Eastern thought than with Western rationalism and empiricism, Pentecostalism has been swimming upstream in North America. The *law of love* regarded as a primary gift of Spirit baptism easily can be eclipsed by an idolatrous *love of law* that worships tradition over relationships. The hegemonic therapeutic culture that Rieff believed was the opposite of charisma in its non-belief, its failure to acknowledge guilt, and its eschewing interdicts has affected both the law of love and the love of law. Those wearing the lens of a therapeutic culture would see the two loves as antithetical, and thus, in the end (Rieff might argue), destroying both. Rather than pit the law of love against the love of law, we use the survey data to explore the potential relationship between them with measures of charisma, interdict, and care-love. Doing so allows us to wrestle with Alexander's description of an "almost Pentecostal" that compromises pentecostal identity, and to explore the role that charisma and law both may play in Godly Love.

A Modern Assessment of a Peculiar People

Throughout their early history Pentecostals practiced the separation from and rejection of the world common to many new religions. They were seen as a "peculiar people" by non-Pentecostal family, neighbors, and friends. As Vinson Synan (1971/1997, 185) notes, this rejection was a mutual one:

> The history of the Pentecostal people in American society is in many respects similar to that of the Methodists and Baptists of the eighteenth and nineteenth centuries. Beginning as total outcasts, they were to gain a status of suspicious toleration, followed eventually with full acceptance by the community. The early history of the Pentecostals in society was in reality a story of mutual rejection. The Pentecostals rejected society because they believed it to be corrupt, wicked, hostile, and hopelessly lost, while society rejected the Pentecostals because it believed them to be insanely fanatical, self-righteous, doctrinally in error, and emotionally unstable. In such an atmosphere it was inevitable that much prejudice, hostility, and suspicion would mar the relationship of the early Pentecostals to society at large.

Early Pentecostalism was rich in norms that ran counter to those of the larger society. With its emphasis on emotional expression and its strange practice of speaking in tongues, its style of worship made Pentecostals vulnerable to charges of emotional instability and fanaticism (Blumhofer 1989). Its catalogue of "social sins," as Synan (1971/1997, 190) summarizes them, included "tobacco in all its forms, secret societies, life insurance, doctors, medicine, liquor, dance halls, theaters, movies, Coca Cola, public swimming, professional sports, beauty parlors, jewelry, church bazaars and makeup." In addition to their peculiar form of worship and list of "social sins," many Pentecostals further defied the norms of most other churches of the day with a pacifist stance against war and support for ordaining women to pastoral ministry.

Over time, the extremes of Pentecostalism have been tempered, with many earlier practices being abandoned or modified. In part, the upward mobility that has graced the Assemblies of God has also eroded some of its distinctiveness. Its adherents are enjoying not only the necessities but also the comforts and pleasures of the world. This success, both individual and denominational, has muted the early Pentecostal call, "Be ye separate," and furthered the accommodation process.[3] In the past, Pentecostalism has been defined—and has at times defined itself—with a focus on dictates of law rather than on the substance of love.

Narratives from the Past

Reports from generations past by AG interviewees in the Flame of Love Project reflect few regrets about the slow demise of the legalism that was once a notable part of Pentecostalism's protest against modernity. Some described situations where prohibitions, taboos, and separatism were anything but loving, leaving them (in the words of one respondent) "still needing to be healed." Others spoke of legalism in a matter-of-fact way, noting simply, "That was the way it was back then," while providing in their narratives details about how negative effects of earlier Pentecostalism were attenuated by intense personal experiences of a loving God and/or the deep and demonstrable love they experienced from their fathers and/or mothers. One exemplar who was reared in a Euro-American ethnic AG community with very strong interdicts contended that older Pentecostals (and ones who have left the fold) need to "grow up and get over it—just get over it," reflecting a stance that old-time Pentecostal mores do not warrant the criticism to which they are commonly subjected.

Amy was a respondent whose recollections of growing up Pentecostal were recounted with humor rather than bitterness. Now in her fifties, Amy was an AG minister in her youth and has served the church all of her adult life—leading worship, preaching, conducting women's retreats, and calling for equality for women in ministry through scholarly writing and in her position as a university administrator. At the age of six she had what she regards as an epiphany—a revelation of God's love that has never left. Even today, as she is battling severe medical problems and financial difficulties and struggling with her career, she looks to that experience of God cradling her in his arms to provide a sense of hope.

Despite the legalistic religious world in which she was raised, Amy says she always knew that God loved her. She attributes this in part to having a very devout mother whom Amy regarded as "the saintliest person I have ever known." When asked about her image of God as a child, Amy replied: "God was soft and safe. For me it is always going back to that initial experience when things do not seem to be gong well—times when God once again gathers me in his arms and holds me close." The interviewer commented: "So, when those ministers preached hellfire and brimstone during your youth it didn't have the same effect on you as it may have had on others?" Amy replied:

> Minimally (hearty laugh). Minimally. I repented at the altar only three hundred times! (more laughter) I always knew God's presence was safe. It was never fearful for me. My greatest fear in life has been disappointing Him—because I loved Him so much that I didn't want to disappoint him.

Roger, an AG minister of Amy's early-boomer generation who now serves extensively outside his own religious tradition, describes the effects of his growing up in a Pentecostal home in less positive terms:

> I was raised in a very conservative, evangelical Pentecostal congregation in a small community. Our home was very ordered. My father had been in the military so he understood protocol, and with a large family, you have to have order to get things done. So that has shaped a lot of my own neurotic approach to keeping all the ducks in a row. We had rituals. Church was no option. We went four times a week—Sunday morning Sunday school, morning worship, and Sunday night service as well as Wednesday night was absolute. So faith was always a huge part of everything that we were a part of in a very simplistic way, very legalistic way, in a highly legalistic church. The love of God was not stressed, but rules and Old Testament theology and always seeking to keep the saints whipped in shape with a lot of fear and guilt is very much part of my memory. If our pastors were sitting here today, they would never say that. That was just the way it was in the middle fifties and early sixties. There was an emphasis on walking a "sanctified life," and it was rules rather than relationships that was stressed.

Although throughout the interview Roger provided occasional illustrations of the negative effect the love of law had on his life, there was at least one positive effect: "The emphasis on order and law," Roger noted, "gave me an incredible work ethic that helped me become who I am today."

Ted is an AG scholar who is nearly a generation older than Amy and Roger. Like Roger, Ted had a strict father and seemed to have little recollection of experiencing a loving God while growing up. He had stories to tell of growing up Pentecostal, but they seemed to revolve around struggling with legalisms that were an integral part of the AG culture while trying to minimize any significance this upbringing might have had on his life. Ted succinctly described his early years as follows:

> For the first eighteen years, the church was my life! It was the old Pentecostal tradition where you didn't go to theaters or other kinds of entertainment. I remember dating and one of my friends saying, "Where are we going to go? We can't go to dances and we can't go to movies—and we can't go to the planetarium every night! (laugh) We went to church Sunday, Sunday night, Tuesday night, and Thursday night. When we didn't do that, we went to Kathryn Kuhlman (a famous evangelist/healer) meetings. That is what we did.

It is safe to say that things have changed. We interviewed no Pentecostal who wanted to return to the past, where love may have been present but legalism seemed to rule the day. AG adherents are no longer the "peculiar people" they were until the 1960s, although some old practices and taboos still remain strong in traditional congregations, particularly in some ethnic churches and for some older members. The legalistic taboos once believed to ward off "worldliness" and to foster "holiness"—taboos against jewelry and makeup for women, and against attendance at "worldly" amusements, sporting events, and movie theaters; proscriptions against alcohol consumption and dancing; and prescriptions that put church involvement at the center of Pentecostal life—have all skied down the slippery slope of a pleasure-seeking, consumerist modern culture that is rarely addressed (as Alexander has astutely noted) by pastors and preachers. In the embracing of the larger culture, religious practices have also suffered. As we have seen, congregational activities, especially extended revival meetings, times for "tarrying" prayer, Sunday evening worship and mid-week gatherings have all lost notable ground in recent decades.

Rieff may be correct in his insistence that charisma cannot exist without interdicts; and thus the legalism of old Pentecostalism (although perhaps excessive) may have played an important role in charismatic identity and community. Rieff (2007, 21) uses the example of the Ten Commandments and ancient Judaism to illustrate the function of interdicts when he states,

"These interdictive instructions drew the Jews out of the welter of individual possibilities and established their corporate identity, their covenant." The empirical question we explore to help us to understand charisma relates to the nature of the "interdictive instructions," the extent to which they are viable in the AG, and how they may operate to establish a "corporate identity" that is Pentecostal. We seek further to explore how interdictive values, norms, and practices may affect the "law of love."

Contextual Measurements of Law and Love

A "love of law" is mirrored, if not captured directly, in the doctrine, teachings, and behavior of a religious community. For Pentecostals it is reflected in prescriptive rituals and belief and in old interdicts against "worldly entertainment" (movie theaters, gambling, and drinking alcohol), as well as in resistance to changes affecting family values (particularly divorce and remarriage and homosexual marriage). Paradoxically, the traditional worldview supported the ordination of women for ministry during a time when the practice was anathema for fundamentalist and mainline churches alike. In reviewing some of these prescriptions and taboos as enlightened by survey data, we are able to develop a clearer picture of the present state of Pentecostal interdicts. We use an index of eight items to construct the *traditional Pentecostal values scale*, which we employ to assess the role of faith and interdicts in fostering charisma and benevolence.

Prescriptive Beliefs and Rituals

Beliefs

As we have seen, the Assemblies of God is committed to the primacy of a fundamentalist/evangelical understanding of the Bible. The AG position paper on "The Inerrancy of Scripture" adopted by the Executive Presbytery in May 1970 begins: "We believe the Bible is the Word of God written; it is the revelation of the truths of God conveyed by inspiration through His servants to us. As such, it is infallible and without error" (General Council 1970/1978). The authors note further, "We conceive the Bible to be in actuality the very Word of God."

The Bible—defined as "inerrant" and "infallible"—is the source of belief for the AG. With the Bible as a plumb line, Pentecostal believers search and study to discern and justify their experiences and practices. Their statement of faith often carries a common, simple understanding reflected in a popular cliché: "The Bible says it, I believe it, and that settles it." In much of the AG, literalism trumps modern hermeneutics and modern biblical scholarship. We measured belief in the Bible through this statement in the congregational survey: "The Bible is the Word of God, true word for word." Eighty percent of the respondents strongly agreed with this statement and another 14 percent agreed, with only 3 percent disagreeing. Another non-negotiable truth gleaned from the Bible, to which the believer assents when being "born again," is the centrality of accepting Jesus as a personal savior. Ninety-six percent of the respondents either strongly agreed (82 percent) or agreed (14 percent) with the statement "Jesus Christ is the only way to salvation." The basic creed is intact and seemingly non-negotiable.

Greater diversity of opinion exists on other beliefs, including some found in the AG Statement of Fundamental Truths. For example, a clear majority of respondents disagreed with the statement that "a person who has never spoken in tongues cannot claim to be Spirit baptized," with 34 percent registering strong disagreement and another 31 percent disagreement. A significant minority (30 percent) either disagreed or strongly disagreed with the popular fundamentalist expectation that "the world will end in a battle between Jesus and the Anti-Christ." Finally, there is some indication that Pentecostalism's shift toward a more responsive role in the social world, both politically and in terms of social outreach, has congregants divided in their responses to a statement that many of their forefathers and mothers would have entirely agreed with. When asked whether "if enough people were brought to Christ, social ills will take care of themselves," half of the respondents disagreed, with another 18 percent reporting they had no opinion. And although pacifism was interpreted as a scriptural mandate in early Pentecostalism, the vast majority of respondents agreed (65 percent)—and another 21 percent had no opinion—that "the U.S. must be able to take preemptive military action against other countries."[4] The Bible may be the infallible and inerrant word of God, but interpretations on many topics clearly differ and are subject to change, as we will continue to demonstrate.

Ritual Activities

Church attendance is frequently used as a measure of religiosity, and the Assemblies of God reports one of the highest rates of regular church participation. In our congregational sample, 79 percent of the respondents indicated that they attended Sunday morning services "four or more times per month," a figure identical to the one reported in *Crossroads* (Poloma 1989, 13). Another 9 percent reported attending Sunday morning services at least three times a month. Regular Sunday school attendance is somewhat lower, with 47 percent reporting weekly attendance. Although regularly gathering for worship is believed to be a biblically based injunction, church membership is not regarded as a biblical mandate and is therefore not stressed in many AG congregations. This is reflected in our survey findings, where adherents—those who attend regularly, support the church, and consider the congregation their home church but are not church members—comprise nearly a third of the sample. Overall, 63 percent of congregants indicated they were members of the congregation, while another 31 percent were regular attendees but not members.

A minority of the respondents were raised in the Assemblies of God: 30 percent reported their denomination to be AG at the age of fifteen; 7 percent were raised in another Pentecostal denomination or in a non-pentecostal Spirit-filled church (3 percent); and 12 percent did not attend church in their mid-teens. The rest were primarily Roman Catholic (20 percent), evangelical (14 percent), or mainline Protestant (13 percent).[5]

Formal rituals, denominational affiliation, and church membership are clearly less important for AG identity than is being born again. As noted earlier, 95 percent of the respondents said they were "born again," having accepted Jesus as their personal Lord and savior. Another important marker of AG beliefs and practices is tithing, or giving at least 10 percent of one's income to the church. A decided majority (82 percent) strongly agreed or agreed that "tithes must be given to the local church." Only a minority reported they had no opinion or disagreed with the statement (17 percent) that allowed for giving the tithe to other religious groups or charities. Significantly, a smaller percent claimed to actually tithe, either to their churches or to a combination of church and other religious charities. Although reported behavior did not match opinion, the figures for tithing were still impressive: 28 percent said they contributed a full 10 percent tithe, and another 42 percent reported giving more than 10 percent; only 29 percent gave less than 10 percent.

Vestiges of Holiness Standards

On most matters, doctrine, behavioral standards, and ritual involvement among congregants are taken for granted rather than imposed through formal rules and regulations on adherents. The vestiges of so-called "holiness" taboos, once a visible sign of the separateness of Pentecostal culture, have likewise been taken for granted with little recent enforcement, thus allowing a slow transformation in practices. A steady accommodation has occurred over the decades at the local church level without repercussion, despite occasional non-enforceable "position" papers drafted by the General Presbytery of the Assemblies of God.

Vestiges of the taboos adhered to by early Pentecostals are still accepted by some of their descendents. Two of the strongest ones—total abstinence from alcohol and gambling—are supported by AG "position papers." "A Biblical Perspective on Abstinence" (General Council 1985, 1) clearly challenges those who would even occasionally use alcohol:

> The General Council of the Assemblies of God has historically opposed the consumption of alcohol in any form. Early documents of the church declare, without reservation or compromise, a position of total abstinence. In more recent years, however, this mark of separation from the world and this token of dedicated service to God has been questioned by some. Yet the continued effective work of reaching the lost and of challenging all believers to be always filled with the Holy Spirit is seriously jeopardized by a careless attitude concerning the consumption of alcoholic beverages.

Despite the unequivocal opposition to alcohol, AG respondents were nearly divided on this issue: 44 percent agreed or strongly agreed with the statement that the "occasional use of alcohol is permissible," while only 41 percent were in solidarity with the official AG position paper. A significant minority (15 percent) claimed having "no opinion" on the issue, suggesting that there are many sipping saints in AG pews despite a strong stance against the use of alcohol by the denomination.

Respondents appeared to be in greater agreement with proscriptions against gambling. In "A Biblical Perspective on Gambling" (General Council 1983, 4) the General Presbytery writes: "When God's Word teaches that we should avoid 'every kind of evil' (1 Thessalonians 5:22) it precludes gambling. There is no way in which a practice can be considered anything other than evil when it violates principles of God's Word concerning stewardship, consideration of others, and the dignity of honest labor." The clear majority of respondents (64 percent) agreed that "gambling should be avoided (even the lottery)," with only 15 percent disagreeing. Taboos against attending movie theaters and social dancing, on the other hand, appear to continue to slide down the slippery slope, allowing adherents to enjoy "worldly entertainment" without guilt.[6]

Clearly Pentecostals are not the peculiar people they once were, and probably few would want to revert to bygone age. But this still leaves us with

Kimberly Alexander's concerns about Pentecostals not questioning the cultural values of materialism and consumerism that were anathema to their forefathers and mothers. We did ask another question that sought to assess the degree to which respondents valued the separatist simple lifestyle rather than the cultural consumerism of modernity in order to gauge the popularity of the "prosperity gospel." Alexander (2007, 141) notes how the Word Faith Movement, which teaches its followers to "name" or acknowledge a specific need or desire and to "claim" or profess in faith that their desired object or goal is theirs, has led many into "identifying gain as godliness." She goes on to say, "The holiness message of *victory*, traditionally understood as a message of victory over sin is now preached by some as a victory over bad health and poverty." We found that AG respondents were divided on whether "God wants all believers to experience material prosperity," with nearly half of the congregants (48 percent) agreeing, one-third (35 percent) disagreeing, and the rest (17 percent) expressing "no opinion." If the prosperity gospel is an indicator of an identity problem in the AG, it is one that may be difficult to resolve. The results of our multivariate statistical test indicate that younger adherents, Euro-Americans, and those with a higher level of education are the most likely to adhere to this position.[7] If Alexander's thesis is correct, our statistics suggest that the prosperity gospel will continue to gain ground at the expense of Pentecostal identity.

"Family Values" and Changing Interdicts

As we have seen in our discussion of holiness standards, some AG norms and values have changed dramatically over the years. However, the basic core of faith—the Bible and Jesus as the only way to salvation—has remained consistently orthodox. Perhaps the biggest change has been the abdication of the simple lifestyle advocated by the movement's founders as descendents moved up the social class ladder and embraced the consumerism and materialism of the larger culture. When interdicts are firmly in place, there is little questioning of them, and Pentecostals assume this is the only biblical way of acting. But changes of interpretation have proven to be inevitable over time.

The Bible may be "in actuality the very Word of God," as the AG position paper on the "Inerrancy of Scripture" (General Council 1970/1978) declares, but it is a Word that has been and continues to be socially interpreted and reconstructed over the centuries. It is no secret to historians that the Bible was used to condone slavery and later to support segregation; that Jesus's prayer for unity was replaced by interpretations of the Bible that condemned church ecumenism (to appease fundamentalists); that Pentecostalism's early interpretation of the Bible calling for pacifism during the popular First World War has been superseded with support for preemptive military action; that it is but an interpretation of Scripture that continues to support the patriarchy found in biblical texts and still blocks women from serving as pastors in many AG churches; and that conservative Christians still interpret the scriptures in ways that depict gays and lesbians as second-class Christians and social deviants. It is instructive to examine some family-values issues to assess the differences among AG congregants' responses to illustrate interdicts that now seem firmly in place but that will most likely shift at least to some extent with the rise of a new generation of believers.

Divorce and Remarriage

Like most conservative Christian denominations and sects, The Assemblies of God has historically proscribed divorce and taken a stand against remarriage. Both the original 1973 version and the 2008 revision of the "position paper" on "Divorce and Remarriage" (General Council 1973/2008) include the following admonition:

> Low standards on marriage and divorce are very hurtful to individuals, to the family, and to the cause of Christ. Therefore, we discourage divorce by all lawful means and teaching. We positively disapprove of Christians getting divorces for any cause except fornication and adultery (Matthew 10:9). Where these exceptional circumstances exist or when a Christian has been divorced by an unbeliever, we recommend that the question of remarriage be resolved by the believer in the light of God's Word. (1 Corinthians 7:15, 27, 28)

Citing a recent figure from Barna Group (a popular conservative Christian polling enterprise) that "among self-professed evangelical Christian believers 26 percent have been divorced" (quoted in General Council 1973/2008, 1), the position paper acknowledges that "the institution of marriage is in crisis."

In our sample of AG congregants, 17 percent said they were divorced or separated from their spouses, with 11 percent being divorced and remarried and 6 percent of divorced persons remaining single.[8] Despite these lower-than-average rates within the denomination, the position paper appears to recognize that divorce is here to stay. The "uncompromising declaration of the sanctity of marriage" as filtered through biblical passages is tempered by the realities of modern life. The position paper concludes (p. 11) with the following statement:

> In all humility, the church today, as did the Early Church, struggles to understand and faithfully to apply the teachings of Scripture as it evangelizes and nurtures people in a secular, materialistic and sensual environment. Realizing there is much we do not know about the ways Jesus and the Apostles would have handled every problem raised by divorce and remarriage, we of the Assemblies of God offer this paper in a sincere effort to affirm and practice the truth of Scripture while also endeavoring "to keep the unity of the Spirit through the bond of peace." (Ephesians 4:3)

While the conciliatory tone of the paper insists that those who are divorced and remarried "not be viewed as second-class saints," it reminds the reader that the scriptures do not permit divorced members (except for certain circumstances, including marital unfaithfulness or a non-believer abandoning a believing spouse) to hold positions of local leadership.

The final decision about whether divorced persons can serve as congregational leaders, however, rests with the local church, where congregants are somewhat more accepting of divorced church elders. In response to the survey statement "Persons who have been divorced and remarried should not be permitted to serve in a leadership position in a local congregation," 67 percent either strongly disagreed or disagreed, and another 17 percent reported they had no opinion, leaving only 16 percent in agreement with an old interdict that clearly has a biblical base, as interpreted in the position paper on "Divorce and Remarriage."

The revised position paper has recently made a long-called-for change to now give limited acceptance to divorced and remarried pastors. While both the 1973 and 2008 versions state that the AG Presbytery disapproves "of any married minister of the Assemblies of God holding credentials if either minister or spouse has a former living spouse," the 2008 version allows for an important exception, namely "divorce occurring prior to conversion or for the scriptural causes of a former spouse's marital unfaithfulness or the abandonment of the believer by an unbeliever." Once again, congregants were more liberal in accepting a divorced and remarried pastor than is the judicatory: nearly half (49 percent) of the congregants were open to having a divorced and remarried pastor, expressing disagreement with the statement "Persons who have been divorced and remarried should not be permitted to pastor." Significantly, another 24 percent indicated "no opinion," leaving only 27 percent in agreement with AG policy.

Homosexuality

The process of accommodating to the reality of divorce and remarriage in American society provides an example of how the AG has been able to profess commitment to the Bible while extending mercy and grace to those active in their congregations. It is significant that on the issue of divorce congregants are more liberal than the General Council, as reflected in the official position paper. Moreover, contrary to the strict reading of the scriptures that once condemned divorce, grace has also quietly been bestowed on the select few who have been granted annulments to marry a partner who has been previously married and divorced. No such mercy, however, has been extended to homosexuals who seek to marry—neither by the denomination nor by most congregants. The AG has accepted an evangelical legalistic interpretation of biblical passages often used to support an anti-gay theology, rather than exploring how these passages may in fact not be as clear as supposed.

There have been times—perhaps most notably in ordaining women—when the Spirit's being poured out in unusual ways and on unlikely people sent Pentecostals back to the scriptures searching for ways to reinterpret biblical injunctions to match their own experiences. Homosexuality has not been the subject of such holy curiosity, despite the fact that the Spirit seems be poured out on gays as well as straights. (It is of note that the Metropolitan Community Church, a gay/lesbian/transgender denomination, was founded by a gay Pentecostal minister.)[9] For the most part, however, leaders and congregants alike are unaware of how the Spirit may be at work among many who have been marginalized by a particular interpretation of select Bible passages.

The gist of the General Council's (1979/2001) position paper on "Homosexuality" is simple and straightforward: "Homosexual behavior is sin" because it is "disobedient to scriptural teachings," "is contrary to God's created order for the family and human relationships," and comes "under divine judgment." The 2001 restatement of the original position paper, prompted as a response to the "increasing political and religious advocacy for homosexuality," clearly cautions against "writers sympathetic to the homosexual community [who] have advanced revisionist interpretations of relevant biblical texts that are biased exegesis and mistranslation." The authors continue:

> Historically, homosexuality often has been defined as an emotional (psychological) or organic (physiological) problem. In recent years, some have lobbied mental health organizations to have homosexuality removed from the list of classified diagnostic pathologies, and many have come to see it as nothing more than a morally neutral personal preference or a naturally

> occurring aspect of human biological diversity. In making moral judgments, we must remember scriptural warnings against depending on our own reasoning or even personal experience to discern truth.

The position paper is firmly in line with the congregational survey data. Respondents overwhelmingly agreed (94 percent) that "marriage should be defined as a union between one man and one woman without exception." Only 3 percent disagreed, with another 3 percent having "no opinion," suggesting minimal acceptance of marriage between homosexual couples among AG congregants. More diversity is found in responses to the statement "Government should insure that homosexuals are treated the same as heterosexuals in employment, housing and privacy." A solid minority (42 percent) agreed or strongly agreed with a position that would extend basic civil rights to gay men and women; 38 percent disagreed or strongly disagreed, with 20 percent reporting "no opinion."

Reflecting general survey findings on the acceptance of homosexuality, younger AG respondents are slightly more tolerant of redefining marriage and more likely to believe that homosexuals deserve to be treated equally under the law than older congregants. In time there may be a shift away from interdict-supporting proclamations toward more dialogue with and acceptance of homosexuality in the AG, but the move appears to be slow at best.

Women and Church Leadership

In writing a popular history of the denomination, Assemblies of God historian Edith Blumhofer (1989, 137) states:

> In the early Pentecostal movement, having the "anointing" was far more important than one's sex. As evangelistic hands carried the full gospel across the country, women who were recognized as having the anointing of the Holy Spirit shared with men in the preaching ministry. Those women who took part in the early development of the Assemblies of God seem to have given relatively little consideration to their "rights" of ministry. Rather they believed that if God gave someone a ministry, he would also give the opportunity to carry it out. A person's call—and how other believers viewed it—was far more important than "papers" (that is, formal denominational licensing).

Unlike some Pentecostal groups, the Assemblies of God did accept the credentials of those few already ordained women who came into the movement. Ambivalence, however, is evident even in the 1914 General Council resolution that granted ministerial status to women evangelists and missionaries, but not the right to be ordained as "elders" (a term that was increasingly interpreted to mean "pastors"). A significant minority of women nonetheless continued to function as AG pastors during these early days, even after further limitations were legislated in 1933. The limitation of women's ministries implied in the 1914 resolution became law in the 1933 revision. Two years later, the 1935 General Council restored to women the right to administer ordinances and permitted them to serve "either as evangelists or pastors as their qualifications warrant" (Barfoot and Sheppard 1980). That the 1933 law was rescinded after only two years demonstrates a healthy tension then existing between the priestly and prophetic forces in the denomination.[10]

Women ministers, however, still do not fare well in the denomination. As an early *prophetic pentecostalism* (which called for a new religious order to replace the old) was replaced by a new *priestly pentecostalism* (which looks increasingly like the fundamentalist old order), women were relegated to being pastors' wives and performing tasks associated with ministry to women and children. When asked whether she was credentialed or ordained in the AG, Sarah, an AG minister and missionary in her mid-forties who was interviewed as an exemplar of Godly Love because of the work she has done to stem human trafficking abroad and now in the United States, had this to say about her experience:

> Let me tell you. I was in ministry with my husband. In those days, they just didn't think that wives needed credentials. Well, I was "called" by God before my husband, but our cultural situation (in the mission field) required for him to be credentialed. I remember when I went to our (AG) district superintendent in northern California and said "I want to get credentialed," the man patted my hand and said, "Well, I think your husband's credentials can cover both of you; but if you feel you really need it, I can get a Christian workers credential for you."

Sarah chose not to pursue this lowest rung on the licensing ladder. It was many years later that she applied for ordination. As she explained: "You see, I had gotten involved in another culture that was hierarchical, and I had forgotten the things my daddy had taught me [i.e., that she "could be anything in life that she chose to be"]. Everything was in my husband's name, and it really didn't bother me at the time. I was doing what I wanted to be doing." It was as a middle-aged student attending an AG university, where she was encouraged by female faculty members, that she said she "recovered what my daddy always said to me." Although Sarah's experience may or may not be typical, there is little question that women are rarely found among church pastors and are not represented on the six-man Executive Leadership Presybytery.[11]

Survey responses indicate that congregants are fairly open to the idea of woman pastors.[12] Only 27 percent agreed with the statement "Women should *not* be encouraged to serve as pastors of local congregations," as compared with 49 percent who disagreed (18 percent reported "no opinion"), indicating support for women pastors. A similar response pattern was found for women as church leaders. A clear majority (66 percent) agreed or strongly agreed that "Women should be actively encouraged to serve on the church board of this congregation," with another 20 percent reporting "no opinion." Nearly a third (30 percent) of the respondents had "no opinion" as to whether more women should be encouraged to assume leadership in the AG at the national and district levels, reflecting the distance many feel toward organizational structures outside the local congregation. A majority (60 percent), however, were supportive of women as part of the governing structure. Opinions, as long known by social scientists, often do not translate into actual policy. Evangelical wariness and prohibitions against women in ministry have taken their toll on women pastors and leaders in the AG.

Because ordination is available to women, there is a crack in the institutional wall through which a few women can squeeze—mostly to take on pastorates of small churches or parachurch ministries that men have passed up. The paucity of women leaders and ministers in the AG, however, can be regarded as a barometer of the rise of a professional "priestly" clergy that jeopardizes the priesthood of all believers that once witnessed the Spirit being "poured out on all flesh." The original enthusiasm found in early Pentecostalism, which recognized the "call" of God rather than social status, continues to give way to a priestly clergy with lines drawn between the leaders and the led.

Measuring Pentecostal Traditional Values

Our discussion thus far has provided a description of interdicts existing in the AG, as well as some of the changes that have taken place in values, rituals, and doctrine, giving us a base to pursue a fuller understanding of charisma and its relationship to Godly Love. In order to take the next step in statistical analysis, we have created a *traditional Pentecostal values scale* comprised of seven survey items: use of alcohol, patronizing movie theaters, social dancing, tongues as initial evidence of Spirit baptism, divorced and remarried pastors, divorced and remarried leaders, and gambling. Another survey item "loaded" on this scale provides a key to what may be at the core the scale, namely, the statement "Assemblies of God congregations must actively seek to revitalize their early Pentecostal roots." Responses to this question were divided, with 53 percent agreeing and only 9 percent strongly disagreeing. (The 38 percent "no opinion" can be interpreted as indifference, thus presenting a picture of a denomination divided over the relevance of its Pentecostal identity.) As can be seen in appendix B, these eight items form a highly reliable scale as a proxy for Rieff's *interdicts* as we continue to explore the relationship between charisma and Godly Love.

What else can we tell from the survey data about those who scored high on traditional Pentecostal values? In order to answer this question, we once again turned to multiple regression analysis.[13] We found that those who scored higher on traditional Pentecostal values tended to be older, female, and non-white; to have a lower income; and to have been raised in a pentecostal denomination. Traditional respondents were likely to report believing without reservation that the Bible is the inerrant word of God and that Jesus is the only way to salvation. They were more likely to attend different church rituals and to attend them more often. They also tithed a larger percentage of their income and were more likely to pray in tongues. While they were also slightly *more* likely to report an abiding sense of the divine presence, they were paradoxically slightly *less* likely to report experiences of prophecy. The last finding possibly reflects the marginality of prophecy as a contemporary Pentecostal practice, with neo-pentecostals being in the forefront of teaching and modeling the functioning of prophecy in congregations.

Finally, we considered the relationship between the four types of congregations and adherence to traditional values. Traditional and evangelical congregations were *more likely* to score higher on traditional values than were renewalist/charismatic and alternative AG congregations. Only 13 percent of the respondents in renewalist/charismatic and 14 percent in alternative congregations scored high on traditional values, compared with 38 percent of both the evangelical and traditional congregations. The same pattern persists when considering the percentage of congregants *least likely* to hold to traditional values and interdicts as measured by the traditional values scale. Slightly over half of the alternative and charismatic church congregants (51 percent) scored in the *lowest* category of the scale, while only one in five of those in traditional churches (19 percent) and approximately one in four in evangelical congregations (27 percent) scored *low* on traditional values. Although clear congregational differences are reflected in the lowest and the highest scores, middle-range scores are fairly evenly distributed throughout the four types of congregations, with 35 percent of alternative, evangelical, and charismatic members and 40 percent of traditional church congregants falling between the two extremes.

AG churches appear to have a solid core of congregants who uphold moderate traditional values and retain a certain level of distinctiveness in their adherence to traditional norms and practices. The influx of new members, however, appears to modulate the distinctiveness provided by traditional Pentecostal values. For example, 41 percent of those who were raised in the AG scored in the highest category of the traditional values scale, compared with only 14 percent of those who were raised charismatic. Converts to the AG from mainline churches were half as likely as those raised in the AG to score high on traditional values—21 percent of former Baptists, 22 percent of former Roman Catholics, and 22 percent of former members of other mainline Protestant churches. Clearly those socialized in Christian denominations outside the AG were less likely to uphold traditional Pentecostal interdicts. With only 30 percent of our AG sample being raised in the AG, the influx of converts appears to be an important factor in the trend away from traditional Pentecostal values. The question remaining is whether the slow erosion of traditional values or interdicts makes any difference for the living out of Godly Love. Specifically, do those who score higher on traditional values, in accord with Rieff's thesis, score higher on charismatic experiences that empower benevolence? Our statistical analysis suggests that traditional values have no effect on benevolent action, and possibly a negative effect on some benevolent attitudes.

Traditional Pentecostal Values and Benevolence

We have used three charismatic measures throughout our analysis—sensing the divine presence, prophecy, and glossolalia—as indicators of charismatic encounters that have been shown to promote benevolence. Our empirical measures of benevolence have been evangelism and healing (either praying with others for healing or seeing oneself as an agent of healing). We now add three more benevolence measures to our original three for testing of the hypothesized multivariate relationship between charisma, interdicts, and benevolent attitudes and behavior.

The *compassion scale*, a measure of benevolence that extends beyond church evangelism, taps the respondent's willingness to reach out to others in the larger community. We drew on five statements from the survey to serve as indicators of this form of benevolence. Items included are "giving away things I need to help someone else" (15 percent strongly agreed), "serving the poor gives me great joy" (29 percent strongly agreed), trying one's best "to respond to the needs of others" (18 percent strongly agreed), willingness to put oneself in "physical danger if it means helping someone in need" (11 percent strongly agreed), and always trying "to have relationships that include the poor and the broken" (8 percent strongly agreed).

The *attitudes toward the poor* scale is made up of four statements to measure benevolent attitudes, with five response choices that range from strongly disagree to strongly agree: "The poor and homeless are reaping what they have sowed" (10 percent agreed); "I cannot truly love a person who does not show gratitude" (18 percent agreed); "I don't understand how anyone can be homeless" (15 percent agreed); and "The poor do not deserve help unless they try to help themselves" (19 percent agreed). The only demographic variable statistically related to supporting the needs of the poor was gender, with women reporting slightly more positive attitudes toward those in need.

The *ecumenism scale* is another indicator of benevolence, this time tapping acceptance of other religions through cooperation with different groups "on issues of common concern." Questions included in this scale asked about the degree (none, limited, or full) to which respondents would like to see their churches cooperate with eight different religious groupings. Respondents were most likely to approve of full cooperation with other Pentecostals (70 percent) and evangelicals (68 percent), followed by mainline (50 percent) and non-denominational Protestants (48 percent). They were somewhat less likely to approve of full cooperation with other pentecostal Christians, both charismatics in mainline churches (39 percent) and in charismatic parachurch ministries (39 percent). Only 30 percent of respondents approved of full cooperation with Catholic churches and 22 percent with non-Christian churches. Of the demographic variables, only age and education show weak but statistically significant correlations. Younger adults and those who are more educated are slightly more likely to be supportive of relations that cross the spectrum of religious groupings.

Evangelism, praying with others for healing, and serving as instruments of healing, as presented in earlier chapters, are specific forms of *behavioral* (rather than attitudinal) benevolent acts commonly found within the congregation. We have argued that evangelism not only can be a catalyst for church growth but also serves as an indicator of spiritual revitalization. The results of our statistical analyses show that both evangelism and healing are empowered by pentecostal spirituality—especially prophecy and an abiding sense of the divine presence (see appendix C, table C.2). Glossolalia, although failing to demonstrate a strong direct effect on benevolence, does appear to have an indirect effect (in that those who are prophetic and abide in a sense of divine presence are also more likely to speak in tongues). The section that follows presents the results for our multivariate analyses of all six of the benevolence measures, testing for the effects of demographics, spiritual experiences, and traditional values.

Interdicts, Spirituality and Benevolence

Evangelism

From our earlier assessment of the impact of charisma on evangelism we raise the additional question of whether traditional Pentecostal values (a proxy for what Rieff has called "interdicts") impact evangelism. (The full results for the multiple regression analyses can be found in appendix C, table C.3). The results of our multivariate analysis continue to support the finding that the divine presence and prophecy scales, both measures of spiritual experiences, are the leading indicators of evangelism. *Interdiction, at least as measured by items included in the traditional Pentecostal values scale, has no impact on whether or not congregants engage in self-giving evangelistic behavior that is potentially congregation building.*

Healing Ministry

Based on our multivariate analyses of healing ministry measures (prayer with another and serving as instruments of divine healing) that include traditional Pentecostal values (see table C.3), maintaining a belief in traditional values *has no direct impact on serving in the healing ministry.* Regular and ongoing experiences of prophecy remain the most powerful descriptor for those who serve as healing agents, while a strong sense of an abiding divine presence is the leading predictor of those who reported more frequently praying with others for healing. Glossolalia has a modest statistical effect on praying with others for healing, but not for serving as an instrument of healing. *It is safe to say that while spiritual experiences do have a positive impact on charismatic healing ministry, adherence to traditional Pentecostal interdicts do not.* Those who strongly uphold traditional Pentecostal values are no more or no less likely to be engaged in the ministry of divine healing.

Compassion

The same pattern whereby spiritual experiences figure prominently in describing a potential empowering source for benevolent action also holds for our analysis of the *compassion scale*, a more general behavioral measure of benevolence. We found that those who frequently experienced a sense of the divine presence and those who were highly prophetic were most likely to be compassionate.[14] *Once again, traditional Pentecostal values do not seem to have any impact on compassion, and those who adhere to them are no more or less likely to be compassionate than their counterparts.*

Attitudes toward the Poor

Evangelism, healing, and compassion are measures of benevolent action, while our last two benevolence indicators reflect attitudes rather than behavior. "Pro-poor" attitudes tap benevolent predispositions toward those in need, with inquiry directed toward the effect traditionalism may have on this measure of benevolence.[15] We found that traditional values, together with two of the spirituality indicators, contribute to our understanding of pro-poor attitudes. As expected, given our earlier findings on benevolent action, those who held benevolent attitudes toward the poor were more likely to report spiritual experiences, including glossolalia, and more likely to have a strong sense of God's abiding presence. Our multiple regression analysis (see table C.3) also shows the pro-poor to be more likely to be female, to pray in tongues, and to have a stronger sense of the divine presence. Maintaining traditional Pentecostal values, however, is the strongest indicator of pro-poor attitudes, but this relationship is a negative one. In other words, *those who hold to more traditional values are significantly less likely to profess attitudes that are empathic toward the needs of the poor and homeless. Those who pray in tongues and who experience an abiding sense of the divine presence, on the other hand, are somewhat more likely to report pro-poor attitudes.* This finding suggests that negative attitudes about the poor are more likely to be held by traditionalists than by those less committed to traditional Pentecostal values.

Ecumenism

Our concluding multiple regression analysis for this chapter seeks to measure religious tolerance—specifically, the extent to which AG respondents expressed favorable attitudes toward cooperating with a range of other religious groups "on issues of common concern." Early Pentecostals tended to be wary of inter-religious cooperation, often even cooperation with other Pentecostals. When Poloma penned *Crossroads* in the 1980s, the AG was still somewhat hostile toward Catholicism, cool towards mainline Protestantism, and suspicious of the charismatic movement. As we saw in an earlier discussion of Pentecostal identity and in presenting the ecumenism scale in this chapter, the pattern found in the 1980s continues as congregants (like their pastors) are most likely to identify with other Pentecostal churches and evangelical congregations. Their sometimes limited view of what makes a Christian—reflecting the common nomenclature of being "born again" or "saved"—can be seen in their reluctance to cooperate with religious groups outside the Pentecostal-evangelical traditions who may express their faith differently, even if they agree on a "common concern." As might be expected, *those who demonstrate greater support for traditional Pentecostal values are also more likely to hold attitudes that disapprove of the AG cooperating with non-evangelical or pentecostal churches.*[16] In this multiple regression equation, only one spiritual experience measure was related to attitudes favoring greater ecumenical cooperation. *Those who reported higher scores on prophecy were slightly more likely to favor ecumenism.*

Charisma, Interdicts, and Godly Love

Like an utterance in tongues at a pentecostal religious ritual, recounting a story with statistics necessarily involves a vernacular interpretation. What do all these statistical findings have to teach about a theory of Godly Love? The findings provide limited but consistent support for our thesis that a perceived two-way love relationship with God is one (but certainly not the only) important factor that empowers benevolence. As we have noted, benevolent acts—especially as measured by evangelism and healing—can be regarded as factors in congregational vitality and growth. Undoubtedly AG congregations grow in part as a result of what Grant Wacker (2001) has called "pragmatism" and sound organizational practices, but "primitive" spiritual experiences are also important for many Pentecostal followers. In accord with our original hypothesis, we contend that spiritual experiences serve as important sources of pentecostal revitalization not only for the individual but also for the congregation.

As Poloma has argued elsewhere (Poloma 2003; Poloma and Hood 2008), experiences of the charismata are a form of mysticism, reflecting one illustration of what Rolf Johnson has called *union-love*. Prayerful interaction between God and the pray-er as described by Pentecostals can deepen union-love with the divine, which in turn empowers *care-love* as it is extended to others. Johnson (2001, 100, 101) contends that through union-love with the divine "the human beloved actually in some sense is divine." He uses Mother Teresa's claims to "see the face of her Beloved in everyone she meets" to illustrate his point. Mystics—those who encounter and are possessed by the divine—come in all shapes and sizes, and we do not mean to suggest that all respondents loved with the intensity of Mother Teresa. In accord with our thesis on Godly Love, however, we do understand many of our AG respondents to be everyday mystics who are empowered for service by divine love.

Johnson's third faces of love, *appreciation-love*, is not a categorical definition of love, but rather an effort to describe an abstract form of "interpersonal love relationships." A*ppreciation-love* can be theoretically regarded as a complement to *union-love* (vertical relationship with God) and *care-love* (horizontal relationship with others). In our analysis of the congregational data, we have conceptualized the "object" (to use Johnson's terms) of *union-love* as "being one with God"; the object of *care-love* as to "seek to benefit" for another; and the object of *appreciation-love* as "ideals, principles, or abstract qualities" (Johnson 2001, 25). Rieff's interdicts, we would argue, can be regarded as a concrete "object" of appreciation-love. Our traditional Pentecostal values scale thus serves as an empirical measure not only of interdicts, but also of appreciation-love. While we have only scratched the surface in our empirical investigation of appreciation-love, we believe this "face of love" mirrors the interdictive "love of law."

In the measures we used to tap benevolent actions—evangelism, healing, and compassion—traditional Pentecostal values have failed to account for the differences in benevolence. Those who scored high on the traditional Pentecostal values scale were no more or less likely to be evangelistic, to serve as healers, or to be more compassionate than those who were less traditional. However, measures of charisma—of experiences of the divine such as prophecy, a sense of the divine presence, and glossolalia—consistently helped explain differences in benevolent behavior.

A somewhat different pattern was found when assessing benevolent attitudes. Although traditional Pentecostal values did account for differences in the two care-love proxies that measured attitudes—attitudes toward the poor and toward other religious faiths—the relationships were surprisingly negative ones. More traditional Pentecostals were *less likely* to report loving attitudes toward the poor, and they were more likely to support limiting church cooperation only to other Pentecostals and evangelicals. Experiences of charisma continued to be positively related to these attitudinal measures, as they had been with the behavioral ones.

Summary

What do these empirical findings on traditional Pentecostal values and benevolence have to say to questions raised by Kimberly Alexander, Rolf Johnson, and Philip Rieff? To Alexander they suggest that abandoning some Pentecostal distinctives could result in the AG becoming "almost Pentecostal." At the same time, as we have seen, indiscriminately seeking to strengthen traditional norms and values could actually have negative consequences (as they did with pro-poor attitudes and ecumenism). The seeming decrease of traditional values, however, may signal a void in interdicts seeking to be filled. One way of filling this void (as Alexander seems to suggest) is to intensify efforts to reconceptualize Spirit baptism as a "baptism of love" and a "baptism for service," rather than focusing on the interdict of speaking in tongues.

To Rolf Johnson we suggest a need to distinguish between forms of appreciation-love that strengthen what we call *Godly Love* and those that may weaken it. The negative findings in our statistical equations that include traditional values are a reminder of a previous ethnographic study of Godly Love. Poloma and Hood's (2008) research on an Atlanta ministry to the homeless observed that a form of appreciation-love that stressed the coming kingdom of God morphed into an idolatrous symbol that led its adherents to lose their focus on caring for the poor and broken. The ever-changing vision presented by the leader became a primary factor in destroying the care-love found in this once-vibrant ministry. While we do not deny that vision is an important component of Godly Love, it can become distorted or, worse, can go amuck, as it did in Poloma and Hood's case study. Although we are careful not to equate attitudes and behavior, the negative findings between loving attitudes and traditional Pentecostal values can be a warning signal. There may be a problem for care-love when Spirit baptism is reduced to glossolalia, serving as a "badge" rather than empowerment for loving service, or when "holiness" is reduced to adhering to the letter of the law rather than seeking love in the law. Appreciation-love clearly has the potential to both facilitate and impede the flow of Godly Love.

To Philip Rieff, we question whether anything more than the interdict of love is needed for charisma. Our statistical findings show the love relationship with God, in direct contrast to traditional Pentecostal interdicts, to be consistently and positively related to measures of care-love. We are left to wonder about the role interdiction plays in enhancing or destroying charisma. It might be that where the "law of love" functions with healthy perceptions of divine–human interaction, it becomes the interdict of a "law to love." Love as divine–human relationship appears to trump law as interdicts when it comes to extending benevolence.

8

Ushering in the Kingdom of God

Religious Values, Godly Love, and Public Affairs

> Historical arguments come and go. I make my case for crucifism theologically—as did the early Pentecostals—not based on a statistically verifiable number of my ancestors who believed a certain way. For the majority is often wrong about all manner of important beliefs and practices (slavery, segregation). The majority, might by numbers, does *not* make right. My historical arguments are simply historical—my theological arguments are much more important because they call us to a faithful way of living regardless of what our ancestors did. (Alexander 2009a, 329)

Paul Alexander represents an example of recent efforts by young Pentecostals to understand the implications of their faith for public affairs. Here, as in other areas, the Assemblies of God confronts a dilemma between the "law of love" and the "love of law" that can encourage different—even contradictory—approaches to public life. On the one hand, distinctive Pentecostal religious experiences can promote a just and compassionate society. On the other hand, the traditional religiosity of Pentecostals can promote a society characterized by traditional moral values. As Alexander notes, these approaches among the Assemblies of God "come and go," and every generation confronts this dilemma in a different context than in the past, often arriving at different conclusions.

The contextual nature of these approaches to public affairs provides an opportunity to investigate many of the theoretical issues raised earlier in this book. It is most relevant to the dilemma of power noted in O'Dea's (1963) notion of the routinization of charisma. Simply put, the institutionalization of the AG now provides a number of opportunities to exercise influence in public affairs. Some of these opportunities may reflect the process of Godly Love, while others may reflect the impact of the traditional interdicts found in Pentecostalism. While we cannot directly measure the processes of Godly Love or the interdicts, we can identify relationships between religious values and various forms of benevolence in public affairs that are consistent with each.

The AG and Contemporary Approaches to Public Affairs

A number of recent observers have found evidence of a renewed interest in poverty and social welfare policies among Pentecostals around the world. Donald E. Miller and Tetsunao Yamamori (2007) have identified the emergence of "progressive Pentecostals," who combine the traditional gifts of the spirit with outreach to the poor. One of the Assemblies of God congregations in our study, Rescue Atlanta, is an example of this approach. Going a step further, theologian Harvey Cox (1995), evangelist Tony Campolo (Campolo and Darling 2007), and young Pentecostal intellectuals such as Alexander, have identified the possibility for progressive politics among Pentecostals. This approach is often seen as a prophetic stance against poverty, racism, and war (Alexander 2009b), and appears to be especially common among African American, ethnic, and immigrant Pentecostal churches, especially in denominations other than AG, such as the Church of God in Christ.

For all these reasons, progressive Pentecostals may have an affinity for the Democratic Party in contemporary American politics, despite holding conservative views on cultural issues such as abortion and homosexuality. A good example of this approach is black Pentecostal minister Joshua Dubois, who was in charge of outreach to religious voters for the Obama presidential campaign in 2008 and then became director of the Office of Faith-Based and Neighborhood Partnerships in the White House (Altman 2009).

Although some scholars claim that such a "pedagogy among the oppressed" was present from the very beginning of Pentecostalism (Johns 1993), most observers see it as new approach to public affairs for most Pentecostals, especially the Assemblies of God. For most of its history, Pentecostalism was largely apolitical and deeply skeptical of large-scale social reform. Indeed, some scholars see its "vision of the disinherited" (Anderson 1979) as discouraging political activity among its lower-status members, and thus supportive of the existing social structure. Even the pacifism of the early Pentecostals during World War I represented a self-conscious detachment from public affairs.

Other scholars have a more positive view of the "social witness" of early Pentecostals (Wacker 2001), but agree that they stressed voluntary charity to needy individuals and abstention from involvement in "worldly" matters.

This "Pentecostal individualism" was closely related to evangelism and missionary work, so that "social uplift" paralleled "spiritual uplift" among converts. In this regard, Pentecostals have contributed to the dense web of civic associations that are an important feature of public affairs in the United States (Smidt et al. 2008). A good contemporary example is the involvement of the Assemblies of God in the "Convoy of Hope," a network of private charitable activities directed at helping the poor (see www.convoyofhope.org). Many of the congregations in this study exhibit elements of this approach.

However, Pentecostals are much better known for another recent innovation in public affairs: active support for traditional morality. Historically, "moral uplift" among converts paralleled "social uplift" and "spiritual uplift" for Pentecostals, a pattern that still finds expression in the traditional Pentecostal values described in the previous chapter, including the strictures against dancing, movies, gambling, and alcohol. In the late 1970s, concern with such traditional values led Pentecostals to play a prominent role in public opposition to abortion and same-sex marriage (Wilcox and Larson 2006). Such "culture war" politics led to engagement in elections, including mobilizing voters within congregations, involvement with the Christian Right, and support for the Republican Party. Good examples of this approach are charismatic televangelist Pat Robertson, founder of the Christian Coalition and Republican presidential candidate in 1988, and former U.S. Attorney General John Ashcroft, the son and grandson of Assemblies of God pastors (Green 2004). This pattern has led scholars to describe Pentecostals as the "ultimate conservative Christians" (Greeley and Hout 2006). Some of the congregations in this study illustrate elements of this approach as well.

This chapter uses our survey of the AG laity to investigate the relationship between religious values and various approaches to public affairs. One focus is the impact of religious experience (divine presence, prophecy, and glossolalia) on benevolent attitudes and behaviors in public affairs. These relationships are often consistent with the process of Godly Love in that they are associated with greater benevolence. Another focus is on the impact of traditional religiosity (doctrinal orthodoxy and church activity) on these same benevolent attitudes and behaviors. These religious variables are related to the traditional interdicts that are part of Pentecostal identity.

In this regard, we will first consider the relationship between the religious values and six measures of benevolent attitudes: belief that Christians should work for social justice, and that Christians should emphasize making converts to solve social problems; support for congregational benevolence and congregational engagement in politics; and attitudes on social welfare programs and cultural issues. These benevolent attitudes will then be included in a second analysis that assesses the impact of the religious measures on four measures of benevolent behavior related to public affairs: volunteering to help the needy; membership in voluntary organizations; participation in politics; and alignment within the broader political system. (See appendix B for more details on all the measures used.) As in the previous chapters, we will describe these relationships using multiple regression analysis (see chapter 6; the full results of these analyses are reported in appendix C, tables C.4, and C.5).

Benevolent Attitudes: Social Theology

A good place to begin is with measures of "social theology" among the Assemblies of God laity, that is, attitudes that connect religious faith to society and politics (Guth et al. 1997, 69–70). Social theology can undergird the various approaches to public affairs by religious people. One example of social theology is relevant to the progressive Pentecostals: "Christians must work to make society more fair and equitable for everyone" (hereafter referred to as the "equitable" measure for ease of presentation). Agreement with this statement, akin to the social gospel long advocated by liberal Christians, implies an active approach to benevolence in public affairs. In contrast, another example of social theology is relevant to Pentecostal individualism: "If enough people were brought to Christ, social ills will take care of themselves" (hereafter referred to as the "social ills" measure). Agreement with this statement puts an emphasis on evangelism and implies a more passive approach to benevolence in public affairs.

Overall, 67 percent of the AG laity agreed with the equitable measure, while 12 percent disagreed (with the remaining 21 percent expressing no opinion). In contrast, 50 percent of the respondents agreed with the "social ills" measure, while 30 percent disagreed. Views on these two statements were negatively related to each other, with those agreeing with the equitable measure tending to disagree with the social ills measure—but perhaps less strongly than one might expect.[1] In fact, 33 percent of the respondents agreed with *both* statements. It is tempting to see such a combination as contradictory, but it need not be: after all, bringing people to Christ could, in fact, make society more equitable. But if not contradictory, the relationship between these two social theology measures reveals a source of the dilemma regarding approaches to public affairs: *the Assemblies of God laity holds attitudes that can encourage both the progressive and conservative approaches to public affairs.*

What kinds of respondents agree with these measures of social theology? The multiple regression analysis reveals that both non-white respondents and those less active in church were more likely to agree with the equitable measure, but respondents who scored high on the divine presence scale were the most likely to agree.[2] Something of an opposite pattern occurred for the social ills measure: the multiple regression analysis reveals that older respondents were more likely to agree with the social ills measure, but people who scored high on the doctrinal orthodoxy scale were most likely to agree.[3]

We can thus conclude that *religious experience is associated with the belief that Christians must work for a more fair and equitable society, while traditional religiosity is associated with the opposite view.* In contrast, traditional religiosity is associated with the belief that bringing people to Christ will solve social ills, while religious experience is not associated with this attitude at all. These findings suggest that the process of Godly Love and traditional interdicts each may play a role in these forms of social theology.

Benevolent Attitudes: Congregational Benevolence

As noted previously, the AG laity is extensively engaged in the life of their congregation, and one form of such engagement is benevolent activities on behalf of people inside and outside of the congregation. Our survey respondents were asked how important it was that their congregation be involved in four such activities: serving the poor and needy; providing services to members; being a leader in the community; and working to improve the community. Overall, 51 percent said it was "extremely important" that the congregation "serve the poor and the needy," and nearly as many, 46 percent, said it was "extremely important" that the congregation "provide services to its members." In addition, 39 percent said it was "extremely important" that the congregation should be "a leader in the community," and 32 percent gave the same response to "work to improve the community." On all four questions, adding in the "very important" responses produced large majorities of the survey respondents.

These four questions form a valid scale of attitudes toward congregational engagement in benevolent activities ("congregational benevolence"; see appendix B). If nothing else, this scale reveals the impact of Pentecostal religiosity on public affairs—namely, the provision of assistance, services, leadership, and change in the local community. In addition, this form of benevolence is quite consistent with Pentecostal individualism because of its stress on voluntary assistance of individuals by other individuals via the agency of the local congregation. In this regard, it is worth noting that the most individualized responses (helping the needy and members of the congregation) were markedly more popular than the more collective responses (being a community leader and improving the community). But whatever its motivation, congregational benevolence is certainly consistent with the official positions of the Assemblies of God.

Who supports congregational benevolence? The multiple regression analysis reveals that younger and less well-educated respondents were most supportive of these types of congregational activities, and so were those who scored high on the divine presence scale. Interestingly, frequent engagement in congregational (religious) activities was negatively associated with support for congregational benevolence.[4] This pattern may reflect a traditional bias toward individual salvation and moral behavior over communal benevolence of any kind—even voluntary, faith-based efforts at the local level. In sum, *religious experience is positively associated with congregational benevolence, while traditional religiosity shows the opposite pattern.* These findings are consistent with the process of Godly Love in that religious experience enlivens both benevolence and the traditional interdicts that remain in Pentecostalism.

The survey respondents were also asked how important it was that their congregation be engaged in political activities that have been common in recent times (Guth et al. 2006). Sixty-seven percent of the respondents said that it was "extremely important" that their congregation "pray for the nation's leaders"; 36 percent said it was "extremely important" that their congregation "work for legislation with Christian morals"; 27 percent reported it was "extremely important" that their congregation help "elect Christians to political office"; and 19 percent gave the same response on "help people register to vote." These four items formed a valid scale of "congregational politics" (see appendix B).

These attitudes on congregational politics raise the issue of political activity by Assemblies of God pastors, who can encourage or discourage such activity in their churches. A 2000 survey of Assemblies of God clergy (Green 2004) found a high level of political activity and a desire for greater personal and denominational engagement in the political process. The clergy were largely focused on cultural issues, on which they personally held very conservative views. These pastors also held conservative positions on government social programs and foreign policy, and were strongly aligned with the Republican Party. In the 2000 election, 68 percent of the clergy surveyed urged their congregation to register and vote; 55 percent prayed publicly for a candidate; 44 percent spoke out on a political issue; and 7 percent actively campaigned for a candidate.[5]

The official position of the Assemblies of God encourages political participation by individual members of the denomination, lay or clergy:

> From this position the Assemblies of God encourages its members and adherents to influence society and the political process by voting, maintaining strong moral convictions and holy lifestyles (Matthew 5:13), praying for government officials (1 Timothy 2:2), encouraging and promoting legislation that strengthens the nation morally, and speaking out both corporately and individually against any political issue that would have an adverse affect upon the kingdom of God or His moral absolutes (www.ag.org/top/Beliefs/contempissues_10_politics.cfm; accessed March 16, 2010).

But this document also includes a cautionary comment about corporate political activity by congregations: "Historically, when *the church* has become involved in partisan politics, the outcome has been disastrous for both the kingdom of God and the system of government it promoted or attacked."

Which respondents were most supportive of congregational politics? Respondents with lesser levels of education were the most supportive of such activities, but so were respondents who scored high on the divine presence and prophetic scale.[6] Thus, *religious experience influences attitudes toward congregational engagement in politics.* These findings are consistent with the process of Godly Love in that religious experience encourages benevolent activities. But as will be discussed below, such political activity can take many forms, some progressive and some conservative. As we have noted earlier, benevolence often lies in the eyes of the beholder. To turn a popular cliché into a question: Is it more benevolent to provide fish for those who are hungry or to teach the hungry person to fish? The choice often rests on different underlying assumptions about the role of government in balancing individual rights with the common good.

Benevolent Attitudes: Social Welfare Issues

One characteristic of progressive Pentecostals is their support for government social welfare policies. Our survey contained four measures of social welfare policy that formed a consistent scale ("social welfare scale"; see appendix B). These policies included charitable choice ("Public funding should be available to churches to provide social services") and national health insurance ("The government should provide health insurance to working people who are not insured"). About three-fifths of our survey respondents (61 and 59 percent, respectively) agreed with both statements, while one-fifth (21 and 19 percent, respectively) opposed them. The additional measures in the scale more evenly divided the respondents, with 42 percent in favor and 37 percent opposed to increased anti-poverty programs ("The government should spend more to fight hunger and poverty"), and 37 percent are in favor of and 30 percent against environmental protection ("Strict rules to protect the environment are necessary even if they cost jobs").

The strong support for charitable choice may reflect progressive Pentecostalism, but it also fits well with Pentecostal individualism; the health insurance item may reflect a similar situation, given its mention of "working people who are not insured." And the more even division of opinions on anti-poverty programs and environmental protection items may reflect the collective emphasis of these items. The official positions of the Assemblies of God help account for this stress on Pentecostal individualism. A good example is the following statement on poverty found on the AG Website:

> If one takes the sociological definition of poverty—below a certain percentage of average income—the number of poor in the United States is large and unlikely to decline, even though more money is dispersed from federal budget programs. The biblical definition of poverty, however, is different. The poor are those who lack minimal survival needs of essential food and clothing. That is why the biblical owners of grape vineyards were to leave some grapes for the poor to gather for themselves (Lev. 19:10), and why owners of grain fields were to leave some grain in the corners of the field for the poor to gather (Lev. 23:22). . . . The spiritual needs of the poor are of primary importance, though essential physical aid should never be neglected. In fact, aid to the needs of the poor can often open a door for meeting a spiritual need. (www.ag.org/top/Beliefs/sptlissues_the_poor.cfm; accessed March 16, 2010)

This document goes on to acknowledge the power of the Holy Spirit in addressing these needs:

> [W]e have found the biblical balance of helping the poor to be a powerful means of fulfilling our primary mission. The Holy Spirit has promised to go with us and to equip us to do that great work. And with humble obedience to the Spirit, we can claim the blessing Jesus gave, "Blessed are the poor in spirit, for theirs is the kingdom of heaven" (Matt. 5:3). The poor in spirit should minister to the poor in physical needs—in the power of the Holy Spirit.

Which respondents support social welfare programs? Younger respondents as well as those who score high on the divine presence scale were most likely to support these programs. Meanwhile, respondents who are engaged in church activity were less supportive.[7] Thus, *religious experience is associated with support for social welfare programs, while traditional religiosity is associated with opposition to them.* These findings on religious experience are consistent with the process of Godly Love in that it enlivens benevolence as subjectively perceived. The traditional interdicts of twentieth-century Pentecostalism may still be at work to slow down the ongoing erosion of traditional Pentecostal values in twenty-first-century America.

Benevolent Attitudes: Cultural Issues

As we have seen, a distinguishing characteristic of Pentecostals is their conservative views on cultural issues. Overall, our survey of the Assemblies of God laity contained six measures of cultural issues that formed a consistent scale ("cultural issues scale"; see appendix B). Two of these are the "hot button" issues of same-sex marriage ("Marriage should be defined as a union between one man and one woman") and abortion ("Abortion should be outlawed except to save the life of the mother"). Some 95 percent of the respondents agreed with the marriage statement, while only 2 percent disagreed; 74 percent agreed with the abortion item, while 16 percent disagreed.

In addition, 85 percent of respondents agreed and 5 percent disagreed with the statement "Local communities should be allowed to post the Ten Commandments." But only 56 percent agreed and 21 percent disagreed with the statement "The government should provide vouchers for private or religious schools." The final two cultural issues are foreign policy matters with strong religious content: 64 percent of respondents agreed that the "U.S. should give top priority to stopping religious persecution around the world," and 59 percent agreed that the "U.S. should support Israel over the Palestinians in the Middle East" (12 and 11 percent disagreed with these statements, respectively).

These opinions fit well with the official positions of the Assemblies of God. Indeed, cultural issues have motivated much of the political activity of Pentecostals over the last three decades. Here is how the denomination officially describes this situation:

> In recent years in America . . . the relationship between church and state has become increasingly complex and estranged. The reason for this change is a growing trend in government to redefine and politicize moral issues. This wholesale sell-out of these once concrete and absolute moral values comes in direct opposition to the message of the church as found in Scripture. . . . The alarming shift from a Judeo-Christian philosophy to secular humanism as the foundation of American government has created profound problems for all Bible-believing churches. More and more, government is defying biblical principles and interpreting sinful behavior as civil rights, i.e. abortion and homosexuality. The church as the body of Christ is obligated to respond. (www.ag.org/top/Beliefs/contempissues_10_politics.cfm; accessed March 16, 2010)

Which respondents held these culturally conservative views? Older respondents as well as those who scored high on doctrinal orthodoxy and church activity supported cultural conservatism. Interestingly, one of the religious experience measures, the prophecy scale, also had a positive association with cultural conservatism.[8] Thus, *traditional religiosity is associated with conservative positions on cultural issues, and religious experience is associated with such positions as well.* From the perspective of traditional religiosity, these conservative issue positions could be interpreted as an expression of "love for sinners"—although many of the people who are the objects of such attention might not experience it as an expression of "love."

One cultural issue included in the survey that did not scale with the other items was a measure of support for gay rights: the "Government should insure that homosexuals are treated the same as heterosexuals." Here the opinion of the respondents was almost evenly divided on the question, with two-fifths agreeing that homosexuals should be treated the same as heterosexuals as a matter of government policy. This pattern represents a sharp contrast with the opinions on marriage, asked in the same battery of questions, which were nearly unanimous in favor of limiting it to traditional (opposite-sex) couples. It seems likely that the wording of the question mattered: the gay rights item was cast in terms of equal treatment of individuals in society rather than an affirmation of appropriate behavior, as in the case of the marriage question. Put this way, the question of rights of gays and lesbians fits with Pentecostal individualism. This unusual finding suggests that Pentecostals may have more complex attitudes on cultural issues than may at first be apparent, with traditional Pentecostal values sometimes generating more progressive policy attitudes.

Benevolent Behavior: Volunteering and Membership in Voluntary Organizations

A prime example of benevolent behavior is private charitable activities, including volunteering to help the needy. This private activity has direct implications for public affairs because of its impact on society. The Assemblies of God's official position on poverty highlights such charitable activities:

> Throughout history literally hundreds if not thousands of local Assemblies of God churches have reached out to the poor through church food banks and clothing centers. Others are now operating "Dream Centers" to help the needy restart their lives—physically, spiritually and economically. Only the Lord knows the full impact that these wonderful ministries and others like them have in reaching the lost and helping the destitute. . . . Local churches form the backbone of this outreach ministry. In other smaller communities, the local churches have independent programs of reaching the poor with the gospel and a tangible expression of Christ's love through help for the homeless and needy. (www.ag.org/top/Beliefs/sptlissues_the_poor.cfm; accessed March 16, 2010)

Our survey of the Assemblies of God laity asked two questions related to charitable activities. The first was how often the respondents volunteered their time to "help the poor or other people." Overall, 15 percent of the respondents reported volunteering once a week or more often, and another 18 percent claimed to volunteer once a month or more often. Meanwhile, 44 percent said they volunteered "occasionally," and 23 percent reported seldom or never volunteering. On the related question, 54 percent of those who reported volunteering did so through their own congregation, 17 percent through another religious organization, and 20 percent through a non-religious organization.

Who reported such volunteering among the AG laity? The multiple regression analysis shows that respondents who scored high on the prophecy scale were most likely to report volunteering. In addition, respondents who scored high on the equitable measures scale also reported high levels of volunteering. And interestingly, respondents engaged in church activities were also likely to volunteer. Apparently participation in congregational life leads to volunteering, although it was negatively associated with support for congregational benevolence.[9] In sum, *religious experience and social theology are associated with volunteering, and so is traditional religiosity.*

The engagement of the Assemblies of God laity in congregational activity is an example of what Robert Putnam (2000, chap. 4) has called "bonding" social capital, that is high levels of trust *within* social organization. Through its religious organizations, the Assemblies of God and other Pentecostal denominations have contributed to the civic life of the country. However, the AG laity was not characterized by a high level of "bridging" social capital, that is, high levels of trust *between* members of social organizations. This pattern can be seen in reported participation in voluntary organizations beyond the congregation. The survey respondents were asked if they are members of twelve types of civic associations, ranging from labor unions to youth groups. The most common group memberships were women's, recreation, youth, professional, and labor organizations, each with about one-tenth of the respondents. However, more than one-half of the survey respondents reported belonging to none of these groups, and another one-quarter reported belonging to one such group. These figures are lower than for the overall population (Putnam 2000, 58–59). A simple additive scale of group memberships allows us to assess this kind of civic engagement in public affairs.

Who was most involved in voluntary association beyond the congregation? The multiple regression analysis shows that younger and higher-income respondents were the most likely to be active in more such groups, as were respondents active in church. However, respondents with high levels of doctrinal orthodoxy were *less likely* to participate, perhaps due to a continuing resistance to "worldly" matters. Religious experience was unrelated to the number of organizational memberships by AG laity.[10] In sum, *neither religious experience nor traditional religiosity encourages this kind of benevolent activity.* Instead, organizational membership is a product of age and social class.

Benevolent Behavior: Participation in Politics

Another important measure of benevolent behavior is participation in politics. Our survey of the AG laity contains seven standard measures of political participation that can be combined into a simple addition scale ("political participation scale"; see appendix B). Overall, 63 percent of the respondents claimed to have voted in the 2004 presidential election, the most common of the political activities. In addition, 41 percent reported signing a petition, 25 percent said they contacted a public official, and 17 percent reported making a campaign contribution. Less than one-tenth claimed to have attended a political meeting (9 percent), attended a demonstration (6 percent), or worked on an election campaign (5 percent). These activities were added together to measure the respondent's level of political activity. Overall, 28 percent of the respondents reported engaging in three or more of these activities, while 28 percent engaged in none at all.

Who was most active in politics? The multiple regression analysis reveals that older, well-educated, white respondents who were raised Pentecostal were the most likely to be active in politics. In addition, respondents active in church and those who scored high on the prophetic scale were more active. In terms of attitudes, cultural conservatives were more active in politics, whereas supporters of social welfare programs were less active. Interestingly, support for congregational politics had no independent impact on the level of political activity.[11] Thus, *religious experience is a source of political participation, but traditional religiosity and cultural conservatism matter as well.* These findings are consistent with the process of Godly Love, but also with the traditional interdicts in Pentecostalism.

These patterns may reflect the effects of the Christian Right in mobilizing Pentecostals to participate in politics. However, it is worth noting that relatively few respondents reported belonging to or being active in the movement. For example, 9 percent of the respondents belonged to a "Christian conservative" organization (4.1 percent were active members), and 5.8 percent claimed to be members of a "pro-family" group (2.3 percent were active members). Active membership in such groups was positively correlated with the political participation scale.

Benevolent Behavior: Political Alignment

Where does the Assemblies of God laity stand on general political attitudes, such as ideology and partisanship, which are central to broader political alignments? Political alignment is a strong measure of context, connecting the individual with broader political aggregations and organizations. A standard seven-point measure of these attitudes was included in our survey, with ideology ranging from "extremely liberal" to "extremely conservative," and partisanship ranging from "strongly Democratic" to "strongly Republican." Overall, 60 percent of the AG survey respondents identified as conservative, about 31 percent as moderate, and 9 percent as liberal. The figures for partisanship were very similar, with 60 percent identifying as Republicans, 26 percent and independents, and 15 percent as Democrats. As one might imagine, these two measures were closely associated.[12] However, extreme positions were somewhat rare: less than one-tenth of the respondents claimed to be "extremely conservative" and just one-sixth to be "strongly Republican."

Political alignment is closely linked to the presidential vote, with conservatives and Republicans being more likely to vote for Republican presidential candidates, and liberals and Democrats being to vote for Democratic presidential candidates. Although our survey of the Assemblies of God laity did not ask respondents who they voted for in the 2004 presidential election, other evidence strongly supports the connection between the active alignment and the vote. For example, analysis of the Pew Forum's Religious Landscape Survey found that four-fifths of the Assemblies of God voted for George W. Bush and one-tenth voted for John F. Kerry in 2004 (http://religions.pewforum.org/; accessed March 16, 2010). Other surveys show similar patterns and reveal that, like other evangelical Protestants, they have shifted toward the Republican Party over the last thirty years, which is reflected in their voting patterns in recent elections (Green 2007).

These strong political patterns are not officially endorsed by the Assemblies of God. Indeed, its position is quite different:

> The Assemblies of God is apolitical; that is, it takes a neutral stance on purely political issues. The role of government and politics is different from the role of the church. While the church and government are both institutions ordained by God (Romans 13:1–7) and should respect each other, it is imperative neither institution overstep its given role. Both serve God's purposes through separate functions. (www.ag.org/top/Beliefs/contempissues_10_politics.cfm; accessed March 16, 2010)

> While the Assemblies of God recognizes government as God's provision and is not opposed to political parties as a part of the American political process, it refrains from becoming embroiled in party politics or promoting a particular system of government for many reasons...Today many Christians are members of different political parties in America. Certainly Christian involvement is appropriate and needed. But political affiliation, by its very nature, divides people into competing groups. There is no room for such division in the church. Therefore the church must never promote any party or system that would be divisive to the body of Christ, but rather contend for the faith that unites every tribe and tongue and people and nation into one glorious Church. (www.ag.org/top/Beliefs/contempissues_09_government.cfm; accessed March 16, 2010)

The AG stance is consistent with the historical position of most Pentecostals, so it is worth exploring the sources of the strong political stands of our survey respondents.

One useful way to assess these general political attitudes is to calculate a "political alignment" scale that combines ideology and partisanship into a single measure, with conservative Republicans at one end of the scale and liberal Democrats at the other. The multiple regression analysis shows that well-educated, white respondents raised Pentecostal were the most likely to be aligned with conservative Republicanism. In addition, respondents who scored high on church activity and doctrinal orthodoxy also tended to be conservative and Republican. Interestingly, religious experience in the form of glossolalia was also associated with a conservative alignment. In terms of attitudes, support for congregational politics and especially cultural conservatism were associated with the conservative and Republican alignment. In contrast, agreement with the equitable measure, support for congregational benevolence, and especially support for social welfare programs was associated with liberal and Democratic alignment.[13]

This analysis can be taken one step further by adding in the level of political participation to calculate an "active political alignment" scale. Here the political alignment scale is weighted by the frequency of political participation, so that the more active respondents' views mattered more—just as happens in the real political process.

Based on this measure of alignment, 10 percent of the survey respondents could be labeled "hyper-active right" (that is, very active politically, very conservative, and strongly Republican); 25 percent could be labeled the "active right"; and another 22 percent could be called the "modestly active right." Thirty-four percent were at the center of the political spectrum, reflecting their ideological moderation and partisan independence as well as lower levels of political participation. These centrist are essentially "nonaligned" in national politics. A total of 9 percent were in the analogous three groupings among liberals and Democrats, with very few in a "hyper-active left" category. This active alignment score showed the same basic patterns of association with the religious and political variables as the simple alignment scale.

In sum, *traditional religiosity, support for congregational politics, and cultural conservatism are associated with active alignment on the right, while social theology, support for congregational benevolence, and support for social welfare programs are associated with centrist and active left alignment. Religious experience has a small, direct impact on rightward alignment.*

Summary

The evidence presented in this chapter reveals that the Assemblies of God faces a dilemma when it comes to public affairs. The "law of love" and the "love of law" pose different—and even contradictory—approaches to "ushering in the kingdom of God," which has been the goal of Pentecostal benevolence. On the one hand, progressive Pentecostals represent an approach that stresses care-love, especially as it pertains to social welfare programs. Progressive Pentecostals, however, also represent a departure from the traditional Pentecostal individualism long exemplified by the AG. Much of this historic approach is still evident in the emphasis on charity being linked with evangelism among Pentecostals. On the other hand, the "cultural war" politics of the last several decades, with its active opposition to same-sex marriage and abortion, also represent a departure from the Pentecostal apolitical past. This path reflects care-love for "sinners."

The distinctive religious experiences of Pentecostalism are an important part of these values. We have seen that divine presence and prophecy are commonly associated with benevolent attitudes and activities exhibited in public affairs, including the equitable measure of social theology, support for congregational benevolence, and support for social welfare programs that are consistent with the process of Godly Love. However, religious experience is also associated with congregational politics, political participation, and political alignment in ways that are less consistent with the process of Godly Love. They are, however, more consistent with the traditional interdicts found in Pentecostalism, where the "love of law" has at times eclipsed the "law of love."

Indeed, other factors matter for public affairs. Measures of traditional religiosity, including congregational activity and doctrinal orthodoxy, are also frequently associated with attitudes and activities related to public affairs. These variables are associated with the "social ills" measure of social theology, opposition to social welfare programs, support for cultural conservatism, volunteering, political participation, and political alignment. Taken together, this evidence is consistent with the traditional interdicts found in Pentecostalism.

In terms of practical politics, attitudes on social welfare and cultural issues help structure the active political alignment of the Assemblies of God laity. Although the magnitudes of these effects are comparable, the overall political alignment of the denomination is presently oriented to the right. This pattern can be seen in our typology of congregations. The evangelical and alternative AG churches are the most aligned with the Republicans, reflecting the combined impact of cultural conservatism, political engagement, and their higher social status. The charismatic/renewal and traditional AG churches were markedly less firm in their alignment with the Republicans. Ethnic congregations were the least likely to align with Republicans, and in fact were mostly centrists and thus effectively "nonaligned."

However, this pattern of alignment may well reflect the salience of cultural issues in national politics over the last thirty years. Social welfare issues could receive higher priority in the future, thus shifting the political alignment of the AG shift to the center and even the left. If so, then the traditional interdicts would be less important, and the process of Godly Love could offer a powerful resource for such a change. As one student of Pentecostalism has argued: "As Pentecostals struggle to develop a mature and authentic Pentecostal identity in the face of rapid accommodation and institutionalization, they must include a concern and a burden for the poor and the oppressed within that Pentecostal identity" (Smalridge 1998).

As with Pentecostal practice and praxis, in matters of politics the AG remains at the crossroads in forging an identity that retains its distinctive primitive qualities while facing the pragmatic demands of the twenty-first century.

9

Covenants, Contracts, and Godly Love

WITH MATTHEW T. LEE

> There it was, then, in pairs: The primitive and the pragmatic. . . . We might think of the two impulses as alternating voices in dialogue, or as contrasting threads in a tapestry, or as complementary plots to the story. . . . The list of possible metaphors does not end here, but by now the point should be clear. No effort to describe the world of early Pentecostalism can be complete without accounting for the impulses and the way they worked together to secure the movement's survival. (Wacker 2001, 14)

Grant Wacker (2001, 15) has identified a process that has gone on throughout the history of Christendom in which groups "have found ways to weave heavenly aspirations with everyday realities." This interchange between primitive experiences and pragmatic practices serves as a foundation for Wacker's historical discussion of Pentecostalism. While taking for granted the primitive or charismatic features inherent in this religious movement, Wacker's analysis focuses on pragmatic practices rather than on charismatic experiences, leading him to wonder whether the tale of early Pentecostals was one in which "heaven had invaded earth or earth had invaded heaven" (p. 15).

Crossroads (Poloma 1989) had a similar focus on pragmatism with its assessment of the institutional dilemmas that seemingly sounded the death knell for mystical charisma. While this book began by revisiting the *Crossroads* thesis, it goes further in presenting a detailed examination of the revitalizing effects of religious experiences through a dynamic process we have called Godly Love. Godly Love—the dynamic interaction between divine and human love that enlivens and expands benevolence—is the engine drives the revitalization process.

In our analyses of the pastoral survey data (framed by Thomas O'Dea's [1961] theory of routinization of charisma) and congregational survey results (framed by the interactive theory of Godly Love), we have sought to describe the two partners in the dialectical dance between primitivism and pragmatism. We have provided narrative and statistical accounts of experiences of the divine to show how "heaven has invaded earth" through spiritually empowered benevolence. Our description of the organizational work in the AG suggests that even if Pentecostals have not "invaded heaven," they have created a bit of heaven here below. The key to understanding revitalization in the AG lies in the tension between the primitive and the pragmatic forces found in its judicatory and in its congregations. In this final chapter we assess the *pragmatic forces* in terms of *contract*, a system of lived-out legal agreements basic to modern organization as found in the AG judicatory, while *primal forces* are discussed in terms of *covenant*, relationships that are rooted in promises and interpersonal relationships commonly believed to be divinely empowered, which are the lifeblood of congregations. We use these concepts as sociological "ideal types"—that is, as heuristic devices to describe a world that does not exist in its pure form, but which serves to demonstrate the rich diversity found in the Assemblies of God. Thus, contractual judicatories also contain elements of congregational covenantal relationships, and covenantal congregations contain varying degrees of contractual leadership. For the most part, however, covenants are expressed within the congregation, where the divine promise of a fresh outpouring of the Holy Spirit is lived out through Godly Love, which facilitates ongoing revitalization within church communities.

The Diamond Model of Godly Love

In order to visualize the process of Godly Love, Figure 1 presents a diamond-shaped diagram with labels of interaction components and arrows designating relationships (see also Lee and Poloma 2009a). At the top is a box labeled "God," the non-empirical divine actor who has customarily been discounted in social-scientific analysis. The boxes featured to the left and right, respectively, are labeled "primary actor" and "collaborating actor(s)" to designate human interaction. As demonstrated by our statistical analysis of the survey data, prophecy has proven to be an important catalyst in accounting for different forms of "benevolence," the box at the bottom of figure 1. Of our three spirituality measures (glossolalia, a sense of divine presence, and prophecy), prophecy provides the best illustration of the interaction represented in the top half of the diamond-shaped model.

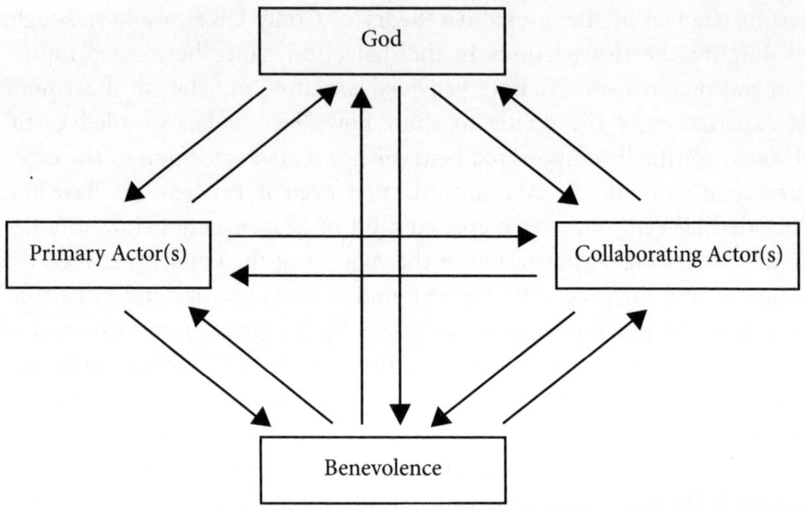

Prophecy begins with the primary actor who believes God has spoken a personal word (usually experienced as a sense or an urge) that requires an active response. As our results demonstrate, the prophetic response often involves the bottom section of the diamond model, as the primary actor may be called to serve others in a beneficial way. Prophecy might be as simple as having a divine "sense" to make a phone call to a friend in need, to write out a check for a special offering, or (as we saw in April's story in chapters 5 and 6) to begin to pray for divine healing for others. Prophecy by definition involves hearing from God and human collaborating actors, those to whom the action or word is directed as well as those who affirm the often wordless but powerful sense or urge to act. To return to April's account, the presiding minister sensed that God was speaking to April as he singled her out with his prophetic word, which confirmed April's perceived divine call to ministry and resulted in her prayer ministry to others. Through this outreach in the congregation, April would tell us in her interview, "many healings were taking place."

April's account is probably much more intense than the divine encounters congregants had in mind when they reported in the survey that they "heard a divine call to perform some specific action" at least daily (6 percent), or that they "received a revelation directly from God" at least daily (8 percent). These measures, two of the four that made up the prophecy scale, suggest that the lines designating interpersonal relationships in figure 1 may be strong or weak, broken or even nonexistent. April's story would be one of strong, unbroken lines between God and the primary collaborator (April), between God and the secondary collaborator (in this case the revival minister), and between April and the minister. The interaction line from April to the recipient(s) of her prayer for healing (benevolence) would vary in strength and intensity.

Guided by this model of Godly Love, we have described how experiences of divine love are significant catalysts of human benevolence within covenantal relationships as found in AG congregations. In so doing we have presented different measures of *union-love* with the divine (glossolalia, prophecy, and sensing the divine presence) together with measures of benevolent *care-love* (including compassion, healing, evangelistic outreach, pro-poor attitudes, ecumenism, social theologies, and political behaviors). Experiences of the divine consistently proved to be significant predictors of increased benevolence that have revitalized the AG, particularly AG congregations. For example, compassionate outreach, evangelism, and healing all promote congregational growth and vitality by exposing new congregants to narratives or first-hand encounters with the fruits of supernatural empowerment, as well as reminding existing church members of the practical effects of God's loving presence.

This basic diamond model can be adapted to describe Godly Love in the judicatory, where interdicts are defined and upheld largely through contractual relations. The "love energy" generated by covenantal interactions by congregants, however, is different from that driving judicatory contractual action. Based on our empirical findings, we thus contend that among members of congregations care-love is likely to be the primary face of love, while in religious organizations love is most likely to be expressed in terms of appreciation-love.

Godly Love and the Judicatory: A Contractual Model

The task of guarding the denomination's vision or mission by defining and enforcing interdictive cultural norms and creating supportive judicatory structures is perhaps best served by appreciation-love rather than interpersonal care-love. Judicatories—even Pentecostal judicatories—commonly function much like secular organizations, where pragmatic rational action is normative. This point can be illustrated by a conversation Margaret Poloma had with Dr. Richard Dobbins, the founder of Emerge Ministries (an AG-affiliated counseling center), when she was collecting data for *Crossroads*. Poloma commented how most counselors at Emerge seemed to be using secular techniques (albeit with biblical injunctions and a prayer at the end of the session that sounded much like a concluding summary statement given by a secular counselor) and, like their secular counterparts, were discouraged from using distinctly pentecostal healing techniques such as prophecy and in-depth prayer with clients. (The comment was intended to raise the issue of how Emerge Ministries' secularly grounded counseling fit with its Pentecostal origins and identity.) Dobbins quickly and succinctly replied, "Emerge is *not* a church; it is a counseling center." The same response could hold for other AG institutions, including its presbytery, universities, publishing house, missionary organizations, and other operations of benevolence. An AG judicatory is not a church—it is a bureaucratic organization (with both the strengths and weaknesses of bureaucracies) that regulates and serves a large denomination. It is more comfortable being solidly grounded in pragmatism than soaring in a world of primal spiritual possibilities.

Unlike most leaders of secular organizations, however, AG judicatory leaders are not strangers to pentecostal experience of the divine. It is important to remember that people commonly participate in both covenantal and contractual relations, and AG leaders are no exception. They are also involved in churches, their families, and friendship networks in which divine–human interactions may be a vital part of their personal social-covenantal interactions. Care-love may also be found in small groups within the administrative organizations. The judicatory itself, however, is driven by a more abstract appreciation-love reflected in denominational vision and values than by the interpersonal love relationships characterized by union- and care-love. In terms of concrete behavior, this means that judicatory decision-making is likely to be preceded by logical and rational debate rather than charismatic ritual or even prayer. To return to our diamond image, the interaction line from actor to God may be weak or nonexistent in a business meeting or committee vote. This is not to suggest that interactions with God are always absent—judicatory leaders may pray about an issue prior to making a decision—just that they do not occur in certain contexts.

The seeds for recognizing this distinction between appreciation-love and care-love were sown in Poloma's first visit to the headquarters of the Assemblies of God in Springfield, Missouri, in the early 1980s. As she approached Dr. Thomas Zimmerman, then General Superintendent of the AG, to request his endorsement of her proposed research, she was taken aback by their introductory exchange. To make her position and needs clear at the onset, she presented herself with "dual citizenship"—as a Spirit-baptized practicing Roman Catholic who worshiped regularly with an AG congregation. Zimmerman's immediate response surprised her: "I owe you an apology for what I have said about Catholics. God has forgiven me; I didn't know any better." It didn't seem appropriate at the time to follow up on this seemingly strange comment as they quickly moved on to talk about the proposal and their understanding of what was to be expected of each party. It wasn't until the next day that she had a serendipitous encounter with a local university professor who was a good friend of the local Catholic bishop of Springfield, Missouri. Bishop Bernard Law, later elevated to a cardinal in the Catholic Church, would make national news headlines years later as he sought to protect the Church against critics of its handling of the pedophile scandal. Poloma asked the professor about the unlikely relationship between Zimmerman and Law, two ecclesial leaders whose denominations were often at odds both globally and nationally. The professor replied, "Zimmerman and Law are much more alike than you might imagine. They both love their institutions." It was not clear that this kind of "love" was something the professor himself valued, but it was apparent that it had the power to make good friends out of potential enemies. That someone could have a powerful and intense love for institutions, culture, religious doctrine, and other seeming abstractions, and that this love operates much like interpersonal love is something Poloma would observe from time to time. The observation took theoretical form as she later read Rolf Johnson's (2002) discussion of appreciation-love as a face of love. Similarly, Philip Rieff's (2007) work is filled with appreciation-love for interdicts, which helped us to see the connections between appreciation-love and the AG judicatory.

Although networks of care-love can and probably do co-exist as secondary forces within formal organizations, the primary object of love for the judicatory rests on an appreciation of the denomination—its principles and values, its well-run organization and structure, and ultimately its size and its influence. In this book we have revisited the routinization of the charisma thesis, in which Pentecostalism originated in a charismatic moment where revival participants experienced a heightened union-love with the divine and care-love relationships with each other that defied social norms of the day. Most pentecostal historians would agree that for at least a short time the revival experiences would level the playing field between blacks and whites, men and women, rich and poor, and young and old. The effects of the charismatic moment, however, would soon lose ground to institutionalization and its attendant dilemmas, with a re-entrenchment of the cultural stratification system of segregated congregations and curtailing of women in leadership. Pentecostalism has not completely lost its identity, but its tendency to self-identify with evangelicalism has certainly blurred its distinctiveness.

Narrated through socio-historical accounts and statistical findings collected from a random sample of AG pastors, we reported how the AG continues to reflect the tension between charisma and its routinization first reported in *Crossroads.* Pastors by and large are committed to being both Pentecostal and evangelical in their support of the AG while holding neopentecostalisms and other faiths at bay. They provided satisfactory evaluations of the core parts of their judicatory system while expressing some reservations about what we judged to be less essential beliefs and practices. Judging from the reluctance of many to explore the revivals of the 1990s, they seemed to use their appreciation-love of the AG to balance the potentially unstable situations that have historically accompanied revivals. The potential downside to this orientation is that it inhibits the revitalizing forces that accompany revivals. Although we have argued that religious experiences have been central to the revitalization of the AG, especially through Godly Love interactions, judicatory leaders and pastors have attempted to close some of the avenues by which congregants might obtain more of these experiences.

There is evidence that it is not unusual for leaders to hold fast to an appreciation-love for their institution (with its particular culture, visions, and values) that is distinct from and sometimes at odds with relational care-love. Appreciation-love appears to be the rudder of much organized benevolence; it is the "love energy" provided by vision that often generates and energizes contractual benevolence. Appreciation-love, for example, played a key role in the assessment that Poloma and Hood (2008) made of Blood and Fire, the now-defunct ministry in Atlanta that sought to create a "church of the poor," in the study that gave birth to the concept of Godly Love. Relationships were tattered by schisms within the ministry as its leader's love for his ever-evolving visions came to take priority over benevolent service. Our statistical portrait of AG pastors relates a much more upbeat story about appreciation-love at work. Pastors, for the most part, gave high marks to the national AG judicatory's values and venues, and even higher marks to their district's leadership and service. Despite minority reports and dissonance around core issues, pastors seemed satisfied with AG leadership and organization. The mixed report card provided by the survey findings did suggest, however, that some "ambiguities around the core" may be symptomatic of an increasing erosion of the charismatic fervor that is at the heart of pentecostal identity.

These ambiguities are further marked by the ongoing fear of newly developing revivals, and by resistance to changes in regulatory rules and practices that Rieff (2007) has called *interdicts*. As measured by a scale we called *tra-*

ditional values, strong interdicts (contrary to Rieff's thesis) are of questionable value for supporting charisma or facilitating benevolence in the AG. Instead, we found that holding strongly to traditional Pentecostal values may be negatively related to some attitudes (e.g., support for the poor or for ecumenism) that are consistent with care-love. Moreover, established organizations often uphold stability and the interdicts that support it long after those interdicts have lost their utility as a cultural glue to hold the community together. Organizational leaders generally prefer holding fast to tradition over less-predictable charisma, which often comes as a dramatic wind with its potential to revolutionize or at least to change old interdicts. It was troubling, for example, for many Pentecostals of the early 1960s to see charismatics in mainline denominations—who often smoked, enjoyed alcohol and an occasional trip to a casino, and went to movies, and whose women wore jewelry and makeup—having spiritual experiences similar to their own, including glossolalia. Since most Pentecostals are no longer a "peculiar people" adhering to these external "holiness" standards, some fear a slippery slope that could wear away the few distinctives that remain.

Many Pentecostals are suspicious of those who would move the AG further away from the status quo of a legal judicatory and traditional and evangelical church models toward the uncertainty of the new postmodern networks reflected in the charismatic and alternate churches. This tension is reflected in the divided response in the pastoral survey, where just over half (54 percent) of the pastors agreed or strongly agreed with the statement that the AG needs to "focus more on being a religious network and less on being a denomination," while nearly half were not in agreement. The desire for more of a relational network than a rigid institutional structure can also be observed in pastors' higher level of support for local district meetings than meetings of the General Assembly, which many reported they preferred not to attend.

Judging from some reports from the August 2009 General Council, however, the Assemblies of God may be in the midst of charting a new course that includes a re-evaluation of some interdicts, a process that began with the 2007 election of General Superintendent Dr. George O. Wood. In our visit to the Assemblies of God Theological School and Headquarters in January 2009, we became aware of what we would describe as a move away from the contractual relations and sometimes harsh interdicts that once dominated the judicatory in Springfield. We took note of the unsolicited but positive comments proffered by university and seminary faculty, students, administrators, and pastors about the national judicatory under the leadership of Superintendent Wood and his new team. The sense that a new day had dawned not only for Springfield but for the national denomination appeared ratified by the enthusiastic support Wood and his leadership team received during the 2009 General Council. It is too early to determine, however, what this shift may mean for pentecostal interdicts and charisma in the AG.

Although all judicatory leaders presumably have accounts to share about their Spirit baptism and call to ministry that have more or less empowered their service as pastors and then judicatory leaders, it is difficult to separate such divine empowerment from rational and pragmatic decision-making. Increasingly pragmatism emerges as the dominant motivator within the judicatory context, while primitive experiences are relegated to the private devotional world. To contrast this with early Pentecostalism, we need only recall that one of the rationales for initiating ordination of ministers, in a sect where priesthood was eschewed and the prophethood of all believers was proclaimed, was to meet a pragmatic need for the railroad discounts given to clergy. The long-standing tension between primitivism and pragmatism can be further illustrated with the account of the founding of Youth With a Mission, one of many stories in which primitive prophets lost out to pragmatic priests within religious organizations.[1]

"Youth With a Mission": Primitivism and Pragmatism in Conflict

In 1956, Loren Cunningham, then an Assemblies of God minister, believed he heard a call from God to tap into the enthusiasm of young people in worldwide evangelism.[2] He recounts the details of this call and his perception of divine guidance in his appropriately titled autobiographical account, *Is That Really You, God?* Cunningham's narration serves as a succinct illustration of the difference between covenantal and contractual relations and the tension that often exists between them. Cunningham (1984, 66) writes:

> The secretary ushered me into the superintendent's office. "Hello, Brother Zimmerman. . . ." *Brother* was a special term of respect in our denomination meant to underline the fact we were brothers and sisters in God's family. Brother Zimmerman shook my hand cordially then sat down and looked at me across the desk. Indeed he had heard about the Bahamian experiment. But if I were expecting a quick endorsement and a blank check to work interdenominationally and still maintain my standing as a minister with my church, I was mistaken. The problem, I gathered as we sat talking quietly, was that new works like ours needed to be brought

> under the organizational umbrella—not outside and autonomous. There was a place for me in the Assemblies, but of course I would have to be a full team player. In the end I was offered a job. A good one, too, there at headquarters complete with a fine salary, a staff, a budget. "You can continue with your vision, Loren, but you'd be taking out a more manageable number—say ten or twenty young people a year."
>
> My heart dropped to my knees as the very gracious offer came out—it sounded so reasonable, so secure. Only it was far from what I believed God had told me to do; send out waves of young people from all denominations into evangelism. I tried to explain what I had felt God was saying to me about what was about to happen. It was much, much bigger than twenty a year, and larger than any one denomination. "Sir," I said, "there's another generation coming. It's different from anything we've ever seen. . . ."
>
> I floundered, for I could hear how foolish it sounded. Brother Zimmerman assured me he had worked with young people for decades and knew them well. As he tried to explain his reservations about my plans, I could truly see his dilemma. If I had his responsibility of leading a large movement, I would need submitted people—ready to play by the rules for the good of the whole. But here I was hearing a different drummer, out of step. That's more or less what Brother Zimmerman said, too. He was sorry, but I would have to leave the team—resign—if I couldn't play by the rules.

Cunningham did leave the AG to establish Youth With a Mission (YWAM), a well-known and respected international organization that embraces volunteers of all ages. YWAM leaders describe the organization as a "family of ministries," rather than a "structured, hierarchical entity." Its thousand-plus centers are largely autonomous and operate indigenously, with international oversight consisting of approximately forty-five leaders from around the world. Although Cunningham's independent ministry is well-regarded by AG ministers and congregations, it is significant for our discussion of the contractual model of Godly Love that YWAM was unable to find a home in the AG.

In sum, divine–human love energy can and probably does infiltrate religious contractual models through a leader's private devotional life, but it is difficult (and perhaps unwise from a management perspective) to integrate experience of the divine into the contractual relations themselves. General Councils are not times of revival; board meetings are not spent praying for supernatural discernment; leaders are not elected for their piety. Experimental Spirit-led ventures like YWAM, and revivals more generally, are difficult to integrate into bureaucratic structures. Furthermore, as we have argued, different objects of love provide the primary energy for covenants and contracts. While in its ideal typical form Godly Love is covenantal, covenants are often nestled within larger contractual organizations. Most of the day-to-day activities of judicatory organizations involve pragmatic and well-defined interactions familiar to social scientists and represented by the bottom half of figure 1. The "love energy" produced by union-love and care-love that dominates the top half of the model does operate on some level in judicatory activities, albeit most often indirectly through private devotion rather than directly through collective spiritual discernment.

Congregational Godly Love: A Covenantal Model

Although some may contend that most churches deviate from being "family" and bear more resemblance to corporations than to communities, there is little question that the vast majority of AG adherents *expect* family-like relationships to prevail in their congregations. Of a list of eleven expectations included in the congregational survey, providing a "family-like atmosphere for members" was ranked first in importance by respondents. More than half (59 percent) of the respondents reported that being part of a family-like congregation was "extremely important," and an additional one-third (36 percent) said it was "very important"; only 5 percent claimed they had no opinion or were indifferent to the issue. Another related question about the importance of the church's "providing service to members" also showed that respondents had high expectations, with 85 percent reporting caring for members to be either "extremely important" or "very important." In time of illness, over half (54 percent) reported that their congregations would help them "a great deal," and another 32 percent expected "some" help; and if they had personal problems, 62 percent believed that they would receive a "great deal" of comfort from their church, with another 28 percent expecting "some." Few expected to receive little or no help or comfort in their hour of need. Although only the most traditional AG congregations continue to use "brother" and "sister" to address one another, as was once a common in the AG, expectations remain that congregational interaction be more familial than the contractual relations that are widespread in modern society.

It is within this covenant of believers that congregants live out their pentecostal identity, which commonly includes alternate spiritual ways of viewing reality. It is here that many experience Spirit baptism, see miracles, learn to pray in tongues, give and receive prophecies, and pray for healing. It is within highly affective revival services that many pentecostals first felt the ecstatic and palpable presence of God. Although some of our qualitative interviews with AG adherents provided examples where the church family may have been spiritually dysfunctional, there are even more examples in which the congregation has played a significant role in developing and affirming the powerful love relationship between the respondent and God. Union-love, as we have examined it experientially within the model of Godly Love, is a significant factor in enhancing benevolence, especially evangelism, healing, and compassion.

Union-love also appears to play a significant role in enhancing interpersonal relations that in turn impact benevolence. As can be seen in table C.1 in appendix C, those who had frequent experiences of personal "inner healing" were also considerably more likely to experience glossolalia, prophecy and a sense of divine presence. They were also more likely to score higher on evangelism, compassion, healing, and ecumenism. Inner healing, as we have seen earlier, involves more than the personal psyche. It extends to "healing" relationships with others, being especially intertwined with forgiveness. As discussed in earlier chapters, God is perceived as a significant other who empowers believers to work together in extending this love to others.

It is important to emphasize that we are not asserting that all congregations mirror the heuristic model of Godly Love found in figure 1. The model is used as a point of departure for comparison and analysis, rather than as a trusted reflection of reality. Based on our four-fold typology of churches (traditional, evangelical AG, charismatic/renewal, and alternative) that reflect the diversity found in the AG, for example, we expect relational ties represented in the model to be of different intensities and frequencies for different congregations. We hypothesize that the basic model of Godly Love found in figure 1 would best fit traditional AG and revivalist congregations where both union-love and care-love are strengthened through revival rituals and experiences. With interdicts that reflect pentecostal parochialism being stronger in traditional churches, we would also expect care-love to be more extensive (ecumenical) in charismatic congregations that are less accepting of the traditional values that separate Pentecostals from other Christians. AG evangelical churches, on the other hand, are more likely to downplay primal religious experiences, to adapt their teachings, and to adopt practices that further the routinization of charisma. We would expect the lines between the "God" and "Collaborating actor(s)" boxes in figure 1 to be weaker for members of congregations that have fewer opportunities to witness and experience pentecostal revitalization.

Alternative congregations, profiled with low scores on both pentecostal identity and experiences, reflect a wide variety of innovative practices that move them further from the intersect of the primal and pragmatic toward an emphasis on the pragmatic. The top half of figure 1 would be less important for understanding benevolence in these congregations, with the lines between God and collaborator being less pronounced. However, alternative congregations, like those in the charismatic quadrant, tend to be marginal to the working of the denomination, and it is doubtful that congregations in these two quadrants of our typology will have any significant impact on the future of the AG. Both types have demonstrated a tendency to revert to other quadrants of the typology or to eventually drop out of the denomination.

Although traditional and evangelical congregations dominate the AG landscape, traditional churches remain more visibly and experientially Pentecostal. Furthermore, traditional churches are significantly more likely to be ethnic churches and less likely to be Euro-American.[3] Ethnic congregations are generally more accepting and encouraging of pentecostal experiences that mirror the Pentecostalism of their native countries. The future of the AG is thus at a crossroads, with the charismatic experiences of the traditional ethnic congregation on one side and the predictability and routinization of the evangelical Euro-American congregation on the other. These two paths are also shaped by the interface of the judicatory and congregational leadership.

The relationship between the judicatory and diverse AG congregations can be described using the analogy of a hot-air balloon ride. When balloon and basket function together, it can provide a breathtaking panoramic view for its riders. When the balloon is left to soar alone, it rides high; but without the tension provided by the rope and basket, it will inevitably self-destruct. The basket without the balloon, on the other hand, will remain bound to the ground, with its riders unable to view the promised panorama. Congregations experiencing primal pentecostal revival need the pragmatism of a basket that controls the hot air to maintain a vital pentecostal congregation; pragmatic judicatories need a balloon to experience afresh the primal stirrings that first brought the AG into existence. Uncoupling the primal from the pragmatic is much like cutting the rope to separate the balloon from the basket; the primal may soar but destruction is its ultimate fate, while the pragmatic will remain solidly grounded but deprived of the panoramic spiritual worldview. The person in charge of navigating between the primal and the pragmatic, deciding how high the congregation is to soar into the realms of Pentecostal possibilities, is generally the AG pastor, who interacts with the judicatory at the district and national levels, as well as with the church boards that can function as local judicatories.

Interactive Model of Godly Love: Pastors as Linchpins

It is the AG pastor who links the denominational structure (where the primary mode of action is corporately pragmatic, interdictive, and contractual, and the primary object of love is appreciation of AG vision and values) with diverse congregational communities (where the primary mode of action is likely to be affective, charismatic, and covenantal, commonly revitalized by the interaction of union-love and care-love). As linchpins between individual congregations and various judicatory systems, it is no surprise that pastors often find themselves between the rock of denominational polity and the hard place of daily pastoral demands. We have heard pastors—including some who have left and others who remain faithful to the AG—lament the seeming incompatibility of the relational networks that foster and sustain their direct experiences of God and the modern organizational structures that provide the denominational context for their spiritual lives.

The tension in negotiating the contradictory dictates of (legal, rational) contract and (relational) covenant often continues within the microcosm of the congregation. To demonstrate this tension between the primal and pragmatic forces that can be found in congregations, we return to a pastoral survey finding reported earlier. When asked about the degree to which the divine presence (e.g., prophetic leadings, tongues, and interpretations) affected the "decision making process of your local congregation," less than one-fifth of the pastors indicated "greatly," while more than one-fourth replied "not at all." In a related question, only one in ten pastors strongly agreed that "the Holy Spirit directly affects the decision making process in most AG administrative agencies." While we do not know why pragmatic decision-making usually takes the lead over primal prophetic experience for most pastors, we do see that the model for congregational government and the perceived model for denominational government, tend toward the pragmatic. Continuing our earlier metaphor, we suspect that those who seek to balance the primal and pragmatic often feel the stretching of the rope that fastens the hot-air balloon to the basket. Sometimes it is easier simply to cut the rope and leave the basket firmly anchored in pragmatism at the expense of primal experiences.

As reflected in the account presented earlier of YWAM, the prophetic visionary and the judicatory leaders can find it difficult to come to agreement when navigating the waters between a divine call and judicatory dictates. A more recent account can be found in Pastor Bill Johnson's Bethel

Church in Redding, California. Like many AG churches in the 1990s, Johnson's congregation experienced a revival—in this case, one that split the congregation and caused half of its members to leave. Johnson supported the revival as a "move of God," and in time his congregation recovered from its loss of members to become a flagship for neo-pentecostals seeking ongoing revival. In 2006, after deciding to leave the AG, Johnson wrote the following:

> This has been an extremely slow, thought-full and care-full process that is not a reaction to conflict but a response to a call. . . . Though we haven't yet articulated it very clearly, we feel called to create a network that helps other networks thrive—to be one of many ongoing catalysts in this continuing revival. Our call feels unique enough theologically and practically from the call on the Assemblies of God that this change is appropriate. We believe we have heard the voice of the Lord very clearly concerning this transition. We are in the process of inviting several apostolic leaders that have had a long-term relationship with us to be integral in the spiritual covering of our church. We look forward to working alongside our brothers and sisters in the Assemblies and are continuing our regular financial and prayer support of the denomination. We thank you for your interest in the ongoing mutual success and respect of the Assemblies of God and Bethel Church of Redding. (www.ibethel.org; accessed on September 1, 2009)

Revivals come at a cost, and they are often countercultural in their demands on personal time and resources. Revivals appear easier to sustain in developing nations than in American society, with its pull toward the very materialistic concerns that early Pentecostals condemned. Pastors often find themselves caught between balloon-like revivalists who want to go all the way with the primal and basket-sitting pragmatists who want order and predictability. How balloon and basket ultimately align in congregations usually depends on pastoral experience with and acceptance of primal spirituality. According to an old cliché, a church cannot rise above its pastor. Individuals may soar with pentecostal experiences found outside the congregation, particularly at charismatic conferences, through itinerant evangelists, and in college-like "schools" that promote the supernatural, but the congregation itself is dependent on pastoral acceptance of the range of the charismatic gifts and leadership skills to monitor them.

A Tentative Sociological Conclusion

Charisma cannot persist without social form and structure. The early Pentecostals soon became aware of this basic sociological premise, and they knew of the dangers of charisma's routinization before sociologists had yet put a label on the process. The AG has always asserted that it is not a denomination. Its Website proclaims: "In keeping with the original intention of the founding body, the Assemblies of God is considered a cooperative fellowship instead of a denomination" (www.ag.org; accessed on September 1, 2009). The "cooperative fellowship" has in fact become layered with judicatory rulings and dictates that many adherents find porous enough for the leading of the Spirit. Others, like Pastor Bill Johnson, seek new "relational networks," neo-pentecostal and evangelical groupings that may well become the new denominations of the twenty-first century.

It is important to stress that not all instances of "routinization" are contrary to charisma (Rieff 2007). Whether the AG's structure is permeable enough to allow a creative tension between primitive experience and pragmatic organization to remain viable is the critical sociological question for the organization's future—and for the future of American Pentecostalism more generally. It would mean making room for failed prophecies, allowing religious services to be more than prepackaged productions, and leaving space for new expressions of charisma, including new waves of revival that seem to roll regularly upon the American continent. Although charisma has long been recognized as a factor in the rise of religious movements, it seems to depart quickly once the task of institution-building has been completed. One can argue that charisma thrives best in relational groups where care-love rather than appreciation-love is center stage.

Some AG judicatory members, particularly among the current leaders in the Executive Presbytery, are aware of this dilemma. A proposal that was defeated in the Fifty-third General Council in August 2009 provides a good illustration. In response to requests from some pastors, the Executive Presbytery proposed a four-year pilot project in which churches would be permitted to depart from membership in traditional geographic and ethnic-language districts. Instead they would be part of a network—a network free of the traditional restraints where AG ministers working for revival could interact primarily through new communications media. This proposal met with considerable resistance from some district superintendents in the General Presbytery, and it was defeated before being sent to the General Council for a vote. As an AG leader in Springfield reported in a personal e-mail (August 29, 2009), "[General Superintendent] George Wood et al. [the Executive Presbytery] had done their homework and were really trying to find a way that they could create a new model. In this case, it was not opposed by Springfield, but initiated by Springfield. It was opposed by some districts for a variety of reasons." Perhaps the most significant reason for this opposition was that some regional and ethnic leaders feared a loss of members to these new networks. When asked what might happen next, the informant responded: "I do think that some form of this non-geographic district initiative will resurface. However, in the meantime, people will create their own non-geographical networks of accountability and influence. The idea that something has been stopped because a resolution wasn't passed simply doesn't mesh with reality. This impetus will find and is finding realization with or without 'officialness.'" The question at hand is whether this new, unofficial network will remain in the AG or take the path of others we have discussed, like YWAM or Bethel Church.

When seen in the light of the overarching patterns of routinization and revitalization evident in our survey data, the fundamental issue currently facing the AG continues to be the lure of pragmatism at the expense of primal experience. This is particularly true in Anglo evangelical AG congregations and in the judicatory, but less so in the traditional ethnic congregations that have accounted for much of the AG's growth in the United States in recent decades. As guardians of the vision and expositors on interdicts, the judicatory leadership (national and district, which, as we have seen, sometimes conflict) has the most power to move toward greater revitalization, but also the biggest stake in not doing so. Scholars in the sociology of organizations would not be surprised by this. They would point out that judicatories always seek a "tight coupling" between their normative structures (e.g., as spelled out in position papers) and the behavioral structures of the other parts of their organization (Perrow 1986, 148). Centralization of control is the goal, and revitalizing experiences of God take a backseat to fidelity to the interdicts. However, this attempt will always fall short because of the "interactive complexity" that always exists in the ever-changing social environment that shapes congregational life (ibid.). In this situation, various forms of "loose coupling" become the norm (as with alternative and revivalist congregations), and some decoupling may occur (as with YWAM and Bethel Church leaving the AG to pursue informal ties with neo-pentecostal networks).

The tension between pragmatism and primitivism plays out against a background of centralization and decentralization. It is easy to see that the primitive will find a more supportive home in decentralized congregations. This suggests that the most vital sectors of the pentecostal movement are likely to be loosely coupled or decoupled from traditional Pentecostal denominations like the AG. Sociologist Richard Sennett's (1998) observations about the shift in the corporate sector from stable, rigid, bureaucratic structures to flexible, innovative, and constantly changing networks applies equally well to the post-denominational environment that characterizes the religious landscape in contemporary America. Regardless of whether the goal is an innovative and prophetic approach to missions, or simply church growth instead of decline, its achievement is more likely in an "archipelago of related activities" rather than a formal "organization" or "denomination" (Sennett 1998, 23). This explains the rise of informal, "apostolic" networks in neo-pentecostal circles, as Pastor Johnson referred to in his letter of withdrawal from the AG.[4]

What can the AG do about this situation? Organizational sociologists would not be optimistic that the judicatory leadership is strategically situated to respond effectively. They would point out that organizations tend to "generate actions unreflectively and nonadaptively" because the "behavior programs" that they create in an attempt to solidify past successes are often the primary causes of current crises (Starbuck 1983, 91–92). Institutionalized programs of behavior create a kind of blindness within bureaucratically structured organizations that directs the attention of leadership to pseudo-problems that are of little concern to the constituencies that they serve, and away from real problems that threaten the ongoing viability of the organization. The AG's failure to establish a new district for revival serves as a case in point. There is an ever-present danger that an organization's behavior programs will shape perceptions of reality in such a way that the judicatory leadership becomes unable to hear the prophetic voices of pastors like Bill Johnson and the young men and women who are trained in schools of the supernatural like the ones found at Bethel Church. The result is likely to be the ongoing dilution of pentecostal distinctives in the AG—as in other classical Pentecostal denominations—to the point that many AG congregations will continue their slide toward a "blander evangelical 'pot of goo' characterized by pop music, well-managed programs, and topical sermons, and from time to time [nostalgia for] that 'old-time religion' of their holy roller grandparents" (Patterson 2007, 201).

The AG is certainly not alone in facing these dilemmas. Other Pentecostal and neo-pentecostal denominations are experiencing similar tensions. In the volatile religious marketplace of the twenty-first century, Godly Love and its support of evangelistic outreach cannot offer a one-size-fits-all solution to the myriad challenges facing religious denominations in general or pentecostalism in particular. But then again, neither can the strong religious interdicts of an earlier era. Our results suggest that interdicts remain relevant in the AG, but that Godly Love has been more central to its recent vitality. Pentecostal experiences of divine love—commonly reflected in glossolalia, prophecy, and sensing the divine presence—are significant catalysts of human benevolence within covenantal relationships as found in AG congregations. This is because profoundly moving experiences of divine love are capable of producing seismic shifts in a person's worldview, core identity, and sense of purpose in life to a degree that few other life experiences seem able (see Lee and Poloma 2009a). When this process happens simultaneously to a group of people within a congregation, the results are amplified and love energy spreads. Congregations that foster emotionally rich and deeply meaningful experiences of union with a loving God *and* benevolent care among a loving community are able to provide an antidote to the disconnection, alienation, and lack of meaning that characterize some portraits of contemporary society (Sennett 1998). Intense personal transformation, the development of a new purpose in life, the creation of a community of love, palpable contact with the Divine: these are the building blocks of congregational revitalization. What else are people looking for in a church, if not these experiences?

Of course, Godly Love by itself does not guarantee organizational success or longevity (see Poloma and Hood 2008). The story of the AG cannot be told, however, without careful attention to this interaction between divine and human love that enlivens benevolence and evangelistic outreach. Our findings demonstrate that the pentecostal gifts of the Spirit do bear benevolent fruit. Whether a pentecostalization of other denominations would have this effect remains to be seen (see Macchia 2006a, for an affirmative theological argument). Our research on the AG thus leaves us both cautious and hopeful about the prospects for revitalization within the movement. We are cautious because we have seen how organizational constraints and routinization can easily stifle the vital energy of religious experience. But we remain hopeful because we have also witnessed how this energy can bring a bit of heaven down to earth and greatly expand benevolence in the process.

Appendix A

Statistical Tables (Pastors Survey)

TABLE A.1. Pentecostal Identity

Pastoral Identity	*Not Important*	*Somewhat Important*	*Very Important*	*Extremely Important*
Assemblies of God	2% (10)	14% (59)	36% (155)	49% (211)
Charismatic	32% (134)	40% (164)	20% (82)	8% (34)
Evangelical	6% (27)	25% (107)	36% (155)	33% (139)
Pentecostal	3% (13)	10% (42)	33% (140)	55% (236)
Revival	4% (18)	10% (44)	32% (139)	54% (234)
Congregational Identity				
Assemblies of God	5% (23)	28% (121)	33% (142)	34% (149)
Charismatic	35% (244)	39% (161)	18% (82)	6% (27)
Evangelical	7% (31)	35% (148)	34% (144)	24% (104)
Pentecostal	4% (16)	19% (81)	35% (150)	42% (184)
Revival	6% (25)	18% (80)	35% (151)	41% (178)

Cooperative Fellowship	*None*	*Limited*	*Full*
Evangelicals	1% (3)	42% (183)	57% (246)
Charismatic Orgs.	8% (36)	65% (278)	27% (113)
Other Pentecostals	—	35% (148)	65% (282)
Non-denominational	4% (17)	65% (276)	32% (135)
Non-Christian groups	56% (24)	39% (166)	5% (20)
Mainline Protestant	5% (26)	70% (299)	24% (103)
Mainline charismatics	8% (33)	66% (279)	26% (110)
Roman Catholic	30% (127)	61% (260)	9% (37)

TABLE A.2. Charismatic Experiences (Pastors)

	Never	Few times	Monthly	Twice monthly	Weekly +
Tongues and interpretations	18% (76)	36% (154)	12% (52)	19% (83)	16% (69)
Prophecy t0 congregation	18% (78)	48% (209)	16% (69)	14% (61)	4% (15)
Used in prayer for physical healing	3% (12)	52% (222)	21% (88)	18% (76)	7% (32)
Used in prayer for mental healing	7% (28)	53% (225)	17% (71)	17% (72)	7% (28)
Used to pray for deliverance	29% (118)	59% (245)	7% (27)	4% (17)	2% (6)
Prayer in tongues	—	7% (29)	4% (17)	7% (30)	82% (361)
Singing in the Spirit	19% (83)	34% (185)	12% (50)	17% (72)	18% (78)
Slain in the Spirit	44% (186)	50% (212)	3% (14)	2% (8)	1% (5)
Physical manifestations	43% (113)	33% (86)	12% (30)	9% (23)	4% (10)
Holy laughter	46% (172)	37% (137)	8% (29)	5% (17)	5% (10)
Dancing in the Spirit	42% (183)	35% (152)	8% (35)	7% (28)	8% (36)

TABLE A.3. Congregational Experiences and Ritual Practices (within the past year)

	Never	Rarely	Sometimes	Regularly
Tongues and interpretation	2% (8)	13% (57)	42% (183)	43% (188)
Prayer for Spirit baptism	1% (3)	9 % (41)	43% (187)	47% (206)
Prayer for healing	—	—	10% (42)	90% (394)
Prophecy	4% (16)	19% (81)	45% (195)	33% (142)
Prayer for deliverance	3% (11)	19% (82)	44% (191)	35% (151)
Altar call for salvation	— (2)	2% (8)	6% (26)	92% (402)
Healing testimonies	— (1)	7% (30)	52% (229)	41% (177)
Salvation testimonies	1% (5)	9% (41)	54% (235)	36% (156)
Dancing in the spirit	20% (86)	39% (176)	32% (139)	10% (43)
Singing in the spirit	10% (43)	31% (134)	33% (143)	26% (115)
Slain in the spirit	10% (43)	30% (129)	47% (205)	14% (60)
Physical manifestations	27% (117)	40% (173)	24% (104)	9% (37)

TABLE A.4. Revival Attitudes and Behavior

Attitudes	*Strong Disagree*	*Disagree*	*Agree*	*Strong Agree*
America is in midst of revival	6% (27)	44% (188)	44% (188)	5% (26)
Must downplay public use of Spirit gifts	61% (265)	34% (150)	3% (14)	2% (8)
Loss of gifts of Holy Spirit in AG	3% (14)	26% (109)	55% (233)	15% (70)
AG must seek revitalization of early roots	2% (10)	13% (55)	45% (192)	39% (174)
AG experiencing loss of Pentecostal ID	6% (25)	34% (140)	48% (202)	12% (51)
Importance of personal ID w/revival	4% (18)	10% (44)	32% (139)	54% (234)
Importance of congreg. ID w/revival	6% (25)	18% (80)	35% (151)	41% (178)

Involvement	*Yes*
Aware of present renewal movement	98% (431)
Read AG articles on revival	100% (422)
Read other Christian articles on R/R	86% (382)
Discussed R/R with AG leaders/pastors	72% (319)
Talked with members who visited	70% (312)
Talked with others who visited	86% (382)
Surfed R/R websites	24% (105)
Visited Toronto revival site	7% (32)
Attended Awake America Crusades	20% (90)
Visited Brownsville Assembly of God	34% (158)
Visited other BAOG-like sites	34% (151)
Other R/R contacts	11% (48)
Church actively involved in renewal	30% (135)
Use renewal music	65% (290)
Invited renewal speakers to church	33% (147)

BAOG = Brownsville Assembly of God; R/R = Renewal/Revival

TABLE A.5. Orthodoxy of Pastors

Theological Beliefs	*Strongly Disagree*	*Disagree*	*Agree*	*Strongly Agree*
Devil actually exists	— (2)	— (1)	94% (411)	5% (23)
Dispensationalism	10% (38)	32% (117)	11% (40)	47% (173)
Scriptures literally accurate	— (3)	1% (6)	85% (371)	13% (58)
Christ only way to salvation	—	—	96% (419)	4% (18)
Premillennial view of history	1% (4)	5% (20)	51% (208)	43% (177)
Immanent rapture	—	1% (5)	77% (329)	22% (94)
Spirit baptism requires tongues	3% (13)	13% (54)	56% (242)	29% (124)
Moral Issues				
Divorced/remarried as congregational leaders	5% (23)	18% (78)	22% (95)	54% (228)
Divorced/remarried as pastors	19% (79)	38% (159)	7% (28)	36% (151)
No dancing	2% (10)	17% (74)	30% (129)	50% (215)
No gambling	1% (5)	— (3)	83% (362)	16% (69)
No movies	6% (26)	43% (183)	15% (62)	36% (152)

Appendix B

Congregational Measurement Scales

An asterisk (*) indicates that the item was reverse-coded, allowing the score to reflect a positive response to a statement that, for methodological reasons, was worded negatively.

Attitudes toward Poor Scale ($\alpha = .577$)

HOW DO YOU FEEL ABOUT THE FOLLOWING STATEMENTS?
(Strongly agree = 1; Agree = 2; No opinion = 3; Disagree = 4; Strongly disagree = 5)

- In general the poor and the homeless are reaping what they have sowed.
- I cannot truly love a person who does not show some gratitude.
- I really don't understand how anyone can be homeless.
- The poor and homeless do not deserve help if they refuse to try to help themselves.

Compassion Scale ($\alpha = .642$)

HOW DO YOU FEEL ABOUT THE FOLLOWING STATEMENTS?
(Strongly agree = 1; Agree = 2; No opinion = 3; Disagree = 4; Strongly disagree = 5)

- There are times I have given away things I needed to help someone else in need.*
- Serving poor and broken people gives me great joy.*
- I have tried my best to respond to the needs of others.*
- I am willing to put myself in physical danger if it means helping someone in need.*
- I always try to have relationships that include the poor and the broken.*

Congregational Activity Scale (α=.654)

INDICATE HOW MANY TIMES IN A TYPICAL MONTH YOU PARTICIPATE IN THE FOLLOWING CHURCH ACTIVITIES.

(0 = 0; 1 = 1; 2 = 2; 3 = 3; 4 = 4 or more times)

- Sunday morning worship participation
- Sunday school participation
- Mid-week church service/activity
- Approximate percentage of annual family income give to congregation and other religious groups (1 = 0–1%; 2 = 2–5%; 3 = 6–9%; 4 = 10%; 5 = more than 10%)

Congregational Benevolence Scale (α = .764)

EACH CONGREGATION HAS A DIFFERENCE SENSE OF WHAT REALLY MATTERS MOST AND WHAT IT SHOULD BE DOING. HOW IMPORTANT IS IT THAT YOUR CHURCH DOES THE FOLLOWING THINGS?

(Not at all important = 1; Somewhat important = 2; Very important =3; Extremely important = 4)

- Being a leader in the community
- Serving the poor and the needy
- Providing counseling and other services for members
- Working with other religious groups to improve the community

Congregational Politics Scale

HOW IMPORTANT IS IT THAT YOUR CHURCH DO THE FOLLOWING THINGS?

(0 = 0; 1 = 1; 2 = 2; 3 = 3; 4 = 4 or more times)

- Help people register to vote
- Help elect Christians to political office
- Work to pass legislation that promotes Christian morals and values
- Pray for the nation's leaders

Cultural Issues Scale (α = .600)

WHAT ARE YOUR VIEWS ON THE FOLLOWING ISSUES?

(Strongly agree = 1; Agree = 2; No opinion = 3; Disagree = 4; Strongly disagree = 5)

- Abortion should be outlawed except to save the life of the mother.*
- Marriage should be defined as a union between one man and one woman without exception.*
- The U.S. should support Israel over the Palestinians in the Middle East.*
- Local communities should be allowed to post the Ten Commandments and other religious symbols in public buildings if the majority agrees.*
- The U.S. should give top priority to stopping religious persecution around the world.*
- The government should provide vouchers to parents to help pay for their children to attend private or religious schools*

Divine Presence Scale (α = .853)

HOW OFTEN DO YOU HAVE THE FOLLOWING KINDS OF SPIRITUAL EXPERIENCES?

(Many times a day = 1; Every day = 2; Most days = 3; Some days = 4; Once in a while = 5; Never or almost never = 6)

- Felt God's love as the greatest power in the universe*
- Felt the unmistakable presence of God during prayer*
- Everything seems to disappear except consciousness of God*
- Deeper insight into a spiritual or biblical truth during prayer*

Ecumenical Cooperation Scale (α = .895)

PLEASE INDICATE TO WHAT EXTENT YOU WOULD LIKE TO SEE YOUR CHURCH COOPERATE WITH THE FOLLOWING GROUPS ON ISSUES OF COMMON CONCERN

(Full cooperation = 1; Limited cooperation = 2; None = 3)

- Evangelical Protestant churches*
- Mainline Protestant churches*
- Other Pentecostal churches*
- Independent-nondenominational churches*
- Roman Catholic churches*
- Independent charismatic organizations*
- Associations of charismatics in mainline Protestantism*
- Non-Christian religious groups*

Evangelism Scale (α = .850)

HOW MANY TIMES HAVE YOU PERFORMED THE FOLLOWING ACTIVITIES WITHIN THE PAST SIX MONTHS?

(0, 1, 2 , 3 , 4, 5 or more)

- Invited non-member to a church event
- Invited an inactive member to a church event
- Offered transportation to church for someone who otherwise would be unable to attend
- Invited children of non-members to attend worship or Sunday school at your church
- Helped a visitor or new member get acquainted with others in the church
- Talked with friends and neighbors about your church
- Visited inactive members of your church to encourage them to be more involved
- Offered the services of your pastor or church to someone in need

Organizational Memberships (Simple Additive Scale)

DO YOU BELONG TO ANY OF THE FOLLOWING KINDS OF GROUPS? (CHECK ALL THAT APPLY.)

- Labor union
- PTA or school group
- Pro-family group
- Women's group
- Professional group
- Business group
- Youth group
- Environmental group
- Gun owners group
- Civic or community group
- Christian conservative group
- Sports or recreation group

Orthodoxy Scale ($\alpha = .592$)

INDICATE HOW STRONGLY YOU AGREE OR DISAGREE WITH THE FOLLOWING STATEMENTS.

(Strongly agree = 1; Agree = 2; No opinion = 3; Disagree = 4; Strongly disagree = 5)

- The Bible is the Word of God, and it is true word for word.
- Belief in Jesus Christ is the only way to salvation.

Political Alignment

Combines two questions: (1) Overall, how would you describe your views on issues? (7 points, from extremely liberal to extremely conservative); and (2) Overall, how would you describe your political affiliation? (7 points from strong Democrat to strong Republican).

Political Participation (Simple Additive Scale)

HAVE YOU ENGAGED IN ANY OF THE FOLLOWING ACTIVITIES IN THE LAST TWO YEARS? (CHECK ALL THAT APPLY.)

- Contacted a public official
- Made a campaign contribution
- Participated in a demonstration or protest
- Worked for a candidate or party
- Signed a petition
- Attended a political meeting
- Voted in the last election

Prophecy Scale ($\alpha = .863$)

HOW OFTEN DO YOU HAVE THE FOLLOWING KINDS OF SPIRITUAL EXPERIENCES?

(Many times a day = 1; Every day = 2; Most days = 3; Some days = 4; Once in a while = 5; Never or almost never = 6)

- Gave a prophecy privately to another person*
- Received a personal revelation from another person*
- Received a revelation directly from God during personal times of prayer*
- Had an experience with God in which you lost awareness of time and things around you*
- Heard a divine call to perform some specific act*

Revival Experience Scale ($\alpha = .797$)

HOW OFTEN HAVE YOU BEEN INVOLVED IN THE FOLLOWING PRACTICES DURING A WORSHIP OR REVIVAL SERVICE AT A CHURCH OR REVIVAL/ RENEWAL MEETING WITHIN THE PAST YEAR?

(Regularly = 1; Sometimes = 2; Rarely = 3; Never = 4)

- Singing in the Spirit*
- Physical manifestations (laughter, shaking, etc.)*
- Being slain or resting in the spirit*
- Dancing in the spirit*

Social Welfare Scale α=.674

WHAT ARE YOUR VIEWS ON THE FOLLOWING ISSUES?

(Strongly agree = 1; Agree = 2; No opinion = 3; Disagree = 4; Strongly disagree = 5)

- The government should spend more to fight hunger and poverty even if it means raising taxes.* ("Anti-poverty program")
- Public funding should be available to churches to provide social services for the needy.* ("Charitable choice")
- The government should provide health insurance to working people who are not insured.* ("Health insurance")
- Strict rules to protect the environment are necessary even if they cost jobs or raise prices.* ("Environmental protection")

Traditional Values Scale ($\alpha = .768$)

INDICATE HOW STRONGLY YOU AGREE OR DISAGREE WITH THE FOLLOWING STATEMENTS.

(Strongly agree = 1; Agree = 2; No opinion = 3; Disagree = 4; Strongly disagree = 5)

- The occasional use of alcoholic beverages is permissible.
- Assemblies of God congregations must actively seek to revitalize its early Pentecostal roots.*
- It is not appropriate for Christians to patronize movie theaters.*
- Christians should not engage in social dancing.*
- Tongues is the initial physical evidence of Spirit baptism.*
- Persons who have been divorced and remarried should not be permitted to be pastors.*
- Persons who have been divorced and remarried should not be permitted to serve in leadership positions in the local congregation.*
- Christians should avoid gambling, including lotteries.*

Appendix C

Statistical Tables (Congregational Survey)

TABLE C.1. Bivariate Correlation Matrix (Chapters 5–7)

	1	2	3	4	5	6	7	8	9	10	11	12	13	14	15	16	17	18
1 Age	1	-01	**16**	03	06	07	-06	**16**	-05	**08**	01	**16**	-05	02	**24**	02	**-08**	**40**
2 Sex		1	-00	**-09**	**-11**	**-07**	09	05	07	**13**	**13**	05	**08**	05	08	01	04	**-07**
3 Race			1	**16**	11	**-12**	**-16**	-04	**-25**	**-20**	**-18**	**-23**	**-17**	**-08**	-03	**-32**	04	-03
4 Education				1	35	-01	**-13**	-04	**-15**	**-09**	**-11**	**-25**	**-09**	00	**-07**	**-24**	06	-05
5 Income					1	03	**-12**	**01**	**-13**	-06	**-10**	**-19**	**-09**	**-08**	**04**	**-18**	-01	**-08**
6 Pentecostal at age 15						1	**.10**	-04	06	-03	07	05	-03	-00	-05	**06**	04	**-19**
7 Revival experience							1	**41**	53	**39**	**28**	32	29	**16**	**25**	38	07	04
8 Tongues								1	**37**	37	**17**	**28**	22	18	33	28	**08**	**28**
9 Prophecy									1	**63**	53	62	**38**	25	31	64	12	09
10 Divine presence										1	54	48	**36**	30	41	46	10	**20**
11 Inner healing											1	**46**	28	**17**	27	**43**	11	04
12 Physical healing												1	29	**14**	27	59	00	**21**
13 Evangelism													1	25	**29**	32	05	05
14 Compassion														1	19	17	13	**10**
15 Prayer healing															1	22	08	**20**
16 Healing instrument																1	-02	**16**
17 Ecumenism																	1	**-10**
18 Traditional values																		1

Coefficients in **bold** are statistically significant.

Dummy Codes: Sex: 0 = male; 1 = female
Race: 0 = non-Anglo; 1 = Anglo/white
Pentecostal at age 15: 0 = yes; 1 = no

TABLE C.2. Multivariate Analysis (Chapter 6)

	Physical Healing		*Inner Healing*		*Healing Instrument*		*Evangelism*		*Compassion*	
	B	*Beta*	*B*	*Beta*	*B*	*beta*	*B*	*beta*	*B*	*beta*
Age	**0.01**	**0.21**	−0.00	−0.01	**0.01**	**0.07**	**−0.01**	**−0.08**	−0.00	−0.04
Sex	−0.05	−0.03	0.12	0.05	−0.14	−0.06	0.12	0.05	0.02	0.02
Race	−0.05	−0.05	0.03	0.02	**−0.15**	**−0.14**	−0.04	−0.04	0.02	0.03
Education	**−0.06**	**−0.07**	−0.01	−0.01	**−0.07**	**−0.06**	−0.01	−0.01	0.03	0.05
Income	**−0.03**	**−0.07**	−0.01	−0.01	−0.01	−0.03	−0.00	−0.00	−0.00	−0.01
Prophecy	**0.66**	**0.51**	**0.53**	**0.34**	**0.72**	**0.49**	**0.23**	**0.16**	**0.10**	**0.13**
Divine presence	**0.11**	**0.11**	**0.40**	**0.35**	**0.11**	**0.10**	**0.11**	**0.11**	**0.10**	**0.17**
Tongues	−0.02	−0.03	**−0.09**	**−0.11**	0.04	0.05	0.04	0.05	0.03	0.08
Physical healing							0.08	0.07	−0.00	−0.00
Inner healing							0.04	0.05	0.01	0.03
Healing instrument							**0.09**	**0.10**	0.01	0.02
Adjusted R square	0.40*		0.33*		0.40*		0.18*		0.10*	

Coefficients in **bold** are statistically significant.
Dummy codes: Sex: 0 = male; 1 = female

TABLE C.3. Multivariate Analysis (Chapter 7)

	Evangelism		*Pray with Others*		*Agent of Healing*		*Pro-Poor Attitudes*		*Compassion*		*Ecumenism*	
	B	*Beta*	*B*	*Beta*	*B*	*Beta*	*B*	*Beta*	*B*	*Beta*	*B*	*Beta*
Age	−0.00	−0.05	**0.01**	**0.14**	0 .00	0.06	0.00	0.04	**−0.00**	**−0.09**	−0.02	−0.08
Pentecostal at age 15	−0.00	−0.02	−0.00	−0.01	−0.00	−0.00	0.01	0.05	0.01	0.04	0.03	0.04
Gender	.011	0.05	0.08	0.04	−0.10	−0.04	**0.19**	**0.14**	0.02	0.01	0.29	0.04
Race	**−0.08**	**−0.08**	0.04	0.04	**−0.16**	**−0.14**	0.02	0.03	0.01	0.02	0.26	0.08
Education	−0.03	−0.03	**0.06**	**0.07**	**−0.08**	**−0.08**	0.05	0.08	0.02	0.04	0.10	0.06
Income	−0.01	−0.02	0.02	0.05	−0.01	−0.02	0.01	0.06	−0.00	−0.02	−0.02	−0.01
Tongues	0.04	0.05	**0.08**	**0.13**	0.03	0.04	**0.05**	**0.13**	0.02	0.06	0.16	0.07
Divine presence	**0.15**	0.15	**0.24**	**0.29**	**0.09**	**0.09**	**0.10**	**0.17**	**0.10**	**0.17**	0.18	0.05
Prophecy	**0.36**	**0.26**	**0.14**	**0.12**	**0.76**	**0.51**	−0.05	−0.06	**0.11**	**0.14**	**0.43**	**0.09**
Traditional values	−0.04	−0.02	0.06	0.05	0.07	0.07	**−0.18**	**−0.21**	0.04	0.05	**−0.57**	**−0.12**
Adjusted R square	0.18		0.25		0.42		0.10		0.10		0.10	

Coefficients in **bold** are statistically significant.

Dummy Codes: Sex: 0 = male; 1 = female
Race: 0 = non-Anglo; 1 = Anglo/white
Pentecostal at age 15: 0 = yes; 1 = no

TABLE C.4. Benevolent Attitudes: Multivariate Analysis (Chapter 8)

	Equitable		*Social Ills*		*Congregational Benevolence*		*Congregational Politics*		*Social Welfare*		*Cultural Issues*	
	B	*Beta*	*B*	*Beta*	*B*	*Beta*	*B*	*Beta*	*B*	*Beta*	*B*	*Beta*
Age	0.00	0.05	**0.05**	**0.10**	**0.00**	**–0.11**	0.00	0.07	**–0.01**	**–0.18**	**0.01**	**0.18**
Pentecostal at age 15	–0.04	–0.02	0.11	0.06	–0.01	–0.01	0.02	0.02	–0.10	–0.09	–0.06	–0.07
Gender	0.02	0.01	0.14	0.06	0.11	0.09	0.01	0.00	0.03	0.02	–0.09	–0.08
Race	**–0.13**	**–0.11**	0.08	0.06	0.06	0.09	0.04	0.05	–0.04	–0.05	0.04	0.06
Education	0.01	0.01	0.05	0.04	**–0.07**	**–0.13**	**–0.15**	**–0.23**	–0.03	–0.04	–0.04	–0.07
Income	–0.02	–0.05	0.02	0.04	0.00	0.00	–0.01	–0.03	–0.03	–0.09	–0.01	–0.02
Tongues	0.10	0.08	0.12	0.08	–0.02	–0.03	–0.05	–0.05	0.01	0.01	–0.03	–0.04
Divine presence	**0.19**	**0.20**	0.09	0.08	**0.13**	**0.23**	**0.13**	**0.19**	**0.16**	**0.22**	–0.03	–0.06
Prophecy	–0.09	–0.07	0.08	0.05	0.08	0.10	**0.13**	**0.13**	0.03	0.03	**0.13**	**0.17**
Orthodoxy	0.04	0.02	**0.35**	**0.14**	0.00	0.00	0.08	0.05	–0.11	–0.07	**0.28**	**0.24**
Church activity	**–0.16**	**–0.16**	0.06	0.05	**–0.08**	**–0.14**	0.04	0.06	**–0.18**	**–0.23**	**0.10**	**0.18**
Adjusted R square	0.06		0.05		0.12		0.16		0.18		0.21	

Coefficients in **bold** are statistically significant.

TABLE C.5. Benevolent Behavior: Multivariate Analysis (Chapter 8)

	Volunteer		*Organizational Memberships*		*Political Participation*		*Political Alignment*	
	B	*Beta*	*B*	*Beta*	*B*	*Beta*	*B*	*Beta*
Age	0.00	0.08	**-0.01**	**-0.11**	**0.02**	**0.17**	0.00	-0.04
Pentecostal at age 15	-0.06	-0.04	0.06	0.03	**-0.23**	**-0.11**	**0.16**	**0.10**
Gender	0.13	0.07	0.15	0.06	0.19	0.06	0.04	0.02
Race	0.03	0.03	0.07	0.05	**0.24**	**0.14**	**0.25**	**0.18**
Education	0.02	0.02	0.10	0.09	**0.30**	**0.23**	**0.10**	**0.10**
Income	0.02	0.06	**0.10**	**0.22**	0.04	0.06	0.03	0.06
Tongues	0.04	0.03	0.08	0.05	0.06	0.03	**0.11**	**0.08**
Divine presence	0.11	0.13	0.20	0.12	-0.07	-0.05	-0.02	-0.02
Prophecy	**0.23**	**0.18**	0.08	0.07	**0.24**	**0.12**	-0.04	-0.02
Orthodoxy	-0.14	-0.08	**-0.35**	**-0.14**	0.03	0.01	**0.20**	**0.09**
Church activity	**0.15**	**0.16**	0.12	0.10	**0.19**	**0.13**	**0.11**	**0.10**
Equitable	**0.09**	**0.10**	0.06	0.05	0.07	0.06	**-0.11**	**-0.10**
Social Ills	0.00	0.00	0.05	0.04	0.01	0.01	0.03	0.03
Church benevolence	0.13	0.08	-0.06	-0.03	0.07	0.03	**-0.20**	**-0.10**
Church politics	-0.10	-0.07	-0.06	-0.04	0.07	0.04	**0.27**	**0.17**
Social welfare	-0.02	-0.02	0.05	0.03	**-0.37**	**-0.19**	**-0.44**	**-0.29**
Cultural issues	0.10	0.06	**0.46**	**0.22**	**0.28**	**0.11**	**0.70**	**0.35**
Adjusted R square	0.13		0.13		0.29		0.48	

Coefficients in **bold** are statistically significant.

Notes

INTRODUCTION

1. It has been often noted that there is no single Pentecostalism but rather many variants and streams of pentecostalisms. When referring to the diverse pentecostal movement (including both historic denominations and neo-pentecostalism), we use the lowercase "pentecostal" and "pentecostalism"; when speaking specifically about classic denominations (of which the Assemblies of God is a prototype), "Pentecostal" and "Pentecostalism" will appear in uppercase.

2. Throughout this work the Assemblies of God (AG) will be used to refer to the Assemblies of God, USA, and to the exclusion of other national bodies known as Assemblies of God.

3. Bethel Assembly of God in Redding, California, withdrew from the denomination to become part of the neo-pentecostal Apostolic Network. On its Website (www.ibethel.org, accessed on September 2, 2009) we read the following: "On January 17, 2006, the membership of Bethel Church of Redding voted to withdraw from our affiliation with the Assemblies of God (AG). However, our heart to bless and celebrate the AG as they continue in their vital role in God's kingdom hasn't changed. The Assemblies has been, and continues to be, one of the great champions of the Gospel in the earth today. We have enjoyed a long and fruitful connection with this organization. Our decision to withdraw from the Assemblies is not due to conflict or broken relationship, but rather because of what we understand to be the call of God on our church and movement."

4. First Assembly of God—Grand Rapids, now known now as Grand Rapids First, is the largest megachurch in a largely Reformed Protestant community A revival broke out in 1996 and continued through 2000 (under the then-pastorate of President Wayne Bensen of Emerge Ministries, an AG-affiliated counseling center in Akron, Ohio) that brought pilgrims from both near and far. Grand Rapids First (now pastored by Sam Rijfkogel) remains a megachurch; its Website (www.grandrapidsfirst.org) identifies it as a "diverse church with people of all ages, races and economic levels worshiping together." As with other evangelical AG congregations, an identification remains (on the Website, if not on the church sign or in the church bulletin) with AG denomination and its statement of faith, but its Sunday services have more of the feel of an evangelical megachurch than a traditional or charismatic pentecostal congregation.

5. Karl D. Strader was senior pastor of The Carpenter's Home Church until it dissolved in 2005. Former associate pastor Stephen R. Strader (Karl Strader's son) began Ignited Church as an Assemblies of God congregation in Lakeland this same year. It was at Ignited Church that the Lakeland Outpouring, a healing revival led by Todd Bentley, occurred.

6. The following congregations were surveyed: Celebration Church (Akron, OH); Central Assembly of God (Springfield, MO); Centro Cristiano (El Camino, CA); Centro

Cristiano Sinai (CA); Christian Life Center (Kent, OH); Church of the Redeemer (Baldwin Park, CA); Crossroads Cathedral (Hartford, CT); Faith Assembly of God (Hartford, CT); Father's House (Norton, OH); First Assembly of God (Akron, OH); First Assembly of God (Strafford, MO); Iglesia Nuevo Vida (Monterey Park, CA); Jesus Power (Columbus, OH); Lighthouse Christian Fellowship (Cuyahoga Falls, OH); Newport Mesa Church (Costa Mesa, CA); New Song Church (Cleveland Heights, OH); New Song Church (Orange Village, OH); Rescue Atlanta (Georgia); Roca Firme (Downey, CA); Temple Bethel (Cypress Park, CA); Victory Christian Fellowship (Trooper, PA).

7. The concluding chapter has been coauthored with Matthew T. Lee, who serves as a co-principal investigator for The Flame of Love Project and is the lead author of *A Sociological Study of the Great Commandment in Pentecostalism: The Practice of Godly Love as Benevolent Service* (Lee and Poloma 2009a).

CHAPTER 1

1. Dr. George O. Wood's interview with Dr. James T. Bradford on the occasion of Bradford's being named to the Executive Presbytery as General Secretary was found at http://ag.org (accessed on February 27, 2009).

2. The statistics cited in this section are from "2006 AG Statistical Reports," www.ag.org (accessed on December 2, 2008).

3. Although Latino/Hispanics have a long history in the AG, they have never been well integrated into the denomination—or into its Website. It was not until May 28, 2008, that *AG News*, the electronic newsletter, announced that "the Assemblies of God site is now available in Spanish."

4. This decline seemed to be a particular concern for the previous AG General Superintendent, Thomas E. Trask. As described by the editor of an issue of *Enrichment* on "Pentecost: Empowerment for Life Changing Ministry," Trask not only "understands his own need to maintain a daily experience in Pentecost" but he "also knows that our Movement must be led and empowered by the Holy Spirit if it is to impact our world for Christ" (Allen 2005, 22). It is too early to tell whether the present leadership is as concerned about the decline of Pentecostal experiences as about failing to be culturally relevant as it seeks to evangelize the postmodern world.

5. An adherence to traditional Pentecostal values and mores may result from what Sánchez-Walsh and Patterson (2007, 73) call "double marginalization." They note: "Not only were they [Latino Pentecostals] disfranchised from the dominant culture, their decision to pursue Pentecostalism immediately thrust them out of their Catholic community. Traditional Catholicism permeated every part of community life and the decision to leave the Catholic Church could result in broken relationships, limits to economic opportunity, and social ostracism." This double marginalization could understandably be responsible for tightly knit and traditionally cohesive Latino Pentecostal communities.

6. With two young women filling four of the other pastoral positions in the congregation, Celebration Church demonstrates an unusual openness to women leaders in the congregation, a topic dealt with in later chapters.

7. This is what seemingly happened to Bethel Assembly of God in Redding, California, a church known worldwide in charismatic circles for its enduring and life-changing revival. In 1991 *Charisma* published an article about the congregation (then an AG

church) and its impact on Redding (Loren 2005). Less than a year later Bethel withdrew from the denomination and changed its name to Bethel Church. Pastor Bill Johnson stressed (in a personal interview) that the congregation withdrew not because it had any major disagreement with the AG, but rather so that its identification would reflect those with whom he was "in ongoing relationship."

8. When Poloma asked Mike Guarnieri following the service whether he had planned to have this altar call, he indicated that he did not have an agenda—it seemed like the right thing to do. Included in the brief biography on the church Website is the following: "Mike is known as a revivalist, apostle and prophet. He has seen the lame walk, the blind see, and terminal cancer healing under his ministry"; (http://mikeonfire.com).

9. Creps (2007, 28) describes his snowball sample of thirty-one individuals and six focus groups as follows: "Most of the interview respondents come from within the Assemblies of God (AG) or from the margins of the denomination. They are virtually all in their twenties or early thirties, most are Anglos, with about one-third being female, and two-thirds being male. The majority are AG ministers."

10. This observation can be supported by the congregational survey in which half (51 percent) of the respondents reported that it was *extremely important* that their church be engaged in "serving the poor and the needy." This was true for 55 percent of Anglo/traditional congregations; 51 percent of Hispanic/traditional congregations; 45 percent of evangelical AG congregations; 56 percent of renewal congregations; and 53 percent of alternative congregations. The differences are statistically negligible.

CHAPTER 2

1. In light of the seemingly unregulated profession of spiritual manifestations and gifts seen in the recent Lakeland Outpouring and the failings of its evangelist Todd Bentley, skepticism and fear seem justified to many. Failings like those of the Lakeland Outpouring only exacerbate the problem for the survival of charisma. Fear seems to lead to a paralysis in pentecostal practices and experiences, as all open manifestations—even those much like ones found in early Pentecostalism—are eschewed. The dilemma between charisma and institutionalization is well illustrated by AG leaders and pastors who claim to want revival (as found in AG articles and confirmed by pastoral surveys) while commonly resisting the forms it has taken in America over the past six decades or so.

2. Recently, a modest position of "methodological agnosticism" (Porpora 2006; Hood 2007; Poloma and Hood 2008) has been proposed that permits some light to pass through reductionist blinders. Methodological agnosticism argues for the adoption of a posture that "remains open to the possibility of supernatural realities [but] neither asserts nor precludes them" (Porpora 2006, 58). For many purposes it has made sense to "bracket" theological claims, but atheistic bracketing has also limited the scope of study with its neglect of spiritual factors (including religious experience). As Porpora (2006, 58) has noted, in making a case for methodological agnosticism, methodological atheism as an a priori general rule is not warranted when religious experience itself is the object of study. See also Lee and Poloma (2009a).

3. "Charismatic Empowerment and Unlimited Love. A Social Psychological Assessment," a longitudinal study with triangulation of observers and methods that sought to study the relationship between the charismata and care-love, was funded by the Institute for Research on Unlimited Love in November 2002.

4. This "dark side" was comprised of web of factors that cannot easily be untangled. Sufficient to say that one aspect of the "dark side" was an appreciation-love gone amuck as the ever-changing vision for Blood and Fire trumped care-love concerns. Appreciation-love, especially the founder's depiction of a supernatural kingdom of God, helped to launch the ministry and to inspire countless followers and beneficiaries. Always a work in process, the "revelations" for the vision came fast and furious as the founder emerged from a period of major depression, changes that significantly altered the direction of the ministry and ultimately led to its demise.

5. "The Flame of Love: Scientific Research on the Experience and Expression of Godly Love in the Pentecostal Tradition," funded by the John Templeton Foundation, has been the catalyst behind the ongoing research on Godly Love. The three-year project included (1) a qualitative study in which more than one hundred exemplars of Godly Love were interviewed, (2) a three-wave national survey on Godly Love conducted by the University of Akron's Bliss Institute of Applied Politics, (3) five subprojects on Godly Love awarded to theologian and social scientist dyads at ten universities in the United States and Canada, and regular meetings with twenty-two scholars representing the social sciences, theology, philosophy, history, and religious studies who provide input for the ongoing projects, share the findings and their implications for the theory, and plan professional meetings and future publications.

CHAPTER 3

1. Pentecostal, when capitalized, will refer to the classical Pentecostal denominations, including the Assemblies of God. Lower-case "pentecostal" refers to the broader movement that includes the three "waves" described in the introductory chapter and the newer emergent groups and their leaders energized by revivals.

2. "By 'pot of goo' I mean to convey the vapid, indistinct, and prophetically fainthearted amalgam that is, unfortunately, only too characteristic of both Evangelical and Classical Pentecostal churches" (Rybarczyk 2007, 7).

3. The heightened primitivism of neo-pentecostal spirituality and its eschewing of traditional organizational structures has led one British sociologist to make the following wager: "I would put my money on the old Pentecostal denominations still to be with us, and thriving at the end of the next century. I'm not prepared to put my shirt on the new churches, and don't relish the long-odds on the Renewal" (Walker 2000, ix).

4. Evangelical identity had a mean score of 3 (on a 4-point scale) while charismatic/third-wave identity scores had a mean score of 2 points.

5. In North America the term "Pentecostal" usually refers to persons in denominations born out of or having some connection with the Azusa Street Revival in Los Angeles (1906–9). "Charismatic" applies to those in mainline and newer (often independent) churches which embraced a pentecostal worldview in the mid-twentieth century or later. In the United States, some 23 percent of all evangelical Protestants, 9 percent of mainline Protestants, 13 percent of Roman Catholics, and 36 percent of black Protestants claim to be "Spirit-filled," another appellation for those persons embracing the Pentecostal-charismatic movement (Green et al. 1997, 228). Americans who claim to be Spirit-filled tend to self-identify as Pentecostal (4.7 percent) or charismatic (6.6 percent), but much less

frequently as "both charismatic and Pentecostal" (.8 percent). It is thus not surprising that these clearly Pentecostal pastors would express some social distance from charismatics. Despite a worldview and theology that is more similar than dissimilar, most pentecostals are likely to identify with a particular stream of the movement.

6. Data from the Cooperative Congregational Studies Project (CCSP) found that "40% of churches estimated that half or less of their members has been baptized in the Holy Spirit with evidence of speaking in other tongues" (Doty and Espinoza 2000).

7. In reviewing these statistics, I was reminded of a comment made by an AG graduate student in one of my courses, during which I was discussing my research on divine healing. The young man commented, "I have heard stories like you are reporting all of my life, but I have never seen one case of such healing in my church. Healing is professed but I have seen little evidence of its being practiced or experienced."

8. It was interesting to review the selection of readings found in the eighty-fifth anniversary edition (1913–98) of the *Pentecostal Evangel*, the weekly publication of the AG. An article on Pentecostal revival was reprinted from the July 12, 1924, issue that lamented how "many folks are blind" to the Pentecostal revival that was still in process. The anniversary issue, published three years after the revival began at BAOG, failed to mention the Pensacola Outpouring (as it is often called) as a significant event in AG history.

9. Ambiguity and ambivalence appear to be heightened by the fact that only 6 percent of the respondents did not believe that the denomination is responsible for promoting revival. Sixty percent of the pastors surveyed believed it was the task of the National Office and another 34 percent reported it was the task of the district offices to promote revival.

CHAPTER 4

1. Under the section on "Leadership and Accountability" on the AG Website (www.ag.org; accessed on March 14, 2009) is found the following statement, which indicates the reluctance of the judicatory to accept a denominational label: "The national church is called 'The General Council of the Assemblies of God.' In keeping with the original intention of the founding body, the Assemblies of God is considered a cooperative fellowship instead of a denomination. As a result the national headquarters operation exists primarily as a service organization – providing educational curriculum, organizing the missions programs, credentialing ministers, overseeing the church's colleges and seminary, producing communication channels for the churched and non-churched publics, and providing leadership for many national programs and ministries of the Assemblies of God (Acts 16:4, 5; Hebrews 13:17)."

2. The interviews conducted with pastors by a team of ORW researchers seem to confirm Menzies's observation about the focus being on the "16 Fundamental Truths," with little concern for "niceties of doctrinal distinctions." It is significant that while some respondents talked about being "big on sound doctrine," it was largely with regard to issues decided at the 1916 Council. Interestingly, none of the twenty-eight pastors interviewed talked about their disagreement with fundamentals of the denomination, not even the somewhat controversial "initial evidence" tenet on glossolalia, which insists that speaking in tongues is *the* evidential sign of Spirit baptism.

3. It is interesting to note the estimate that only 35 percent of Pentecostals speak in tongues. In other words, only one in three members of churches who teach that glossolalia is the "initial evidence" of Spirit baptism actually are glossolalic. Hollenweger (1999, 147) comments on this statistic: "If we add to this number those Pentecostal denominations who refuse to subscribe to the doctrine of 'initial sign' (for instance, the very strong Chilean movement), the percentage is even higher." Based on our congregational survey data and other observations, the 35 percent figure seems somewhat low for AG members/adherents (see chapter 5), where a slight majority are regular users of glossolalia.

4. At least some pastors have quietly been neglecting to check the box asking about a belief in tongues as "initial physical evidence" of Spirit baptism, noting that the constitution and bylaws do not authorize the collection of such information. Those seeking ordination papers for the first time are caught in the most precarious position. Reportedly, the Executive Presbytery has added the term "immediate," so that it reads "tongues as the immediate initial physical evidence," to close in on those who have been acquiescing to the words but not the spirit of increasing doctrinal rigidity.

5. The percentage of those disagreeing with the tongues doctrine represents a significant increase over the 2 percent figure reported from a 1985 data set on pastors for the same question (Poloma 1989, 40). Also of interest from the study of congregations and pastors in the mid-1980s is the gap between the pastoral and congregational responses to the issue of tongues as initial evidence. At that time, 39 percent of the congregants did not agree with this fundamental doctrine (as compared with 2 percent of the pastors).

6. One interesting caveat may be found in testimony by J. Roswell Flower, the first General Superintendent of the AG, on his Spirit baptism. In the original article, which appeared in the *Pentecostal Evangel* in 1933, it is clear that Flower, while believing in the Fundamental about glossolalia, regarded himself as having received the baptism some months before he actually spoke in tongues, and *after* leading evangelistic crusades deemed to be Spirit-empowered. When the article was reprinted in the *Pentecostal Evangel* in 1993, it was abridged to make it appear that Flower actually spoke in tongues on the occasion of his Spirit baptism, which he reports empowered him for the crusades. For an AG defense against critiques of the existing doctrine on tongues, see Bridges (2000).

7. See the video *Go Inside the Toronto Blessing* (Canton, OH: Fresh Start Marketing, Inc., 1997), an account of the outbreak of revival at the Toronto Airport Christian Fellowship in 1994.

8. Perhaps the story of an egalitarian Pentecostalism is a myth (as some historians have suggested), but religious myth can be a powerful propellant for change. What is significant here is that the myth of early equality has been eroded with the aging of Pentecostalism. The vision of God's pouring out his Spirit on all people, as foretold in the book of Joel and reiterated by Peter on Pentecost, often fails to find modern expression.

9. In an interview with one of the authors, Robeck shared in detail how despite his efforts to stay within the guidelines of the AG with regard to ecumenical activities, "there was a group that was really after my credentials. They published articles in which they were really hammering against me and against our general superintendent for allowing me to do these kinds of things. It was a very painful period." The inquisition was mounted that included a meeting with the then Executive Presbytery, who vindicated him of wrongdoing. Robeck noted that he was told that the Presbytery "had agreed not to minute

anything about this meeting to avoid it becoming part of the Executive Presbytery minutes." He then added laughingly, "You know that was disappointing to me as a historian, but understandable to me in terms of politics of the institution."

10. David J. Moore, director of the AG Center for Ethnic Relations, provided figures showing an increase of black (from 111 to 213), Hispanic (from 1457 to 1885), Native American (from 168 to 178), and "other" (from 53 to 125) congregations. "In 1990 ethnic minority congregations and those with no single majority represented 20.2% of all A/G churches. In ten years that has grown to 26.7%. If the current trend remains constant in 2010 they will account for one third of our churches."

11. The overwhelming majority of respondents, reflecting their Anglo affiliation, either disagreed (61 percent) or strongly disagreed (28 percent) with the item stating that these special language districts have been detrimental to the AG. A significant minority of pastors, most of whom are themselves "on the margin," do seem to recognize the problems presented by the present structural arrangement.

12. The survey question providing this information read: "Which of the following tasks are best performed by the national office, which by the district office, and which are not appropriate for either denominational administrative office by placing a check for each of them in the appropriate column. (National, District, Not Appropriate)." Information provided by the Hartford Institute for Religious Research, Hartford, Connecticut.

13. The question providing this information read: "What kind of job are these denominational services/outreach doing? (Excellent, Good, Fair, Poor, Don't Know.)" Information provided by the Hartford Institute for Religious Research.

CHAPTER 5

1. The narratives used as illustrations in this and the following four chapters come from AG adherents or former adherents who experienced Spirit baptism within the AG and were interviewed for the Flame of Love Project (see Lee and Poloma 2009a).

2. Of those who claimed to be Spirit baptized, more than half reported that they underwent the experience in a church or church-like setting—28 percent in response to a church altar call, and 23 percent during a renewal or revival meeting. Another 12 percent had the experience while attending a youth camp meeting. A minority experienced Spirit baptism while they were praying alone (18 percent) or with a family member or friend (10 percent).

3. This total of 74 percent comes close to the 77 percent who were certain they had been baptized in the Spirit. Another 8 percent were "uncertain" about whether or not they had received the baptism in the Spirit, a figure nearly identical to the 7 percent of the congregational sample who indicated that they were unable to identify the precise time of their baptism.

4. In using a multivariate equation to test for the possible effects of demographic variables—age, gender, race, income, and education—on the experience of Spirit baptism and glossolalia measures, only age was found to have a statistically significant relationship. Younger congregants were less likely to agree with the AG doctrinal stance on the relationship between tongues and Spirit baptism (beta = –.24), and also less likely to report that they had experienced Spirit baptism (beta = –.10). Not surprisingly, they are

less likely to report praying in tongues (beta = –.15). Support for the AG position on glossolalia was not affected by race, or socio-economic status (income and education). Younger respondents were less likely, however, both to be glossolalic and to support the doctrine than were older respondents.

5. For further discussion and an overview of studies of glossolalia, see Cartledge (2006), Malony and Lovekin (1985), and Mills (1986).

6. These respondents were even less likely to give an interpretation of the tongues message. Eighty-three percent said they had never done so, with another 9 percent reporting it was rare for them to do so.

7. Previous research on prayer experience began with a survey of residents of Akron, Ohio, in 1985 (see Poloma and Pendleton 1991a, 1991b) that served as the testing ground for a national survey (Poloma and Gallup 1991).

8. The bivariate correlations with glossolalia and the spiritual experiences are as follows: experiencing the unmistakable presence of God (r = .40), obtaining deeper insights into spiritual truths (r = .37), receiving revelations directly from God (r = .40), receiving answers to a specific prayer requests (r = .31), and hearing divine calls to perform a specific actions (r = .31).

9. The correlations for the general mysticism measures and glossolalia are as follows: feeling everything disappear except consciousness of God (r = .32), having experiences of God that no words could express (r = .31), feeling oneself merge with God (r = .33), and having experienced God and lost awareness of time (r = .34).

10. For an account of the bodily manifestations found in the 1990s revival known as the Toronto Blessing, see Poloma (1998a, 2003).

11. The wariness of many pentecostals to accept a range of embodied experiences, it can be argued, reflects what we have discussed as the routinization of charisma and the drift toward evangelicalism. This drift has resulted in a Pentecostal theology that is more evangelical than pentecostal in that it "seeks to convey an arid, rationalistic, formalistic, unemotional, nonexperiential and non-charismatic approach to religious life that is unacceptable" (see Baker 1995: 62).

12. The statistically significant correlations found between frequently speaking in tongues and embodied experiences are as follows: experiencing physical manifestations (r = .33), being slain or resting in the spirit (r = .40), dancing in the spirit (r = .35), and singing in the spirit (r = .34). When the physical manifestations are combined into a single scale, the bivariate relationship shows that those who experience a wider range of embodied experiences are also more likely to pray in tongues (r = .41).

13. For items used to construct the scales, and for the results of reliability analyses of these scales, see Appendix B. For relationships between items or *bivariate correlations* and their statistical significance, see Appendix C, Table 1.

14. In a multiple regression analysis with the evangelism scale as the dependent variable *and* glossolalia and revival manifestations (together with demographic controls) as the independent variables, glossolalia (beta = .14) and revival manifestations (beta = .20) were the leading predictors of evangelism. Of the demographic measures, only race (i.e., being "non-white") helped to account for the explained variance (beta = –.12). Since the bivariate relationship between race and evangelism is not statistically significant (see Appendix C, Table 1), it would appear that the profile of a highly evangelistic AG congregant is a person of color who is also highly glossolalic and experiences revival manifestations.

CHAPTER 6

1. For an illustration of the process of social constructionism and reconstructionism of Pentecostal history (especially in the Church of God, Cleveland, Tennessee), as well as a comprehensive and thoroughly researched account of how Mark 16:17–18 has been understood by serpent handlers as evaluated through social-scientific lenses, see Hood and Williamson (2008).

2. The bivariate correlations for the healing items are as follows: receiving prayer for healing (r = .18), praying for the healing of family and friends (r = .20), hearing accounts about miraculous healings (r = .12), and personally witnessing a miraculous healing (r = .16).

3. The results reported in Appendix C, Table 1 are correlations or numbers indicating a relationship between two variables. A perfect relationship is shown as "1," as when the item is correlated with itself in the table. The closer a decimal figure is to "1," the higher the correlation or stronger the relationship. The .62 correlation between physical healing and prophecy, for example, is much stronger than the .16 correlation between age and physical healing.

4. Details for all scales, including the questions, response choices for individual items, and the reliability co-efficients, are found in Appendix B.

5. Non-whites (r = –.25) and those with less education (r = –.15) and less income (r = –.13) appear to be *more* prophetic than whites and more prosperous respondents. Those who are highly prophetic are more likely to pray for deliverance (r = .36), to pray with others for healing (r = .31), to be prayed with for healing (r = .33), to pray for family and friends for healing (r = .20), and to have witnessed a miraculous healing (r = .42).

6. Women were slightly more likely than men to score higher on the divine presence scale (r = .13), as were non-whites (r = –.20) and those with less education (r = –.09). Those who scored higher on divine presence were also more likely to pray for deliverance (r = .36), to pray for healing for family and friends (r = .37), to pray with others for healing (r = .41), to have been prayed with for healing (r = .33), and to have witnessed a miraculous healing (r = .48).

7. In a multiple regression equation for physical healing, we were able to explain 40 percent of the variance through the use of demographic and spirituality measures. The strongest relationship was found between prophecy and healing (beta = .52). Other significant relationships included being older (beta = –.21), having a strong sense of the divine presence (beta = .11), having less education (beta = –.07), and having less income (beta =. –07).

8. In a multiple regression equation for inner or emotional healing we were able to explain 34 percent of the variance. The leading predictors were spirituality measures—the prophetic scale (beta = .33) and the divine presence (scale (beta = .35). Those who were more prophetic and had a sense of an abiding divine presence were more likely to experience inner healing. Glossolalia demonstrated a smaller statistically significant relationship (beta = –.11). The demographic variables were not statistically significant.

9. A multivariate equation with "prayer with others for healing" as the dependent ("outcome") variable and glossolalia, divine presence scale, prophetic scale, plus six demographics as independent variables (potential "causes") was found to be statistically significant in explaining 25 percent of the variance, with statistically significant partial

correlations for three of the nine independent variables. To summarize our findings, those who prayed most frequently with others for healing were older (beta = .15), scored higher on the divine presence scale (beta = .26), and more frequently prayed in tongues (beta = .15). The remaining variables in the equation (prophecy scale, gender, race, education, and income) were not statistically significant in accounting for differences found in praying with others for healing.

CHAPTER 7

1. Rieff's attack on the "therapeutic culture" was cast in *Freud: The Mind of the Moralist* (1959), further developed in *The Triumph of the Therapeutic: Uses of Faith after Freud* (1968), and expanded in *My Life among the Deathworks: Illustrations of the Aesthetics of Authority* (Rieff 2006).

2. Rieff regards much of Protestantism as having lost charisma to the forces of a therapeutic culture that dominants the West. He does not necessarily have more hope for Catholicism's ability to retain charisma, but he seems to find examples of charisma more readily in the Catholic faith than in later Protestant streams of Christianity born out of Enlightenment thought. Pentecostalism, as we have noted elsewhere (Poloma 1982; 1989), has been regarded as a "third force" within Christianity, a stream different from both Catholicism and Protestantism. A theme that continues to run through this assessment of the AG is whether or not this distinct identity is in jeopardy.

3. A dissonance between vestiges of Pentecostal distinctiveness and forces of accommodation could be seen throughout much of the media coverage of Sarah Palin, the Alaskan governor and Republican vice-presidential candidate in 2008 (Lukins 2009). Although she no longer belongs to an AG church, Palin was raised in the AG and seems to navigate easily in its culture. A video of her addressing members of Wasilla AG, the church in which she grew up, reflected a traditional Pentecostal understanding of the world. (The video was quickly pulled from the church Website when it attracted media attention.) Spending $350,000 on a wardrobe (as Palin allegedly did with campaign funds) would have been a serious violation of early Pentecostal taboos calling for simplicity of dress for women, as would her implying that sending U.S. military forces around the world was "a task that is from God" (Lukins 2009, 28). The AG's taboos against modern dress and makeup and its early pacifism have long been abandoned and even forgotten. Yet secular reporters were as distraught by the thought that Sarah Palin might "speak in tongues" as they were by her passionate Pentecostal preaching that reflected fundamentalist "end-times" visions.

4. For further discussion see Paul Alexander (2009a), in which the theologian documents the transformation of the American Assemblies of God over the course of the twentieth century "from its roots as an antiwar, pacifistic, and peace-seeking church into a nationalistic, militaristic, and Americanist denomination."

5. The figures for those with Pentecostal background in this sample were identical to those in *Crossroads*. Due to the deliberate sampling of Hispanic congregations, more came from Catholic background (19 percent vs. 9 percent) in this sample. A higher percentage (10 percent vs. 2 percent) reported that they did not attend church in their mid-teens when compared with the *Crossroads* sample.

6. In a multimedia age of the Internet, DVDs, and television, only 18 percent of respondents still agreed with the old prohibition that it was "best to avoid movie theaters." In a multivariate equation that regressed attending movies against demographic variables, demographic variables were found to account for 10 percent of the explained variance, with (not surprisingly) older adherents (beta = .25) being the most likely to agree with the statement. A greater number of respondents (26 percent) agreed with the position that "Christians should not engage in social dancing." A regression equation was able to account for 16 percent of the explained variance, with age (beta = .35) being the leading predictor, followed by being raised Pentecostal (beta = .19).

7. The multivariate analysis explained 10 percent of the variance: younger adherents (beta = –.09), Anglo/whites (beta = .23), and those with a higher level of education (beta = .16) are the most likely to adhere to the belief that God wants all to experience material prosperity.

8. The figures for this AG sample of congregants were remarkably similar to those reported in *Crossroads*, where 5 percent were divorced or separated and 11 percent were divorced and remarried.

9. The first congregation was founded in Los Angeles by Troy Perry in 1968. It has since grown to have a presence in 23 countries with 250 affiliated churches. Perry served as moderator of the Metropolitan Community Church until 2005.

10. One example from the period is Mary Watford Stabler, who launched her ministry at the age of sixteen in Franklin, Alabama,. Stabler, now eighty-seven years old, was recently interviewed by General Superintendent George Wood, who proclaimed her the AG's "longest serving continuing pastor" (www.ag.org; accessed on November 9, 2009). Stabler's ministry began with a "divine call" to preach, fueled by revival and a populist acceptance of her call, and resulting in an ongoing ministry to a single church that has lasted for over seventy years. Her advice to women who are now entering AG ministry: "Keep before the Lord and obey him."

11. None of the top six "executive presbytery leadership" positions has ever been held by a woman. In August 2009, Dr. Beth Grant was chosen to serve on the fourteen-person "non-resident executive presbytery" to represent ordained female ministers. Dr. Grant is heralded as the first woman to serve on the AG presbytery.

12. Only one congregation in our study was pastored by a woman—a Hispanic church in which the founding pastor died and the congregation agreed that his widow was "called" to lead the church. We did approach one church founded by a woman (with the help of the AG congregation in which she had served as an associate), but she declined to be part of the study. We saw no evidence that the status of women has changed in the AG from the analysis Poloma (1989, esp. 101–21) presented in *Crossroads*.

13. When traditional values was regressed against the demographics measures, orthodoxy, religious ritual, praying in tongues, the divine presence scale, and the prophetic scale, the multivariate equation was able to explain 40 percent of the variance. Those who scored higher on traditional Pentecostal values were likely to be older (beta = .40), female (beta = –.13), lower-income (beta = –.09), and non-white (beta = –.10), and to have been Pentecostal at age fifteen (beta = –.21)

14. When the demographics, spirituality measures, and Pentecostal values were regressed against the scores for the compassion scale, we found the multivariate equation accounted for 10 percent of the explained variance. Of the demographic measures only

age shows a small partial negative correlation (beta = –.08). A sense of divine presence (beta = .17) and prophetic experiences (r = .14) were the primary predictors of higher compassion scores.

15. Using our multivariate model, this time with attitudes toward the poor as the outcome measure, the model explains 10 percent of the variance. Two demographic measures were statistically significant predictors of these pro-social attitudes, indicating that women (beta = .14) and those with more education (beta = .08) were more likely to have higher scores on the pro-poor measures. The spirituality measures of divine presence scale (beta = .17) and praying in tongues (beta = .13) contributed to the explained variance. The leading predictor of pro-poor attitudes was the traditional Pentecostal values scale (beta = –21), but the relationship was a negative one. Those who scored high on the values scale were significantly less likely to report a compassionate attitude toward the poor and homeless.

16. Although statistically significant, the results for the multivariate model with ecumenism as the outcome measure were somewhat smaller (adjusted R square = .05). Those who were younger (beta = –.08) and Euro-American (beta = .09) were slightly more likely to be supportive of religious groups outside Pentecostalism and Evangelicalism. Of the pentecostal spirituality measures, only the prophecy scale (beta = .09) demonstrated a weak statistical significance—those who scored higher on prophetic measures were more likely to be more ecumenical. Once again the traditional Pentecostal values scale was the leading predictor of the outcome measure (beta = –.12)—and once again the relationship was a negative one. Those who scored higher on traditional values were less likely to be supportive of cooperation with churches other than Pentecostal or evangelical ones.

CHAPTER 8

1. For all respondents, the correlation between the equitable and social ills measure was –.17.

2. The multiple regression analysis of the equitable measure shows that race (beta = –.11), church activity (beta = –.16), and the divine presence (beta = .20) were statistically significant (adjusted R-squared = .06).

3. The multiple regression analysis of the social ills measure shows that doctrinal orthodoxy (beta = .14) was statistically significant (adjusted R-squared = –.05).

4. The multiple regression analysis of the congregational benevolence scale found that age (beta = –.11), education (beta = –.13), divine presence (beta = .23), and church activity (beta = –.14) were statistically significant (adjusted R-squared = .12).

5. See chapter 4 for similar information from another survey of AG clergy taken in the same time frame.

6. The multiple regression analysis of the congregational politics scale found that education (beta = –.23), the divine presence (beta = .19), and prophetic scales (beta = .13) were statistically significant (adjusted R-square = .16).

7. The multiple regression analysis of the social welfare scale found that age (beta = –.18), divine presence (beta = .22), and church activity (beta = –.23) were statistically significant (adjusted R-squared = .18).

8. The multiple regression analysis of the culture issue scale found that age (beta = .18), prophecy (beta = .17), doctrinal orthodoxy (beta = .24), and church activity (beta = .18) were statistically significant (adjusted R-squared = .21).

9. The multiple regression analysis of the four-point volunteering measure found that prophecy (beta = .18), church activity (beta = .16), and the equitable measure (beta = .10) were statistically significant (adjusted R-squared = .13).

10. The multiple regression analysis of the organizational membership scale found that age (beta = –.11), income (beta = .22), and doctrinal orthodoxy (beta = –.14) were statistically significant (adjusted R-squared = .13).

11. The multiple regression analysis of the political participation scale found that age (beta = .17), having been raised Pentecostal (beta = –.11), race (beta = .14), education (beta = .23), prophecy (beta = .12), church activity (beta = .13), social welfare (beta = –.19), and cultural issues (beta = .11) were statistically significant (adjusted R-squared = .29)

12. The correlation between ideology and partisanship was .66.

13. The multiple regression analysis of the political alignment scale found that having been raised Pentecostal (beta = .10), race (beta = .18), education (beta = .10), praying in tongues (beta = .08), doctrinal orthodoxy (beta = .09), church activity (beta = .10), the equitable measure (beta = –.10), church benevolence (beta = –.10), church politics (beta = .17), social welfare (beta = –.29), and cultural issues (beta = .35) were statistically significant (adjusted R-squared = .48).

CHAPTER 9

1. Other similar accounts can be found in *Crossroads*, including that of David du Plessis (commonly known as "Mr. Pentecost" because of his extensive work with the World Council of Churches and the charismatic movement), who was defrocked because of his ecumenical activities (although reinstated some twenty years later). See also chapter 4 for a short account of Cecil M. Robeck's struggle to remain true to his prophetic call while avoiding denominational dismissal because of his ecumenical activities.

2. As a twenty-year-old college student traveling in the Bahamas, Cunningham had a vision of waves breaking over the earth that turned into young people taking the gospel into all the nations. It was this vision that served as the mystical seed for YWAM, a loose-knit network of YWAMs in over 130 countries served by over 11,000 staff and thousands more volunteers. Its major training center, University of the Nations, encompasses training programs in hundreds of YWAM locations.

3. All eight of the ethnic congregations included in this sample—six Hispanic, one Caribbean, and one African—were traditional churches.

4. Leaders of "apostolic networks" commonly call for the restoration of the "five-fold ministry" of pastor, teacher, evangelist, prophet, and apostle, a teaching that gained both followers and detractors during the mid-twentieth-century Latter Rain movement. In the 1980s the "office of the prophet" (often with long predictions about the future) and prophets were identified in some sectors of the neo-pentecostal movement; the "office of the apostle" gained ground in the 1990s. Just as the AG rejected early Latter Rain teachings about the "offices" of prophets and apostles, it does not support the theology that underlies new apostolic networks.

References

Albrecht, Daniel E. 1999. *Ties in the Spirit: A Ritual Approach to Pentecostal/Charismatic Spirituality*. Sheffield, U.K.: Sheffield Academic Press.

Alexander, Kimberly Ervin. 2007. "The 'Almost Pentecostal': The Future of the Church of God in the United States." Pp. 137–56 in E. Patterson and E. Rybarczyk, eds. *The Future of Pentecostalism in the United States*. Lanham, MD: Lexington Books.

Alexander, Paul. 2009a. *Peace and War: Shifting Allegiances in the Assemblies of God*. Telford, PA: Cascade Publishing House.

———. 2009b. *Signs and Wonders*. New York: Jossey-Bass.

Allen, Gary R. 2005. "Interview with Thomas E. Trask." *Enrichment*: 22–23.

Altman, Alex. 2009. "Joshua DuBois: Obama's Pastor-in-Chief." *Time*, February 6.

Anderson, A. 2004. *An Introduction to Pentecostalism*. Cambridge, U.K.: Cambridge University Press.

Anderson, R. M. 1979. *Vision of the Disinherited*. New York: Oxford University Press.

Baker, Heidi. 1995. "Pentecostal Experience: Towards a Reconstructive Theology of Glossolalia." Ph.D. dissertation. King's College, University of London.

———. 2008. *Compelled by Love*. Lake Mary, FL: Charisma House.

Barfoot, Charles H., and Gerald T. Sheppard. 1980. "Prophetic vs. Priestly Religion: The Changing Role of Women Clergy in Classical Pentecostal Churches." *Review of Religious Research* 22 (1): 2–17.

Barnes, L. L., and S. S. Sered, eds. 2005. *Religion and Healing in America*. New York. Oxford University Press.

Benvenutti, Sherilyn. 1995. "Anointed, Gifted and Called: Pentecostal Women in Ministry." *Pneuma: The Journal of the Society for Pentecostal Studies* 17 (Fall): 229–36.

Bernard, David K. 2007. "The Future of Oneness Pentecostalism." Pp. 123–36 in E. Patterson and E. Rybarczyk, eds., *The Future of Pentecostalism in the United States*. Lanham, MD: Lexington Books.

Blumhofer, Edith.1989. *The Assemblies of God: A Chapter in the Story of American Pentecostalism, Vol. 2 (Since 1941)*. Springfield, MO: Gospel Publishing House.

———. 1993. *Restoring the Faith: The Assemblies of God, Pentecostalism, and American Culture*. Champaign: University of Illinois Press.

———. 1995. "Reflections on the Source of Aimee Semple McPherson's Voice." *Pneuma: The Journal of the Society for Pentecostal Studies* 17 (Spring): 19–24.

Bridges, James K. 2000. "The Full Consummation of the Baptism in the Holy Spirit." *Theological Enrichment* (2000): 92–95.

Bueno, Ronald N. 1999. "Listening to the Margins: Re-Historicizing Pentecostal Experiences and Identities." Pp. 268–88 in M. W. Dempster, B. D. Klaus, and D. Petersen, eds. *The Globalization of Pentecostalism: A Religion Made to Travel*. Carlisle, CA: Regnum Books International (Paternoster Publishing).

Cagel, Timothy B. 1993. "Beyond the Fundamentalist–Modernist Controversy: Pentecostals and Hermeneutics in a Postmodern Age." *Pneuma: The Journal for Pentecostal Studies* 15 (Fall): 163–87.

Campolo, Tony. 1994. *How to Be Pentecostal without Speaking in Tongues*. Dallas: Word Books.

Campolo, Tony, and Mary Albert Darling. 2007. *The God of Intimacy and Action: Reconnecting Ancient Spiritual Practices, Evangelism, and Justice*. San Francisco: John Wiley.

Cartledge, Mark J., ed. 2006. *Speaking in Tongues: Multi-Disciplinary Perspectives*. Waynesboro, GA: Paternoster Press.

Cerillo, Augustus. 1997. "Interpretive Approaches to the History of American Pentecostal Origins." *Pneuma: The Journal for Pentecostal Studies* 19 (Spring): 29–52.

Chappell, F. C. 1988. "Healing Movements." Pp. 353–74 in S. M. Burgess and G. B. McGee, eds., *Dictionary of Pentecostal and Charismatic Movements*. Grand Rapids, MI: Regency Reference Library.

Chavda, Mahesh. 2003. *The Hidden Power of Speaking in Tongues*. Shippensburg, PA: Destiny Image.

Cole, John. 1996. "Gallup Poll Again Shows Confusion." *NCSE Reports* (Spring): 9. Cited in Brown (2006).

Collins, Randall. 2004. *Interaction Ritual Chains*. Princeton: Princeton University Press.

Corum, Fred T., and Hazel E. Bakewell. 1983. *The Sparkling Fountain*. Windsor, OH: Corum and Associates.

Coser, Lewis A. 1956. *Functions of Social Conflict*. Glencoe, IL: Free Press.

———. 1967. *Continuities in the Study of Social Conflict*. Glencoe, IL: Free Press.

Cox, Harvey. 1995. *Fire from Heaven: The Rise of Pentecostal Spirituality and the Reshaping of Religion in the Twenty-first Century*. Reading, MA: Addison-Wesley.

Creps, Earl. 2007. "Postmodern Pentecostals? Emerging Subcultures among Young Pentecostal Leaders." Pp. 27–48 in E. Patterson and E. Rybarczyk, eds., *The Future of Pentecostalism in the United States*. Lanham, MD: Lexington Books.

Cunningham, Loren (with Janice Rogers). 1984. *Is That Really You, God?* Grand Rapids, MI: Chosen Books.

Curtis, Heather D. 2007. *Faith in the Great Physician: Suffering and Divine Healing in American Culture, 1860–1900*. Baltimore: Johns Hopkins University Press.

Daniels, David D. 1999. "'Everybody Bids You Welcome': A Multicultural Approach to North American Pentecostalism." Pp. 222–52 in M. W. Dempster, B. D. Klaus, and D. Petersen, eds., *The Globalization of Pentecostalism: A Religion Made to Travel*. Carlisle, CA: Regnum Books International (Paternoster Publishing).

Darling, F. C. 1992. *The Restoration of Christian Healing: New Freedom in the Church since the Reformation*. Boulder, CO: Vista Publications.

Dempster, Murray W., Byron D. Klaus, and Douglas Petersen, eds. 1999. *The Globalization of Pentecostalism: A Religion Made to Travel*. Carlisle, CA: Regnum Books International (Paternoster Publishing).

Deutscher, Irwin. 1973. *What We Say/What We Do: Sentiments and Acts*. New York: Aldine de Gruyter.

Deutscher, Irwin, Fred P. Pestello, and Frances G. Pestello. 1993. *Sentiments and Acts*. New York: Aldine de Gruyter.
Di Sabatino, David. 1999. *The Jesus People Movement: An Annotated Bibliography and General Resource*. Westport, CT: Greenwood Press.
Doty, Sherri, and Efraim Espinoza. 2000. "FACT Survey Analysis: A 2000 Survey of Assemblies of God Churches." The General Council of the Assemblies of God.
Durkheim, Émile. 1915/1968. *The Elementary Forms of the Religious Life*. Translated by Joseph Ward Swain. London: George Allen and Unwin.
Eisenstadt, S. N., ed. 1968. *Max Weber on Charisma and Institution Building: Selected Papers*. Chicago: University of Chicago Press.
Espinosa, Gaston. 2008. "Liberated and Empowered: The Uphill History of Hispanic Assemblies of God Women in Ministry, 1915–1950." *The Assemblies of God Heritage* 28: 44–48.
Everts, Janet Meyer. 1995. "Brokenness as the Center of a Woman's Ministry." *Pneuma: The Journal of the Society for Pentecostal Studies* 17 (Fall): 237–44.
———. 1999. "'Your Daughters Shall Prophesy' Pentecostal Hermeneutics and the Empowerment of Women." Pp. 313–37 in M. W. Dempster, B. D. Klaus, and D. Petersen, eds., *The Globalization of Pentecostalism: A Religion Made to Travel*. Carlisle, CA: Regnum Books International (Paternoster Publishing).
Ford, Marcia. 1995. "Trask Puts New Face on Assemblies." *Charisma* (July): 62–63.
Garzon, Fernando, and Margaret M. Poloma. 2005. "Theophostic Ministry: Preliminary Practitioner Survey." *Pastoral Psychology* 53 (5): 387–96.
General Council of the Assemblies of God. 1970/1978. "The Inerrancy of Scripture" (1978; original report approved in 1970). Position paper, http://ag.org (accessed on December 29, 2008).
———. 1973/2008. "Divorce and Remarriage" (2008; original report approved in 1973). Position paper, http://ag.org (accessed on December 29, 2008).
———. 1979/2001. "Homosexuality" (2001; original report approved in 1979). Position paper, http://ag.org (accessed on December 29, 2008).
———. 1983. "A Biblical Perspective on Gambling." Position paper, http://ag.org (accessed on December 29, 2008).
———. 1985. "A Biblical Perspective on Abstinence." Position paper, http://ag.org (accessed on December 29, 2008).
———. 2000. "The Baptism in the Holy Spirit: The Initial Experience and Continuing Evidences of Spirit-Filled Life." Position paper, http://ag.org (accessed on December 29, 2008).
———. n.d. "View of Ordination." Position paper, http://ag.org (accessed on December 29, 2008).
Gibbs, Eddie, and Ryan K. Bolger. 2005. *Emerging Churches: Creating Christian Community in Postmodern Culture*. Grand Rapids, MI: Baker Academic.
Gill, Deborah M. 1995. "The Contemporary State of Women in Ministry in the Assemblies of God." *Pneuma: The Journal of the Society for Pentecostal Studies* 17 (Spring): 33–36.
Goff, J. R., Jr. 2002. "Parham, Charles Fox." Pp. 955–57 in S. M. Burgess, ed., *New International Dictionary of the Pentecostal and Charismatic Movements*. Grand Rapids, MI: Zondervan.
Goffman, Erving. 1961. *Encounters: Two Studies of the Sociology of Interaction*. Indianapolis: Bobbs-Merrill.

———. 1963. *Behavior in Public Places: Notes on the Social Organization of Gatherings.* Glencoe, IL: Free Press.

———. 1971. *Relations in Public.* New York: Harper Colophon.

———. 1974. *Frame Analysis: An Essay on the Organization of Experience.* New York: Harper Colophon.

Gold, Malcolm. 2003. *The Hybridization of an Assembly of God Church: Proselytism, Retention, and Re-Affiliation.* Lewiston, NY: Edwin Mellen Press.

Greeley, Andrew, and Michael Hout. 2006. *The Truth about Conservative Christians.* Chicago: University of Chicago Press.

Green, John C. 2004. "Assemblies of God." Pp. 179–94 in Corwin E. Smidt, ed., *Pulpit and Politics: Clergy in American Politics at the Advent of the Millennium.* Waco, TX: Baylor University Press.

———. 2007. *The Faith Factor: How Religion Influences the Vote.* Westport, CT: Praeger.

Green, John C., James L. Guth, Corwin E. Smidt, and Lyman A. Kellstedt. 1997. *Religion and the Culture Wars.* Lanham, MD: Rowman and Littlefield.

Grudem, Wayne, ed. 1996. *Are Miraculous Gifts for Today? Four Views.* Grand Rapids, MI: Zondervan.

Guarnieri, Mike. 2008. "How the River Changed Our Church." Spread the Fire (January), www.tacf.org/about/revival/spread-the-fire (accessed on April 7, 2010).Guth, James L., John C. Green, Corwin E. Smidt, Lyman A. Kellstedt, and Margaret M. Poloma. 1997. *The Bully Pulpit: The Politics of Protestant Clergy.* Lawrence: University of Kansas Press.

Guth, James L., John C. Green, Corwin E. Smidt, Lyman A. Kellstedt, and Margaret Poloma. 1997. *The Bully Pulpit: The Politics of Protestant Clergy.* Lawrence, KS: University Press of Kansas.

Guth, James L., Lyman A. Kellstedt, John C. Green, and Corwin E. Smidt. 2006. "Getting the Spirit? Religious and Partisan Mobilization in the 2004 Elections." Pp. 157–81 in Allan J. Cigler and Burdett A. Loomis, eds., *Interest Group Politics*, 7th ed. Washington, DC: Congressional Quarterly Press.

Hefner, Philip. 2006. "Spiritual Transformation and Healing: An Encounter with the Sacred." Pp.119–33 in J. D. Koss-Chionino and P. Hefner, eds., *Spiritual Transformation and Healing.* Lanham, MD: AltaMira Press.

Hollenweger, Walter J. 1997. *Pentecostalism: Origins and Developments Worldwide.* Peabody, MA: Hendrickson Publishers.

———. 1999. "Roman Catholics and Pentecostals in Dialogue." *Pneuma: The Journal for Pentecostal Studies* 21 (Spring): 135–54.

Hood, Ralph W., Jr. 2007. "Conceptual Paper: Methodological Atheism, Methodological Agnosticism, and Religious Experience." *Spirituality and Health International.* Published online in Wiley InterScience (http://www.interscience.wiley.com).

Hood, Ralph W., Jr., and W. Paul Williamson. 2008. *Them That Believe: The Power and Meaning of the Christian Serpent-Handling Tradition.* Berkeley: University of California Press.

Hunter, James Davison. 1983. *American Evangelicalism: Conservative Religion and the Quandary of Modernity.* New Brunswick, NJ: Rutgers University Press.

———. 1987. *Evangelicalism: The Coming Generation.* Chicago: University of Chicago Press.

Johns, Cheryl Bridges. 1993. *Pentecostal Formation: A Pedagogy among the Oppressed.* Sheffield, UK: Sheffield Academic Press.

Johns, Jackie David. 1999. "Yielding to the Spirit: The Dynamics of a Pentecostal Model of Praxis." Pp. 70–84 in M. W. Dempster, B. D. Klaus, and D. Petersen, eds., *The Globalization of Pentecostalism: A Religion Made to Travel*. Carlisle, CA: Regnum Books International (Paternoster Publishing).

Johnson, Rolf M. 2001. *Three Faces of Love*. DeKalb: Northern Illinois University Press.

Kalb, Claudia. 2003. "Faith and Healing." *Newsweek*, November 10.

Kennedy, John W. 2005. "Fellowship Celebrates Ethnic and Linguistic Diversity." *Pentecostal Evangel* (September 18): 6–7.

Koss-Chioino, Joan D., and Philip Hefner, eds. 2006. *Spiritual Transformation and Healing: Anthropological, Theological, Neuroscientific, and Clinical Perspectives*. Lanham, MD: AltaMira Press.

Land, Steven. 1993. *Pentecostal Spirituality: A Passion for the Kingdom*. Sheffield, U.K.: Sheffield Academic Press.

Lee, John A. 1976. "Social Change and Marginal Therapeutic Systems." Pp. 23–41 in Roy Wallis and Peter Morley, eds., *Marginal Medicine*. London: Peter Owen.

Lee, Matthew T., and Margaret M. Poloma. 2009a. *A Sociological Study of the Great Commandment in Pentecostalism: The Practice of Godly Love as Benevolent Service*. New York: Edwin Mellen Press.

———. 2009b. "Has Charisma Been Taken from Us? An Empirical Examination of Rieff's Theory." Paper presented at the annual meeting of the Society for the Scientific Study of Religion. Denver, Colorado, November.

Loren, Julia. 2005. "California Fire." *Charisma* (March): 44–47, 78.

Lukins, Julian. 2009. "The Faith of Sarah Palin." *Charisma* (January): 26–32.

Ma, Wonsuk. 1999. "Biblical Studies in the Pentecostal Tradition: Yesterday, Today and Tomorrow." Pp. 52–69 in M. W. Dempster, B. D. Klaus and D. Petersen, eds., *The Globalization of Pentecostalism: A Religion Made to Travel*. Carlisle, CA: Regnum Books International (Paternoster Publishing).

Macchia, Frank D. 1999. "The Struggle for Global Witness: Shifting Paradigms in Pentecostal Theology." Pp. 8–29 in M. W. Dempster, B. D. Klaus, and D. Petersen, eds., *The Globalization of Pentecostalism*. Carlisle, CA. Regnum Books International (Paternoster Publishing).

———. 2006a. *Baptized in the Spirit: A Global Pentecostal Theology*. Grand Rapids, MI: Zondervan.

———. 2006b. "Babel and the Tongues of Pentecost: Reversal or Fulfillment?—A Theological Perspective." Pp. 34–51 in M. J. Cartledge, ed., *Speaking in Tongues: Multi-Disciplinary Perspectives*. Waynesboro, GA: Paternoster.

———. 2006c. "The Kingdom and the Power: Spirit Baptism in Pentecostal and Ecumenical Perspective." Pp. 109–25 in M. Welker, ed., *The Work of the Spirit: Pneumatology and Pentecostalism*. Grand Rapids, MI: William B. Eerdmans.

MacNutt, F. S. 2005. *The Nearly Perfect Crime: How the Church Almost Killed the Ministry of Healing*. Grand Rapids, MI: Chosen Books.

McClymond, Michael. 2007. *Encyclopedia of Religious Revivals*. Westport, CT: Greenwood Press.

McGee, Gary B. 2002. "Initial Evidence." Pp. 784–91 in S. M. Burgess, ed., *New International Dictionary of the Pentecostal and Charismatic Movements*. Grand Rapids, MI: Zondervan.

———. 2005. "'More than Evangelical': The Challenge of Evolving Identity in the Assemblies of God." Pp. 35–44 in D. A. Roozen and J. R. Nieman, eds., *Church, Identity and Change*. Grand Rapids, MI: William B. Eerdmans.

———. 2008. "The New World of Realities in Which We Live: How Speaking in Tongues Empowered Early Pentecostals." *Pneuma* 30 (1): 108–35.

McGuire, Meredith B. 1988. *Ritual Healing in Suburban America*. New Brunswick, NJ: Rutgers University Press.

———. 1993. "Health and Healing in New Religious Movements." Pp. 139–55 in D. G. Bromley and J. K. Hadden, eds., *Religion and the Social Order*, vol. 3, part B. Greenwich, CT: JAI Press.

———. 2008. *Lived Religion: Faith and Practice in Everyday Life*. New York: Oxford University Press.

Malony, H. Newton, and A. Adams Lovekin. 1985. *Glossolalia: Behavioral Science Perspectives on Speaking in Tongues*. New York: Oxford.

Maslow, Abraham H. 1970. *Religions, Values, and Peak-Experiences*. New York: Viking Press.

May, L. C. 1956. "A Survey of Glossolalia and Related Phenomena in Non-Christian Religions." *American Anthropologist* 58: 75–96; reprinted in W. E. Mills, ed., *Speaking in Tongues: A Guide to Research* (Grand Rapids, MI: William B. Eerdmans 1986), 53–82.

Menzies, Glen. 1998. "Tongues as 'The Initial Physical Sign' of Spirit Baptism in the Thought of D. W. Kerr." *Pneuma: The Journal of the Society for Pentecostal Studies* 20 (Fall): 174–89.

Menzies, William W. 1971. *Anointed to Serve: The Story of the Assemblies of God*. Springfield, MO: Gospel Publishing House.

———. 2005. "The Challenges of Organization and Spirit in the Implementation of Theology and the Assemblies of God." Pp. 97–131 in D. R. Roozen and James R. Nieman, eds., *Church, Identity, and Change: Theology and Denominational Structure in Unsettled Times*. Grand Rapids, MI: William B. Eerdmans.

Meyer, Donald A. 1988. *The Positive Thinkers: Popular Religion Psychology from Mary Baker Eddy to Norman Vincent Peale and Ronald Reagan*. Middletown, CT: Wesleyan University Press.

Miller, Donald E. 1997. *Reinventing American Protestantism*. Berkeley: University of California Press.

Miller, Donald E., and Tetsunao Yamamori. 2007. *Global Pentecostalism: The New Face of Christian Social Engagement*. Berkeley: University of California Press.

Mills, Watson E., ed. 1986. *Speaking in Tongues: A Guide to Research on Glossolalia*. Grand Rapids, MI: William B. Eerdmans.

Newman, Joe. 2007. *Race and the Assemblies of God*. Youngstown, NY: Cambria Press.

O'Dea, Thomas. 1961. "Five Dilemmas of the Institutionalization of Religion." *Journal for the Scientific Study of Religion* 1: 30–41.

———. 1963. "Sociological Dilemmas: Five Paradoxes of Institutionalization." Pp.71–89 in Edward A. Teryadian, ed., *Sociological Theory, Values, and Sociocultural Change*. Glencoe, IL: Free Press.

O'Dea, Thomas, and Janet O'Dea Aviad. 1983. *The Sociology of Religion*, 2d ed. Englewood Cliffs, NJ: Prentice-Hall.

Patterson, Eric. 2007. "Conclusion: Back to the Future: U.S. Pentecostalism in the 21st Century." Pp. 189–209 in E. Patterson and E. Rybarczyk, eds., *The Future of Pentecostalism in the United States*. Lanham, MD: Lexington Books.

Perrow, Charles. 1986. *Complex Organizations: A Critical Essay*, 3d ed. New York: McGraw-Hill.
Petersen, Douglas. 1999. "Changing Paradigms: An Introductory Overview." Pp. 3–8 in M. W. Dempster, B. D. Klaus, and D. Petersen, eds., *The Globalization of Pentecostalism: A Religion Made to Travel*. Carlisle, CA: Regnum Books International (Paternoster Publishing).
Pollner, Marvin. 1989. "Divine Relations, Social Relations, and Well-Being." *Journal of Health and Social Behavior* 30: 92–104.
Poloma, Margaret M. 1982. *The Charismatic Movement: Is There a New Pentecost?* Boston: Twayne.
———. 1989. *The Assemblies of God at the Crossroads: Charisma and Institutional Dilemmas*. Knoxville: University of Tennessee Press.
———. 1995. "Charisma, Institutionalization and Social Change." *Pneuma: The Journal of the Society for Pentecostal Studies* 17 (Fall): 245–52.
———. 1997. "The 'Toronto Blessing': Charisma, Institutionalization and Revival." *Journal for the Scientific Study of Religion* 37 (2): 257–71.
———. 1998a "Inspecting the Fruit of the 'Toronto Blessing': A Sociological Assessment." *Pneuma: The Journal for the Society for Pentecostal Studies* 20 (1): 43–70.
———. 1998b "The Spirit Movement in North America at the Millennium: From Azusa Street to Toronto, Pensacola and Beyond." *Journal of Pentecostal Theology* 37 (2): 253–73.
———. 2001. "Mysticism as a Social Construct: Religious Experience in Pentecostal/Charismatic Context." Paper presented at the annual meetings of the Association for the Sociology of Religion, Anaheim, CA.
———. 2003. *Main Street Mystics: The Toronto Blessing and Reviving Pentecostalism*. Walnut Creek, CA: AltaMira Press.
———. 2005. "Charisma and Structure in the Assemblies of God: Revisiting O'Dea's Five Dilemmas." Pp. 97–131 in D. A. Roozen and J. R. Nieman, eds., *Church, Identity and Change*. Grand Rapids, MI: William B. Eerdmans.
———. 2006a. "Pensacola (Brownsville) Revival." Pp. 320–23 in Michael McClymond, ed., *Encyclopedia of Religious Revivals in America*, vol. 1. Westport, CT: Greenwood Press.
———. 2006b. "Toronto Blessing." Pp. 440–42 in Michael McClymond, ed., *Encyclopedia of Religious Revivals in America*, vol. 1.Westport, CT: Greenwood Press.
———. 2006c. "Old Wine, New Wineskins: The Rise of Healing Rooms in Revival Pentecostalism." *Pneuma: The Journal for Pentecostal Studies* 28 (1): 59–71.
Poloma, Margaret M., and George H. Gallup, Jr. 1991. *Varieties of Prayer: A Survey Report*. Philadelphia: Trinity Press International.
Poloma, Margaret M., and Lynette F. Hoelter. 1998. "The 'Toronto Blessing': A Holistic Model of Healing." *Journal for the Scientific Study of Religion* 37: 258–73.
Poloma, Margaret M., and Ralph W. Hood, Jr. 2008. *Blood and Fire: Godly Love in a Pentecostal Emerging Church*. New York: New York University Press.
Poloma, Margaret M., and Brian F. Pendleton. 1989. "Religious Experiences and Institutional Growth within the Assemblies of God." *Journal for the Scientific Study of Religion* 24: 415–31.
———. 1991a. *Exploring Neglected Dimensions of Religion in Quality of Life Research*. Lewiston, NY: Edwin Mellen Press.

———. 1991b. "The Effects of Prayer and Prayer Experiences on Measures of General Well-Being." *Journal of Psychology and Theology* 19: 71–83.

Porpora, Douglas V. 2006. "Methodological Atheism, Methodological Agnosticism, and Religious Experience." *Journal for the Theory of Social Behavior* 36: 1–57.

Porterfield, Amanda. 2005. *Healing in the History of Christianity*. Oxford: Oxford University Press.

Putnam, Robert D. 2000. *Bowling Alone: The Collapse and Revival of American Community*. New York: Simon and Schuster.

Rabey, Steve. 1998. *Revival in Brownsville: Pensacola, Pentecostalism, and the Power of American Revivalism*. Nashville: Thomas Nelson.

Rieff, Philip. 1959. *Freud: The Mind of the Moralist*. New York: Viking.

———. 1968. *The Triumph of the Therapeutic: Uses of Faith after Freud*. New York: Harper and Row.

———. 2006. *My Life among the Deathworks: Illustrations of the Aesthetics of Authority*. Charlottesville: University of Virginia Press.

———. 2007. *Charisma: The Gift of Grace, and How It Has Been Taken Away from Us*. New York: Vintage Books.

Robeck, Cecil M., Jr. 1997. "The Assemblies of God and Ecumenical Cooperation: 1920–1965." Pp. 107–50 in Wonsuk Ma and Robert P. Menzies, eds., *Pentecostalism in Context: Essays in Honor of William W. Menzies*. Eugene, OR: WIPF and Stock.

———. 1999a. "Toward Healing Our Divisions. Reflecting on Pentecostal Diversity and Common Witness." Paper presented at the 28th Annual Meeting of the Society for Pentecostal Studies, Springfield, MO, March 11–13.

———. 1999b. "The Holy Spirit and Ecumenism." Paper presented at a symposium on The Holy Spirit and Ecumenism, Sponsored by the Cardinal Suenans Foundation, Leuven, Belgium, December.

———. 2002. "Seymour, William Joseph." Pp. 1053–58 in S. M. Burgess, ed., *New International Dictionary of the Pentecostal and Charismatic Movements*. Grand Rapids, MI: Zondervan.

Rodgers, Darrin. 2008. "The Assemblies of God and the Long Journey toward Racial Reconciliation." *Assemblies of God Heritage* 28: 50–59.

Roozen, David A., and James R. Nieman, eds. 2005. *Church Identity and Change: Theology and Denominational Structures in Unsettled Times*. Grand Rapids, MI: William B. Eerdmans.

Ruthven, Jon. 1999. "Review of *Are Miraculous Gifts for Today?* by Wayne Gruden, ed." *Pneuma: The Journal for the Society of Pentecostal Studies* 21 (1): 155–58.

Rybarczyk, Edmund J. 2007. "Introduction: American Pentecostalism: Challenges and Temptations." Pp. 1–14 in E. Patterson and E. Rybarczyk, eds., *The Future of Pentecostalism in the United States*. Lanham, MD: Lexington Books.

Samarin, W. J. 1969. "Glossolalia as Learned Behavior." *Canadian Journal of Theology* 15: 60–64.

Sánchez-Walsh, Arlene M., and Erick Dean Patterson. 2007. "Latino Pentecostalism: Globalized Pentecostalism and the United States." Pp. 71–82 in E. Patterson and E. Rybarczyk, eds., *The Future of Pentecostalism in the United States*. Lanham, MD: Lexington Books.

Sargeant, Kimon. 2000. *Seeker Churches: Promoting Traditional Religion in a Nontraditional Way*. New Brunswick, NJ: Rutgers University Press.

Sennett, Richard. 1998. *The Corrosion of Character: The Personal Consequences of Work in the New Capitalism*. New York: W. W. Norton.
Sheppard, Gerald T. 1984. "Pentecostals and the Hermeneutics of Dispensationalism: The Anatomy of an Uneasy Relationship." *Pneuma: The Journal of the Society for Pentecostal Studies* 6 (Fall): 5–33.
———. 2002. "Prophecy from Ancient Israel to Pentecostals at the End of the Modern Age." *The Spirit and the Church* 3 (1): 47–70.
Smalridge, Scott. 1998. "Early American Pentecostalism and the Issues of Race, Gender, War, and Poverty: A History of the Belief System and Social Witness of Early Twentieth Century Pentecostalism and Its Nineteenth Century Holiness Roots." Masters Thesis, Faculty of Religious Studies, McGill University, Montreal.
Smidt, Corwin E., Kevin R. den Dulk, James M. Penning, Stephen V. Monsma, and Douglas L. Koopman. 2008. *Pews, Prayers, and Participation: Religion and Civic Responsibility in America*. Washington, DC: Georgetown University Press.
Sorokin, Pitirim A. 1954/2002. *The Ways and Power of Love: Types, Factors, and Techniques of Moral Transformation*. Philadelphia: Templeton Foundation Press.
Spittler, Russell P. 1994. "Are Pentecostals and Charismatics Fundamentalists? A Review of American Uses of These Categories." In Karla Poewe, ed., *Charismatic Christianity as a Global Culture*. Columbia: University of South Carolina Press.
———. 2002, "Glossolalia." Pp. 670–71 in S. M. Burgess, ed., *International Dictionary of Pentecostal and Charismatic Movements*. Grand Rapids, MI: Zondervan.
Starbuck, William H. 1983. "Organizations as Action Generators." *American Sociological Review* 48: 91–102.
Synan, Vinson. 1971/1997. *The Holiness-Pentecostal Movement in the United States*. Grand Rapids, MI: William B. Eerdmans.
Taves, Ann. 1999. *Fits, Trances, and Visions: Experiencing Religion and Explaining Experience from Wesley to James*. Princeton: Princeton University Press.
Tinlin, Paul B., and Edith L. Blumhofer. 1991. "Decade of Decline or Harvest? Dilemmas of the Assemblies of God." *The Christian Century*, July 10–17: 684–87.
Wacker, Grant. 2001. *Heaven Below: Early Pentecostals and American Culture*. Cambridge: Harvard University Press.
Wagner, C. Peter. 2002. "Third Wave." P. 1141 in S. M. Burgess, ed., *New International Dictionary of the Pentecostal and Charismatic Movements*. Grand Rapids, MI: Zondervan.
Walker, Andrew. 2000. "Foreword." Pp. vii–ix in William K. Kay, *Pentecostals in Britain*. Carlisle, CA: Pater Noster Press.
Wilcox, Clyde, and Carin Larson. 2006. *Onward Christian Soldiers? The Religious Right in American Politics*, 3d ed. Boulder, CO: Westview.
Wilkinson, Michael, and Peter Althouse. 2010. "The Place of Soaking Prayer in the Charismatic Renewal." Paper presented at the Thirty-ninth Annual Meeting of the Society for Pentecostal Studies. Minneapolis: North Central University.
Wilson, Everett A. 1999. "They Crossed the Red Sea, Didn't They? Critical History and Pentecostal Beginnings." Pp. 85–115 in M. W. Dempster, B. D. Klaus, and D. Petersen, eds., *The Globalization of Pentecostalism: A Religion Made to Travel*. Carlisle, CA: Regnum Books International (Paternoster Publishing).

Index

About the Authors

MARGARET M. POLOMA is Professor Emeritus at the University of Akron. She has authored many books, including *Blood and Fire*; *Main Street Mystics*; and *The Assemblies of God at the Crossroads*.

JOHN C. GREEN is Distinguished Professor of Political Science at the University of Akron and a Senior Fellow with the Pew Forum on Religion and Public Life. He is co-author of *The Bully Pulpit: The Politics of Protestant Clergy; Religion and the Culture Wars: Dispatches from the Front*; and *The Diminishing Divide: Religion's Changing Role in American Politics.*

About the Author